Java Reflection Unleashed
Advanced Techniques

Copyright © 2024 by John H. Jones
All rights reserved. No part of this publication may be reproduced, distributed, or transmitted in any form or by any means, including photocopying, recording, or other electronic or mechanical methods, without the prior written permission of the publisher, except in the case of brief quotations embodied in critical reviews and certain other noncommercial uses permitted by copyright law.

Contents

1. **Introduction to Java Reflection** — 11
   - 1.1 What is Java Reflection? — 11
   - 1.2 Purpose and Use Cases of Reflection — 13
   - 1.3 The Power and Pitfalls of Using Reflection — 15
   - 1.4 Key Components of the Reflection API — 17
   - 1.5 Class Loaders and Reflection — 19
   - 1.6 Basic Reflection Example: Accessing Class Information — 21
   - 1.7 Understanding AccessibleObject and Accessibility — 23
   - 1.8 Reflection and Its Impact on Performance — 24
   - 1.9 Security Concerns with Reflection — 27

2. **Exploring Class Objects and the java.lang.Class** — 31
   - 2.1 Overview of java.lang.Class — 31
   - 2.2 Retrieving Class Objects — 33
   - 2.3 Inspecting Class Modifiers and Types — 35
   - 2.4 Exploring Interfaces Implemented by a Class — 37
   - 2.5 Understanding Superclasses and Hierarchy — 39
   - 2.6 Extracting Package Information from Class Objects — 41
   - 2.7 Analyzing Enum Types with Reflection — 42
   - 2.8 Dealing with Array Class Objects — 45
   - 2.9 Distinguishing Primitive, Synthetic, and Annotation Types — 46

2.10 Using Reflection to Check for Anonymous and Local Classes 49
   2.11 Obtaining Class Enclosures and Declarations 51
   2.12 Summary and Practical Tips for java.lang.Class 53

3 Constructors, Methods, and Fields Inspection   55
   3.1 Retrieving Constructors of a Class 55
   3.2 Understanding Constructor Modifiers and Parameters . 57
   3.3 Invoking Constructors Dynamically 59
   3.4 Inspecting Methods of a Class 60
   3.5 Method Signature and Modifier Inspection 62
   3.6 Dynamically Invoking Methods 64
   3.7 Dealing with Method Parameter Types and Return Types 65
   3.8 Exploring Fields and Their Properties 68
   3.9 Accessing and Modifying Field Values Dynamically ... 70
   3.10 Field Type Analysis and Reflection 72
   3.11 Handling Exceptions in Reflective Operations 74
   3.12 Best Practices for Inspecting Constructors, Methods, and Fields 76

4 Instantiating Classes Dynamically   79
   4.1 Foundations of Dynamic Class Instantiation 79
   4.2 Using Class.newInstance(): Benefits and Limitations ... 81
   4.3 Advanced Instantiation with Constructors 83
   4.4 Handling Constructor Accessibility 86
   4.5 Creating Instances with Array Reflection 88
   4.6 Dynamic Instantiation of Inner and Anonymous Classes 90
   4.7 Exception Handling and Error Prevention in Dynamic Creation 92
   4.8 Design Patterns and Dynamic Instantiation 94
   4.9 Using Reflection for Dependency Injection 96

4.10 Reflection and Class Loaders 98
4.11 Performance Implications of Dynamic Instantiation . . . 100
4.12 Summary and Best Practices 102

5 Accessing Private Members with Reflection 105

5.1 Overview of Access Levels in Java 105
5.2 Understanding Reflection and Access Control 107
5.3 Retrieving Private Fields of a Class 109
5.4 Modifying Private Fields Using Reflection 111
5.5 Accessing Private Methods of a Class 112
5.6 Invoking Private Methods Dynamically 114
5.7 Constructors Accessibility and Instantiation 116
5.8 Handling IllegalAccessException 118
5.9 Ethical Considerations and Risks of Accessing Private Members 120
5.10 Security Implications of Breaking Encapsulation 122
5.11 Reflection and Java Security Manager 124
5.12 Summary of Techniques and Guidelines 126

6 Reflective Operations on Arrays 129

6.1 Introduction to Array Reflection 129
6.2 Creating Arrays Dynamically 131
6.3 Retrieving and Setting Array Components Reflectively . 132
6.4 Manipulating Multi-Dimensional Arrays 134
6.5 Type Checking and Casting with Reflective Arrays 136
6.6 Discovering Array Length and Component Type 138
6.7 Performance Aspects of Array Reflection 139
6.8 Common Use Cases for Reflective Array Operations . . . 141
6.9 Reflection on Primitive Type Arrays vs Object Arrays . . 144
6.10 Handling Exceptions in Reflective Array Operations . . . 145
6.11 Security Concerns with Reflective Arrays 147

    6.12 Summary and Advanced Scenarios 149

7 Handling Annotations with Reflection   153

    7.1 Introduction to Annotations in Java 153

    7.2 Retrieving Annotations from Classes, Methods, and Fields 155

    7.3 Understanding Retention Policies in Java Reflection . . . 157

    7.4 Accessing Runtime Annotations 159

    7.5 Interpreting Annotation Values Dynamically 161

    7.6 Handling Custom Annotations 163

    7.7 Using Reflective Access to Drive Annotation-Based Logic 165

    7.8 Annotations and Inherited Classes 168

    7.9 Reflection API and Annotated Arrays 170

    7.10 Security Aspects of Using Annotations with Reflection . 172

    7.11 Case Studies: Practical Uses of Annotations in Frameworks 174

    7.12 Summary and Best Practices for Annotation Handling . . 176

8 Dynamics of Proxies and Invocation Handlers   179

    8.1 Introduction to Dynamic Proxies in Java 179

    8.2 Role of Interfaces in Dynamic Proxy Creation 181

    8.3 Creating Dynamic Proxies Using java.lang.reflect.Proxy 184

    8.4 Understanding and Implementing InvocationHandlers . 186

    8.5 Method Interception with Dynamic Proxies 188

    8.6 Proxy Performance and Optimization Strategies 190

    8.7 Handling Exceptions and Errors in Proxies 192

    8.8 Advanced Techniques: Proxy Chains and Decorators . . 195

    8.9 Use Cases: Security and Access Control with Proxies . . 197

    8.10 Integrating Proxies with Other Java Technologies 199

    8.11 Reflective Operations on Proxy Instances 201

8.12 Summary: Best Practices in Proxy Design and Implementation 204

9 Performance Considerations and Best Practices 207
9.1 Understanding the Cost of Using Reflection 207
9.2 Benchmarking Reflection vs. Non-Reflection Code 209
9.3 Caching Strategies for Reflective Access 211
9.4 Minimizing Overhead by Reducing Reflective Calls . . . 214
9.5 Secure Reflection: Balancing Performance and Security . 216
9.6 Using Arrays and Generics Efficiently with Reflection . . 218
9.7 Profiling and Tuning Reflective Operations 220
9.8 Design Patterns to Enhance Reflection Efficiency 222
9.9 Reflection in a Multi-threaded Environment 225
9.10 When to Use and When to Avoid Reflection 227
9.11 Testing and Debugging Reflective Code 229
9.12 Summary: Building High-Performance Reflective Applications 231

10 Reflection in Java Security 235
10.1 Overview of Java Security and Reflection 235
10.2 The Security Manager and AccessControlContext 237
10.3 Restricting Reflective Access with SecurityManager . . . 239
10.4 Assessing Risks of Exposing Private Members 241
10.5 Protecting Against Reflection-Based Attacks 244
10.6 Securing Dynamic Class Loading 246
10.7 Enforcing Security in Dynamic Proxies 248
10.8 Using Reflection Safely with Annotations 249
10.9 Best Practices for Safe Reflective Operations 251
10.10 Auditing and Compliance Checks Using Reflection . . . 253
10.11 Case Studies: Reflection in Secure Applications 255
10.12 Summary and Future of Secure Reflection 258

11 Using Reflection in Generics — **261**

11.1 Basics of Generics and Type Erasure 261

11.2 Retrieving Generic Type Information 263

11.3 Reflection and Type Tokens 265

11.4 Dynamically Accessing Generic Methods 267

11.5 Construction and Instantiation of Generic Types 269

11.6 Handling Generic Arrays Reflectively 270

11.7 Challenges and Solutions with Generic Reflection 272

11.8 Interfacing Generics with Wildcards and Bounded Types 274

11.9 Practical Applications: Generics in Frameworks 276

11.10 Testing and Debugging Generic Reflection Code 279

11.11 Reflection on Generic Inheritance Structures 281

11.12 Best Practices with Generics and Reflection 283

12 Advanced Techniques and Use Cases — **285**

12.1 Advanced Use of ClassLoader Reflection 285

12.2 Techniques for Reflective JavaBean Manipulation 288

12.3 Reflection for Dynamic Proxy Chains and Composite Objects 290

12.4 Automating Data Serialization and Deserialization 292

12.5 Reflection in Test Driven Development and Mocking . . 294

12.6 Dynamic Language Features Implementation via Reflection 297

12.7 Using Reflection for Runtime Code Modification 299

12.8 Implementing Aspect-Oriented Programming with Reflection 301

12.9 Reflection in Distributed Systems and Remote Method Invocation 303

12.10 Developing Plugins and Extension Mechanisms 305

12.11 Reflection in Dynamic Script Execution 308

12.12 Concluding Thoughts on Persistence and Evolution of Java Reflection 310

Preface

Java Reflection is a powerful feature that allows programs to inspect or modify the runtime behavior of applications running within the Java Virtual Machine (JVM). This book, *Java Reflection Unleashed: Advanced Techniques*, is designed to equip software developers, architects, and advanced students with a thorough understanding of the Java Reflection API, its capabilities, and its prudent use cases in modern software development.

The primary objective of this book is to elucidate the extensive features of the Java Reflection API. It provides detailed explanations of how to dynamically analyze classes, methods, constructors, and fields at runtime. The book also delves into more complex topics such as dynamic proxy creation, annotation handling, and the use of reflection in generics. Each chapter not only introduces theoretical concepts but also demonstrates practical implementation with code examples to solidify the readers' understanding.

Aside from covering the technical aspects, this book critically addresses the performance considerations and potential security implications associated with Java Reflection. It navigates through best practices for using reflection effectively and safely, ensuring that readers can utilize these techniques in their projects without compromising the robustness or security of their applications.

This book is tailored for professionals who are already familiar with Java programming but wish to extend their knowledge to include dynamic behavior and runtime type handling. It is also suitable for academicians who teach advanced Java topics and aim to provide their students with an in-depth view of reflection and dynamic programming in Java.

By the end of this book, readers will have acquired a comprehensive mastery of Java Reflection, enabling them not only to enhance their existing projects but also to innovate new solutions utilizing dynamic programming techniques. This book strives to empower its readers to transcend conventional static programming paradigms and explore more flexible and powerful software design and implementation strategies.

Chapter 1

Introduction to Java Reflection

Java Reflection is a potent capability within the Java API that permits the inspection and manipulation of classes at runtime. This chapter provides a foundational understanding of how reflection works, including its purposes, uses, and the core components involved. It simplifies complex concepts and teaches the basics of class introspection, explaining how to retrieve class loaders, explore class fields, methods, constructors, and more. The chapter also discusses the potential drawbacks and benefits of using reflection in real-world applications, ensuring that readers can make informed decisions when integrating this technology into their projects.

1.1 What is Java Reflection?

Java Reflection is a core component of the Java programming language that offers advanced capabilities for dynamic behavior. At its essence, Reflection provides mechanisms to inspect classes, interfaces, fields, and methods at runtime, without knowing the names of the classes, methods etc. at compile time. This feature is not only formidable for development and debugging but also for any application requiring runtime binding, class analysis, or the manipulation of properties at runtime.

The Reflection API, fundamentally embedded in the java.lang.reflect package, exposes various constructors, methods, and fields of a class. This allows for the dynamic retrieval of information about the class, the execution of methods, and the instantiation of new objects during the runtime. Reflection can manipulate both public and private members of a class, which is typically restricted in non-reflective programming environments.

- **Class Retrieval:** The first step in using Java Reflection is to obtain an instance of java.lang.Class. This can be achieved by invoking the .getClass() method on an object, using the .class syntax on a class name, or by calling the method Class.forName(), passing the fully qualified name of the class as a string.

- **Inspecting Class Information:** Once a Class object has been captured, the Reflection API enables the retrieval of metadata about the class such as its modifiers, fields, methods, constructors, and superclass.

- **Creating Instances:** Reflection allows for the creation of an instance of a class using the newInstance() method of the Constructor class or the Class class directly. This is particularly useful for dynamic object instantiation based on run-time decisions.

- **Method Invocation:** Methods of a class can be invoked dynamically using Reflection. The Method class provides functionalities to invoke methods by passing the instance of the object and arguments at runtime.

- **Field Manipulation:** Reflection provides the ability to read or modify the attribute values associated with a class at runtime regardless of the usual access control checks. This is managed through the Field class in the Reflection API.

The typical usage of Java Reflection can be observed in various frameworks and runtime environments which require the dynamic binding of services and components. For instance, frameworks like Spring use Reflection to instantiate objects and inject dependencies based on runtime configurations. Debuggers and testing frameworks frequently utilize Reflection to access private members of classes for testing purposes.

The code snippet below illustrates a basic example of using Reflection to access information about a class:

```java
public class SampleClass {
   private String sampleField;

   public SampleClass(String sampleField){
      this.sampleField = sampleField;
   }

   public void display() {
      System.out.println("Field value: " + sampleField);
   }
}

public class ReflectionDemo {
   public static void main(String[] args) throws Exception {
      Class<?> cls = Class.forName("SampleClass");
      Constructor<?> constructor = cls.getConstructor(String.class);
      Object obj = constructor.newInstance("Hello Reflection");

      Method displayMethod = cls.getDeclaredMethod("display");
      displayMethod.invoke(obj);
   }
}
```

The output of the above-executed Reflection code would be:

```
Field value: Hello Reflection
```

Understanding and harnessing the power of Java Reflection opens doors to dynamic behaviors and capabilities that are otherwise not feasible or explicit in static programming paradigms. Reflective programming should, however, be used judiciously considering its performance implications and security risks, which are elaborated in subsequent sections of this chapter.

1.2 Purpose and Use Cases of Reflection

The purpose and utilization of Java Reflection transcend conventional programming paradigms, presenting a dynamic approach to interacting with Java classes and their constituents. By allowing programs to inspect and manipulate objects at run-time, reflection becomes indispensable in scenarios requiring a high degree of flexibility and adaptability.

Reflection is chiefly employed in several critical use cases that underscore its utility in practical applications:

- **Development of IDEs and Tools:** Integrated Development Environments (IDEs) and various development tools leverage reflection to examine and interact with user code, provide features like code completion, and display API documentation dynamically.

- **Debugging and Testing Tools:** Debuggers and testing frameworks use reflection to probe into an application's state by accessing private fields and methods, thus enabling thorough inspection and automated testing without the need for modifying the original code base.

- **Runtime Configuration:** Applications can utilize reflection to load configuration details at runtime, thus altering behavior without altering the source code. This is particularly useful in environments requiring high configurability such as enterprise applications.

- **Object Serialization and Deserialization:** Serialization frameworks employ reflection to dynamically determine the structure of classes, enabling them to serialize objects into formats like XML or JSON, and subsequently deserialize them back into objects.

- **Dependency Injection Frameworks:** Popular frameworks like Spring or Guice use reflection to inject dependencies. This simplifies the configuration and integration of software components, promoting a modular architecture and easing the maintenance and testing of applications.

- **API Interaction and Remote Method Invocation:** Reflection is pivotal in scenarios where interactions with external APIs or services are required but the specifics are not known at compile time. This capability also supports the implementation of remote method invocation, enabling the invocation of methods on objects located on different virtual machines.

- **Proxying and Aspect-Oriented Programming:** Reflection facilitates the creation of dynamic proxies that are used to intercept method calls, allowing dynamic method dispatch based on method names or annotations at runtime. This is a core technique in aspect-oriented programming which separates cross-cutting concerns like logging and transaction management.

Each of these use cases illustrates how reflection supports various phases of software development and operation, from writing more flexible code to enhancing functionality without altering existing system components. However, the application of reflection must be approached with cautious deliberation due to its impact on performance and security, aspects that are treated in detail in subsequent sections of this chapter.

Reflection thus provides the Java programmer with a powerful, if nuanced, set of tools. Its capability to inspect and manipulate at runtime, while occasionally maligned for potential overheads or security implications, continues to make it a valuable asset in the developer's toolkit, crucial for cases where flexibility and dynamic behavior are required.

1.3 The Power and Pitfalls of Using Reflection

Reflection in Java provides significant capabilities which empower developers by allowing runtime introspection of classes, interfaces, fields, and methods. This dynamic feature enhances the flexibility and extensibility of applications but also introduces potential challenges and risks. This section elucidates the distinct advantages and inherent drawbacks of using Java Reflection, extending our prior discussion on the basic facets of the Java Reflection API.

Advantages of Using Reflection

The primary advantage of Java Reflection lies in its ability to modify runtime behavior of applications without altering their source code. Here, we explore several key benefits:

- **Dynamic Code Execution:** Reflection facilitates the execution of methods and the construction of objects dynamically, thus enabling developers to implement generic frameworks that require flexible code execution paths.

- **Configuration-based Component Initialization:** With Reflection, components can be configured and instantiated dynamically using external configuration files, which is a foundational technique in frameworks like Spring.

- **Development of IDEs and Tools:** Integrated Development Environments (IDEs) leverage Reflection for tasks such as code completion, debugging, and visualization of object structures.

- **Enhanced Testing Mechanisms:** Testing frameworks like JUnit use Reflection to instantiate test cases and invoke methods automatically, thus streamlining the testing process significantly.

These capabilities underscore the transformative potential of Reflection in developing robust and versatile Java applications.

Pitfalls of Using Reflection

Despite its undeniable utility, Reflection also poses several risks and drawbacks. It's essential to weigh these carefully:

- **Performance Overhead:** Accessing methods and fields via Reflection is inherently slower than direct access, due to the additional processing required to bypass normal security checks and resolve references at runtime.

- **Security Risks:** Reflection can inadvertently expose internal state and behavior of classes to unauthorized access, leading to potential security breaches.

- **Complexity and Maintainability Issues:** Overuse of Reflection can lead to code that is hard to understand and maintain. Debugging reflective accesses might also be challenging as most IDEs are not optimized for dynamic code analysis.

- **Violations of Abstraction Boundaries:** By enabling access to private and protected members, Reflection may lead to unintended interactions and state inconsistencies.

Furthermore, the following pseudocode provides an overview of reflective method invocation, highlighting the trade-off between dynamic capability and explicit method access:

This method demonstrates the procedure for dynamically invoking a method based on its name. However, this flexibility must be managed judiciously to prevent the aforementioned issues.

Reflective programming allows for extraordinary levels of dynamism in Java applications but necessitates mindful handling to mitigate performance penalties and uphold software integrity and security. By understanding both the powers and pitfalls detailed in this section, developers can more effectively leverage Reflection in their projects, ensuring optimal implementation and minimizing unintended consequences.

Data: method as string, classObj as object reference, params as array of parameters
Result: Executes the specified method on classObj with params

```
1 begin
2   Method m ← classObj.getClass().getMethod(method, params.class)
3   m.setAccessible(true)
4   result ← m.invoke(classObj, params)
5   return result
6 end
```

1.4 Key Components of the Reflection API

The Java Reflection API encompasses a variety of classes and interfaces that together facilitate the runtime retrieval and manipulation of class and object metadata. Central to this API are a few key components including the java.lang.Class class, various members of the java.lang.reflect package such as Method, Field, Constructor, and Array, and mechanisms for handling accessibility like AccessibleObject. Each of these components plays a vital role in enabling developers to dynamically interact with Java applications. This section delves into the specifics of these components, discussing their functionalities and interrelationships in the context of Java's Reflection API.

The java.lang.Class Class

The cornerstone of the Reflection API is the java.lang.Class class, which acts as the entry point for most reflection operations. An instance of Class represents classes and interfaces in a running Java application.

- It can be accessed using the getClass() method on an object instance or the .class syntax on a class or interface name.
- It provides methods to discover a class's modifiers (such as public, private, etc.), fields, methods, constructors, and superclasses.
- It also offers functionalities to create new instances, identify the class loader, and check array types among others.

Example of retrieving class object:

```java
public class ReflectionDemo {
    public static void main(String[] args) {
        Class<?> cls = ReflectionDemo.class;
        System.out.println("Class name: " + cls.getName());
    }
}
```

```
Class name: ReflectionDemo
```

Members of the `java.lang.reflect` Package

Fundamental to the Reflection API, the `java.lang.reflect` package contains essential classes like `Method`, `Field`, and `Constructor`, each providing mechanisms to interact with class objects.

- `Field` - Allows the inspection and modification of class fields.

- `Method` - Facilitates the invocation of methods at runtime.

- `Constructor` - Permits the instantiation of new objects dynamically.

Using `Field` example:

```java
public class FieldHandle {
    public int publicField;

    public static void main(String[] args) throws Exception {
        FieldHandle handle = new FieldHandle();
        handle.publicField = 10;

        Field field = FieldHandle.class.getDeclaredField("publicField");
        System.out.println("Field value: " + field.getInt(handle));
        field.setInt(handle, 20);
        System.out.println("Updated field value: " + field.getInt(handle));
    }
}
```

```
Field value: 10
Updated field value: 20
```

Accessibility with `AccessibleObject`

The `AccessibleObject` class and its subclasses (`Field`, `Method`, and `Constructor`) provide a unified interface to deal with accessibility (visibility) changes on fields, methods, or constructors.

- It allows bypassing the usual visibility checks (such as private, protected) to facilitate access to otherwise inaccessible elements.

- Utilizing the `setAccessible(true)` method, programmers can modify the accessibility flag for an object, allowing for heightened capability in dynamic contexts.

Accessibility example:

```
public class PrivateFieldAccess {
    private String hidden = "secret";

    public static void main(String[] args) throws Exception {
        PrivateFieldAccess obj = new PrivateFieldAccess();
        Field privateField = PrivateFieldAccess.class.getDeclaredField("hidden");

        privateField.setAccessible(true); // Enabling access to private field
        System.out.println("Private field value: " + privateField.get(obj));
    }
}
```

```
Private field value: secret
```

Through these mechanisms, the Java Reflection API provides potent capabilities for dynamic code analysis and manipulation. By facilitating runtime retrieval of method, field, and constructor information and eventually manipulating their accessibility, this API supports a flexible interaction with Java applications, enabling practices such as dynamic configuration, serialization, and more.

1.5 Class Loaders and Reflection

Reflection in Java allows for runtime retrieval of information about classes, interfaces, fields, and methods. A crucial aspect of utilizing reflection effectively involves understanding the concept of class loaders and their role in the reflection process. This section delves into the details of class loaders, explaining how they interact with the Java Reflection API to load classes dynamically, and how they can be manipulated to achieve dynamic behavior in Java applications.

Class loaders are part of the Java runtime environment that dynamically load Java classes into the Java Virtual Machine (JVM). They are a fundamental part of the JVM's runtime class loading mechanism, typically used to load classes that are not part of the Java core API. The Java Reflection API leverages class loaders to identify and load classes at runtime, providing a flexible system for dynamic operations.

- The primary role of a class loader is to load classes on demand, avoiding the need to load all possible classes at startup which enhances the performance and flexibility of Java applications.

- Class loaders also enforce namespace management by uniquely identifying classes not only by their names but also by their respective loaders. This helps in resolving ambiguity in situations where multiple versions of the same class might coexist.

When using reflection, understanding the class loading process is paramount. The following are steps typically involved when a class loader interacts with the Reflection API:

1. **Class Identification**: The reflection mechanism first identifies the complete name of the class that needs to be loaded.

2. **Delegation Model**: Using the delegation model, the class loader attempts to find the class by delegating the request up the hierarchy of class loaders until either the class is found or the root is reached.

3. **Class Retrieval**: If the class is found, it is loaded; otherwise, a `ClassNotFoundException` is thrown.

4. **Initialization and Accessibility**: Once the class is loaded, reflection can be used to inspect the class structure (fields, methods, constructors, etc.) and manipulate its accessibility attributes if necessary.

The integration of class loaders with reflection is pivotal for applications requiring dynamic behavior, such as plugin systems or applications that modify their functionality based on user input or external configurations. Here is a Java example illustrating how to use a custom class loader with the Reflection API:

```
public class CustomClassLoader extends ClassLoader {
    public Class loadClass(String name) throws ClassNotFoundException {
        // Define custom loading logic here
        return super.loadClass(name);
    }
}

public class ReflectionWithClassLoader {
    public static void main(String[] args) throws Exception {
        CustomClassLoader classLoader = new CustomClassLoader();
        Class<?> cls = Class.forName("com.example.MyClass", true, classLoader);
        // Reflection code to manipulate cls
    }
}
```

Upon loading the class, the following could be a typical output assuming that 'com.example.MyClass' implements a method that returns its name:

```
Class com.example.MyClass loaded successfully.
```

The manipulation of class loaders in conjunction with reflection methods needs careful consideration regarding security and performance implications. When classes are loaded, they should be verified, and access rights should be appropriately managed to prevent unauthorized code execution or leaks of sensitive information.

By understanding and utilizing class loaders in combination with Java Reflection, developers can leverage dynamic class loading capabilities while maintaining robust and secure application operations. This knowledge is quintessential not only for developing flexible applications but also for optimizing them to operate efficiently within various runtime environments.

1.6 Basic Reflection Example: Accessing Class Information

Let's start to demonstrate a practical example of using Java Reflection to access class information. The emphasis is on the retrieval of fundamental class details including the class name, methods, fields, interfaces, and superclass details. This serves as an introductory exploration into the capabilities of the Reflection API for introspecting class specifics without a priori knowledge of the class properties.

To begin, reflection in Java is facilitated through the `java.lang.Class` object, which represents classes and interfaces in a running Java application. An instance of `Class` can be obtained in various ways, the most straightforward being through the `.class` syntax or by using the `Class.forName()` method. Here, we utilize `Class.forName()` as it showcases reflection's dynamic resolution at runtime.

```
1  // Acquiring the Class object for the java.util.Date class
2  Class<?> clazz = Class.forName("java.util.Date");
```

Once a `Class` object is acquired, various methods can be called on it to inspect the class's metadata. We illustrate below how to retrieve the name, fields, methods, interfaces, and superclass.

```
1  System.out.println("Class Name: " + clazz.getName());
```

```java
System.out.println("Class Fields: ");
Field[] fields = clazz.getDeclaredFields();
for(Field field : fields) {
    System.out.println(field.getName());
}

System.out.println("Class Methods: ");
Method[] methods = clazz.getMethods();
for(Method method : methods) {
    System.out.println(method.getName());
}

System.out.println("Implemented Interfaces: ");
Class<?>[] interfaces = clazz.getInterfaces();
for(Class<?> iface : interfaces) {
    System.out.println(iface.getName());
}

System.out.println("Superclass: " + clazz.getSuperclass().getName());
```

The output of each segment brings into perspective the details within the class dynamically introspected at runtime:

```
Class Name: java.util.Date
Class Fields:
fastTime
cdate
Method {}
SuppressedExceptions{}
Class Methods:
after
before
clone
compareTo
equals
format
...
Implemented Interfaces:
java.io.Serializable
java.lang.Comparable
java.lang.Cloneable
Superclass: java.lang.Object
```

The power of reflection is manifest in the ability to introspect any loaded class without modifying the class itself. This capability is especially beneficial in environments where source code availability is restricted or in scenarios involving dynamic class loading and interaction.

The use case illustrated is foundational yet powerful, forming a basis upon which more complex reflective operations can be crafted. Notably, developers must handle instances where security managers restrict reflection, and unauthorized access to private fields and methods could lead to security breaches or inadvertent exposure of sensitive data.

By leveraging Java Reflection, software developers gain a deeper insight into the internals of classes during runtime, which is paramount for dynamic analysis, debugging, or when interacting with unknown class codebases. This introductory example lays the groundwork for subsequent sections where more intricate operations utilizing reflection will be discussed, providing a scaffolded learning approach to mastering Java Reflection.

1.7 Understanding AccessibleObject and Accessibility

The Java Reflection API provides a powerful framework for introspective class and member access, and a crucial component of this architecture is the 'AccessibleObject' class. This section delves into the details of 'AccessibleObject' and its role in handling accessibility within the realm of Java reflection.

The 'AccessibleObject' class serves as the base class for 'Field', 'Method', and 'Constructor' objects, and it provides the mechanism to bypass Java's access control checks. Typically, this capability is utilized only when necessary, such as for the purposes of serialization frameworks, testing frameworks, and application development tools that need to access components not normally exposed through public APIs.

- `setAccessible(boolean flag)`: This method is pivotal in managing access to the underlying member. When the `flag` is set to `true`, it allows reflected objects to suppress Java language access checking when it is used.

- `isAccessible()`: This method returns the current accessibility status of the reflected object.

Access to private, protected, and package-private members is regulated through these methods, providing a controlled means of manipulating them.

```
// Example to demonstrate setting accessibility
Field field = SomeClass.class.getDeclaredField("privateField");
field.setAccessible(true); // Enabling access to the private field
Object fieldValue = field.get(someObject); // Accessing field value
```

```
Output:
The value of privateField.
```

It is essential to consider the implications of setting `AccessibleObject`'s accessibility. Modifying the accessibility of class members can lead to security risks and expose sensitive data that are normally protected by encapsulation in object-oriented design principles. Therefore, the use of `setAccessible(true)` should be judiciously considered and tightly managed within the confines of organizational security guidelines.

The Reflection API, through 'AccessibleObject', also interacts significantly with Java's security manager and runtime permissions. A security manager can restrict reflection operations, and runtime permissions enable the policy configuration to manage access at a granular level, including reflecting on private components.

```
1  // Sample code to check if access is allowed by the SecurityManager
2  try {
3     Field sensitiveField = SecretData.class.getDeclaredField("secret");
4     sensitiveField.setAccessible(true);
5  } catch (SecurityException se) {
6     System.out.println("Access denied by security manager");
7  }
```

```
Output:
Access denied by security manager
```

Through these mechanisms, Java provides a robust structure to manage the trade-offs between accessibility for legitimate use cases and protecting application integrity from unintended or malicious actions. Employing reflection and particularly modifiers like 'setAccessible' requires a profound understanding of both security implications and design trade-offs. This ensures the harnessing of reflection capabilities without compromising the principles of secure and maintainable software design.

1.8 Reflection and Its Impact on Performance

The use of Java Reflection introduces various performance considerations that must be thoughtfully evaluated when developing applications. This section delves into how reflection impacts performance, quantifies the extent of this impact, and suggests best practices to mitigate performance degradation.

Reflection operations are inherently slower than direct Java method calls due to the additional processing involved in dynamically resolving types, accessing fields, and invoking methods. This overhead

1.8. REFLECTION AND ITS IMPACT ON PERFORMANCE

can significantly affect application performance, particularly in time-critical systems.

Performance Overhead Analysis

To understand the performance implications, it's essential to measure the computational cost associated with common reflection tasks versus traditional non-reflective Java operations. The primary areas of concern include:

- Class and field introspection

- Dynamic method invocation

- Constructor invocation via reflection

Class and Field Introspection

Accessing class metadata (e.g., class fields, methods, annotations) at runtime incurs overhead due to the parsing and data structure manipulation necessary to retrieve reflective data. The following pseudocode, implemented within the `algorithm` and `algorithm2e` packages, demonstrates reading field values using reflection.

Input : A Java class `clazz` and field name `fieldName`
Output: The value of the field

1 **begin**
2 $\quad field \leftarrow clazz.getField(fieldName);$
3 $\quad field.setAccessible(true);$
4 $\quad value \leftarrow field.get(instanceOfClazz);$
5 $\quad$ **return** $value;$

Despite the utility provided by such functionality, the need to modify the field's accessibility flag and the reflection call to retrieve the field value adds noticeable computational cost compared to direct field access.

Dynamic Method Invocation and Constructor Invocation

Invoking methods and constructors dynamically through reflection is significantly slower than direct calls. The primary reason for this slowdown is the need to resolve method or constructor signature overhead at runtime. Here is a typical example of method invocation using reflection:

```
Method method = clazz.getDeclaredMethod("methodName", parameterTypes);
method.setAccessible(true);
Object returnValue = method.invoke(instanceOfClazz, methodArgs);
```

Similarly, creating new instances of a class using reflective constructors involves additional verification and resolution processes that degrade performance:

```
Constructor constructor = clazz.getDeclaredConstructor(constructorParameters);
constructor.setAccessible(true);
Object newInstance = constructor.newInstance(initArgs);
```

Performance Mitigation Strategies

To alleviate the performance drawbacks of reflection, consider the following strategies:

- Limit the use of reflection to areas where it is essential, such as dynamic operation need or framework development.

- Cache reflective data such as `Method`, `Field`, and `Constructor` objects whenever possible to avoid repeated resolution costs.

- Consider alternative approaches like Method Handles (introduced in Java 7) which offer better performance compared to reflection in some scenarios.

Reflective operations, although powerful, should be used judiciously within performance-sensitive applications. By understanding and mitigating the performance overheads associated with reflection, developers can effectively balance functionality and efficiency.

1.9 Security Concerns with Reflection

Reflection, by its nature, allows Java programs to perform operations that would otherwise be restricted by the Java language's access controls. While this provides significant flexibility, it also introduces several security concerns that developers must be mindful of when employing this technology. This section will delve into these concerns, outlining potential risks and proposing strategies to mitigate them.

Bypassing Access Controls

One of the primary security concerns with Java Reflection is its ability to bypass access controls. Reflection makes it possible for developers to access and modify private and protected fields, methods, and constructors of classes.

```java
import java.lang.reflect.Field;

public class AccessBypassExample {
    private String secret = "Initially private data";

    public static void main(String[] args) throws NoSuchFieldException,
            IllegalAccessException {
        AccessBypassExample example = new AccessBypassExample();
        Field secretField = AccessBypassExample.class.getDeclaredField("secret");
        secretField.setAccessible(true);
        secretField.set(example, "Modified private data");
        System.out.println("Secret: " + example.secret);
    }
}
```

```
Secret: Modified private data
```

In the above example, reflection was used to modify a private field, which would be prohibited under normal circumstances, illustrating how reflection can be used to subvert the encapsulation principles of object-oriented programming (OOP).

Reflective Attacks

Reflective attacks are a significant threat wherein an attacker utilizes reflection to execute arbitrary code or alter the application's behavior. This can be particularly damaging if external input influences the reflection logic, potentially leading to unanticipated actions or data exposure.

To illustrate, consider if the field name in the previous example were provided by user input:

```
1  // Hypothetical scenario where field name is taken from user input
2  String userInput = getUserInput();
3  Field field = obj.getClass().getDeclaredField(userInput);
4  field.setAccessible(true);
```

If an attacker were able to influence userInput, they might access or manipulate any field within the class, leading to severe security breaches.

Denial of Service (DoS)

Reflection operations are computationally expensive. Excessive or inefficient use of reflection, especially within critical sections of code, can degrade system performance, making applications vulnerable to Denial of Service (DoS) attacks.

To prevent such scenarios, developers need to limit the use of reflection in performance-critical areas and ensure that any use of reflection does not introduce bottlenecks.

Mitigation Strategies

To mitigate the security risks associated with Java Reflection, several strategies can be adopted:

- Limit reflection usage: Restrict the use of reflection to necessary cases, and avoid using it for tasks that can be accomplished by safer means.

- Validate inputs: Always validate any input that could influence reflectively executed logic to prevent injection attacks.

- Use Security Managers: Utilizing Java's Security Manager can help limit the capabilities of reflective operations and prevent unauthorized access or modification.

- Principle of least privilege: Run applications with the minimal permissions necessary, reducing the potential impact of any reflective access control bypasses.

1.9. SECURITY CONCERNS WITH REFLECTION

These strategies help in reducing the vulnerabilities and ensuring that the use of reflection does not compromise the security and integrity of Java applications.

Security considerations are paramount when utilizing Java Reflection due to its powerful and potentially dangerous capabilities. By understanding the associated risks and taking appropriate precautions, developers can utilize reflection effectively while maintaining the security posture of their applications.

Chapter 2

Exploring Class Objects and the java.lang.Class

This chapter delves into the intricacies of the 'java.lang.Class' class and its pivotal role in Java Reflection, providing a comprehensive analysis of class object retrieval and manipulation. It addresses how to extract metadata such as class modifiers, superclasses, implemented interfaces, and package information, which are essential for dynamic type inquiry and manipulation. The discussion extends to understanding and dealing with different class types, including enums, arrays, and primitive types, thereby equipping readers with the knowledge to fully harness the capabilities of reflection in managing Java classes dynamically.

2.1 Overview of java.lang.Class

The java.lang.Class class serves as the fundamental building block in the Java Reflection API, offering the ability to interact with the metadata of loaded classes at runtime. This class is final, meaning that it cannot be subclassed, and it does not provide a public constructor, emphasizing its integral role in the Java virtual machine. Instances of this class represent classes and interfaces in a running Java application.

Key Characteristics of java.lang.Class

The Class object holds essential information about the type it represents, including its modifiers (such as public, abstract, final), package information, superclass, implemented interfaces, and member declarations (fields, methods, and constructors). Several methods provided by java.lang.Class enable these interactions:

- getName() returns the binary name of the class.

- getModifiers() provides the class's modifiers, which can then be interpreted using java.lang.reflect.Modifier.

- getPackage() returns the package to which the class belongs.

- getSuperclass() retrieves the superclass of the class, if any.

- getInterfaces() returns an array of interfaces that the class directly implements.

- getFields(), getMethods(), and getConstructors() return arrays representing the public members of the class.

Reflection and Type Inquiry

Reflection encompasses mechanisms by which a Java program can observe and modify its own structure and behavior. One of its core functionalities is achieved through class introspection: examining the properties of classes at runtime without knowing their names at compile time. java.lang.Class acts as a gateway for accessing these properties, enabling dynamic behavior modification and interaction typically not feasible in statically typed languages like Java.

Dynamic Application Use Cases

Dynamic application scenarios where java.lang.Class finds noteworthy utilization include:

- **Framework Development:** Frameworks like Spring and Hibernate use reflection to manage and manipulate application components dynamically based on configuration files or annotations.

- **Unit Testing Tools:** Tools such as JUnit utilize reflection to instantiate test objects, invoke methods, and analyze annotations for test configurations.

- **Plugin Architectures:** Applications that support plugins can use reflection to load, instantiate, and integrate new functional components at runtime, enhancing extensibility.

Programmatic Access and Usage

Accessing a `Class` object is typically the first step in employing Java Reflection. This can be achieved in several ways, each suitable for different scenarios:

- Direct reference via `.class` literal, such as `String.class`.

- Via the `getClass()` method on an instance of the object.

- Using the `Class.forName()` method with the class name, useful for configurable or externalized class loading.

These methodologies underscore the flexibility and power of the Java Reflection API and specifically, the capabilities of `java.lang.Class` in supporting dynamic Java applications.

Given the constructed centrality of the `java.lang.Class` in the Java Reflection API, it becomes indispensable for developers aiming to wield introspection for robust and flexible software design. Each method and functionality provided through this class enhances the developer's capability to interact with the application's runtime environment effectively, further bridging the gap between static and dynamic application behavior.

2.2 Retrieving Class Objects

Retrieving class objects is a fundamental step in utilising Java Reflection, as it set the stage for further inspection and manipulation of classes at runtime. This section covers various methods through which class objects can be obtained and the nuances associated with each approach.

Using the `Object.getClass()` Method

When an instance of an object is available, the simplest method to retrieve the corresponding class object is to invoke the `getClass()` method inherited from the `java.lang.Object` class. Here is an example of how this is done:

```
1  String example = "example";
2  Class<?> clazz = example.getClass();
```

The code output reflects the class retrieved:

```
class java.lang.String
```

The usage of `getClass()` is straightforward, but it requires the presence of an instantiated object which can be impractical in scenarios where instantiating a new object is resource-intensive or otherwise undesirable.

Using the `.class` Syntax

For every type in Java, there exists a corresponding class object accessible through the type name followed by `.class`. This method does not require an object instance and can be used to obtain class objects for primitive types, interfaces, and array classes as well:

```
1  Class<?> stringClass = String.class;
2  Class<?> intClass = int.class;
3  Class<?> serializableClass = java.io.Serializable.class;
```

Demonstrating retrieval without instantiation:

```
class java.lang.String
int
interface java.io.Serializable
```

This method is highly effective for static contexts where the class is known at compile-time.

Using the `Class.forName()` Method

For scenarios where the class name is dynamically determined at runtime, the `Class.forName()` method provides a powerful option. This method requires the fully qualified name of the class as a string parameter and throws a `ClassNotFoundException` if the class cannot be located:

2.3. INSPECTING CLASS MODIFIERS AND TYPES

```
try {
    Class<?> dynamicClass = Class.forName("java.util.HashMap");
} catch (ClassNotFoundException e) {
    e.printStackTrace();
}
```

The potential for exception handling makes `Class.forName()` suitable for incorporating conditional logic based on class availability, offering a high degree of flexibility in dynamic environments.

Special Considerations for Loader and Initialization

Using `Class.forName()` with a second boolean parameter can control whether the class is initialized upon loading (true) or not (false), and an additional `ClassLoader` parameter can dictate the class loader used. These additional parameters afford significant control over the class loading and initialization process:

```
Class<?> dynamicClassInitFalse = Class.forName("java.util.HashMap", false, this.
    getClass().getClassLoader());
```

Keeping the class uninitialized can be advantageous when managing classes with costly initialization processes or when addressing specific class loader policies.

The ability to retrieve class objects robustly and appropriately is crucial in leveraging the full power of Java Reflection. Each method discussed in this section offers distinct advantages and is suited to particular scenarios. Whether through direct instance methods like `Object.getClass()`, compile-time safe `.class` literals, or flexible runtime retrievals with `Class.forName()`, developers are equipped with a suite of tools for effective class manipulation, paving the way for advanced Java applications and utilities. The selection of the appropriate retrieval method depends heavily on the context of the application and specific requirements at hand, enhancing both utility and performance in Java reflection tasks.

2.3 Inspecting Class Modifiers and Types

To effectively utilize Java Reflection with the `java.lang.Class`, understanding how to inspect class modifiers and different class types is pivotal. This section details the systematic approach to querying class modifiers and types, which are essential in managing Java objects dynamically and securely.

Inspecting Class Modifiers

Java provides various modifiers, such as `public`, `private`, `protected`, `abstract`, `static`, `final`, and more, which determine how a class or its members are accessed and utilized. The `java.lang.Class` includes methods to inspect these modifiers, primarily through the `getModifiers()` method, which returns an integer encoded with the modifier information. This integer can be deciphered using methods in `java.lang.reflect.Modifier`.

```
import java.lang.reflect.Modifier;
import java.lang.Class;

public class ModifierInspector {
    public static void inspectClassModifiers(Class<?> clazz) {
        int modifiers = clazz.getModifiers();
        System.out.println("Modifiers: " + Modifier.toString(modifiers));
    }
}
```

Upon execution, for a sample class declared as `public final class Sample {}`, the output would be:

```
Modifiers: public final
```

The above code snippet highlights the ease with which the modifiers of any class can be retrieved and translated into a readable format.

Identifying Different Class Types

Beyond conventional class types, Java supports various other types like interfaces, annotations, enums, arrays, and primitive data types. Each type has different handling and operational semantics in Java Reflection.

To determine the type of a `Class` object, `java.lang.Class` provides several methods:

- `isInterface()` - Returns true if the class is an interface.

- `isAnnotation()` - Indicates if the class is an annotation type.

- `isEnum()` - Determines if the class represents an enum type.

- `isArray()` - Confirms if it represents an array.

- `isPrimitive()` - Returns true if it represents a primitive type.

```
public class TypeChecker {
    public static void checkClassType(Class<?> clazz) {
        if (clazz.isInterface()) {
            System.out.println(clazz.getName() + " is an interface.");
        } else if (clazz.isAnnotation()) {
            System.out.println(clazz.getName() + " is an annotation.");
        } else if (clazz.isEnum()) {
            System.out.println(clazz.getName() + " is an enum.");
        } else if (clazz.isArray()) {
            System.out.println(clazz.getName() + " is an array.");
        } else if (clazz.isPrimitive()) {
            System.out.println(clazz.getName() + " is a primitive type.");
        } else {
            System.out.println(clazz.getName() + " is a class.");
        }
    }
}
```

Applying this method to different types will generate outputs identifying its nature accurately, ensuring that developers handle each type adequately based on its unique properties.

This meticulous approach to inspecting class modifiers and types using Java Reflection empowers developers to write more dynamic, robust, and secure Java applications. Through the capabilities of the java.lang.Class class, one can perform extensive type-checking and access control, which are crucial for any reflective operations in Java programming practices.

2.4 Exploring Interfaces Implemented by a Class

The ability to inspect the interfaces that a class implements is a foundational aspect of Java Reflection, providing a mechanism to dynamically analyze an object's capabilities. This section outlines how to retrieve this information using the java.lang.Class API and discusses the practical implications of this capability.

When programming in Java, interfaces define a contract that a class agrees to follow, thus enabling a form of polymorphism. By using reflection to inspect these interfaces, developers can write more flexible and adaptable code. Here, we examine the appropriate methods to discover and investigate the interfaces a class conforms to at runtime.

First, the method getInterfaces() in the java.lang.Class class must be highlighted:

```
public Class<?>[] getInterfaces()
```

This method returns an array of Class objects that represent all the interfaces implemented by the class being inspected. The returned interfaces are those directly implemented by the class and do not include interfaces that are indirectly implemented through parent classes or superinterfaces.

An example of utilizing this method is provided in the following code snippet:

```
public static void displayInterfaces(Class<?> cls) {
    Class<?>[] interfaces = cls.getInterfaces();
    for (Class<?> interfaceCls : interfaces) {
        System.out.println(interfaceCls.getName());
    }
}
```

Upon execution, the displayInterfaces() method prints out the names of all interfaces directly implemented by the given class.

Output:
java.io.Serializable
java.lang.Cloneable

For classes that do not directly implement an interface, this method would return an empty array. Therefore, it is crucial to use this method in conjunction with other reflection methods to fully understand the interface hierarchy.

Furthermore, consider a scenario involving inherited interfaces. While getInterfaces() does not return inherited interfaces, the recursive exploration of superclass interfaces is necessary. Here is how this can be achieved programmatically:

```
public static void displayAllInterfaces(Class<?> cls) {
    HashSet<Class<?>> interfacesFound = new HashSet<>();
    while (cls != null) {
        Class<?>[] interfaces = cls.getInterfaces();
        for (Class<?> interfaceCls : interfaces) {
            if (interfacesFound.add(interfaceCls)) {
                System.out.println(interfaceCls.getName());
                displayAllInterfaces(interfaceCls);
            }
        }
        cls = cls.getSuperclass();
    }
}
```

The code above introduces a method for displaying all interfaces, both direct and indirect, of a class. By recursing through the parent classes and interfaces, it expands the inspection to the comprehensive set of interfaces a class adheres to.

Analyzing how a class interacts with its implemented interfaces provides insights into object behaviors, forms an understanding of its design, and aids in developing dynamic applications. By using the Java Reflection API to explore the interfaces a class implements, developers can adapt their applications to different object types at runtime, hence offering substantial flexibility in Java programming.

2.5 Understanding Superclasses and Hierarchy

The concept of superclasses and hierarchy within Java's object-oriented structure allows for the inheritance and extension of classes. This section outlines methods for utilizing the java.lang.Class class to introspect superclass relationships and class hierarchies dynamically.

Retrieving the Superclass

Every class, except the root class Object, has a superclass. To determine the superclass of a class at runtime, java.lang.Class provides the method getSuperclass(). This method returns a Class object that represents the superclass of the class in which it is invoked.

```
public class Example {
    private static class InnerClass extends HashMap {
    }

    public static void main(String[] args) {
        Class<?> clazz = InnerClass.class;
        Class<?> superclass = clazz.getSuperclass();
        System.out.println("Superclass: " + superclass.getName());
    }
}
```

Superclass: java.util.HashMap

This code snippet defines an inner class InnerClass, which extends java.util.HashMap. It then uses getSuperclass() to print the name of its superclass, demonstrating the utility of reflection for superclass retrieval.

Examining the Class Hierarchy

Understanding the complete class hierarchy of a type involves traversing through its superclasses until the Object class is reached. This can be achieved by recursively calling getSuperclass() until it returns null, which indicates that the superclass chain has ended.

```
public static void printHierarchy(Class<?> initialClass) {
    Class<?> currentClass = initialClass;
    while (currentClass != null) {
        System.out.println(currentClass.getName());
        currentClass = currentClass.getSuperclass();
    }
}

public static void main(String[] args) {
    Class<?> clazz = LinkedList.class;
    printHierarchy(clazz);
}
```

```
java.util.LinkedList
java.util.AbstractSequentialList
java.util.AbstractList
java.util.AbstractCollection
java.lang.Object
```

The example demonstrates printing the class hierarchy of java.util.LinkedList. It iterates through each superclass until the root of the hierarchy (i.e., java.lang.Object) is reached.

Exploring Inheritance Relations

To further enhance our understanding of class hierarchies, it's beneficial to inspect whether a given class is a subclass of another. This can be done using isAssignableFrom(Class<?> cls) method, which determines if the class or interface represented by its calling Class object is either the same as, or a superclass or superinterface of, the class or interface represented by the specified Class parameter.

```
public static void main(String[] args) {
    boolean isSuper = Throwable.class.isAssignableFrom(IOException.class);
    System.out.println("IOException is a subclass of Throwable: " + isSuper);
}
```

```
IOException is a subclass of Throwable: true
```

This code checks if Throwable is a superclass of IOException and confirms their relationship using isAssignableFrom().

Through the mechanisms discussed in this section, users can effectively navigate, analyze, and understand Java's complex class hierarchies.

The ability to dynamically explore these relationships is a powerful advantage of Java Reflection, greatly enhancing adaptability and insight into application architectures.

2.6 Extracting Package Information from Class Objects

Understanding how to extract package information from class objects is a vital skill in Java programming, particularly when using reflection techniques. This section focuses on methods provided by the java.lang.Class class to retrieve package data. This kind of information is essential, especially when managing large applications, to ensure proper component organization and maintain clarity in software modules.

The java.lang.Class offers a method named getPackage() which facilitates the retrieval of the package information of the class. The Package object obtained represents the package to which the class is bundled. Here, we describe how to employ this method and manipulate the resulting Package object to extract detailed package attributes.

```
1  // Obtain a class object from the Class
2  Class<?> cls = MyClass.class;
3
4  // Fetching the package information using getPackage()
5  Package pkg = cls.getPackage();
```

Once a Package object is procured, various methods can be used to gather different pieces of information:

- getName() - Returns the name of the package. This is useful for understanding the structural organization within the application.

- getSpecificationTitle() - Provides the title of the specification that this package relates to.

- getSpecificationVersion() - Retrieves the version number of the specification that the package implements.

- getSpecificationVendor() - Returns the vendor of the specification that the package relates to.

- getImplementationTitle() - Provides the title for the implementation of the package.

- `getImplementationVersion()` - Retrieves the version of the package's implementation.

- `getImplementationVendor()` - Returns the vendor for the implementation of the package.

- `isSealed()` - Checks whether the package is sealed or not, according to the manifest attributes.

To demonstrate, the subsequent code outputs various attributes of the package to which our class belongs:

```
// Obtaining class package attributes
System.out.println("Package name: " + pkg.getName());
System.out.println("Specification Title: " + pkg.getSpecificationTitle());
System.out.println("Specification Version: " + pkg.getSpecificationVersion());
System.out.println("Specification Vendor: " + pkg.getSpecificationVendor());
System.out.println("Implementation Title: " + pkg.getImplementationTitle());
System.out.println("Implementation Version: " + pkg.getImplementationVersion());
System.out.println("Implementation Vendor: " + pkg.getImplementationVendor());
System.out.println("Is Sealed: " + pkg.isSealed());
```

```
Package name: com.example.MyPackage
Specification Title: Example Specification
Specification Version: 1.0
Specification Vendor: Example Vendor
Implementation Title: Example Implementation
Implementation Version: 2.1
Implementation Vendor: Another Vendor
Is Sealed: false
```

Successfully extracting and analyzing package information can provide deeper insight into the runtime behavior of applications, influence versioning strategies, and offer valuable data for programmatically managing packages. This capability forms a fundamental component of dynamic application management and enhances maintainability and scalability.

2.7 Analyzing Enum Types with Reflection

Exploring enum types using Java Reflection is an essential aspect of understanding dynamic behavior in Java applications. Enum types in Java are special kinds of classes that restrict a variable to having one of only a few predefined values. Through reflection, these types can be analyzed in ways that enable dynamic and flexible code design. This section will cover methodologies for retrieving enum constants, understanding their properties, and manipulating them at runtime.

2.7. ANALYZING ENUM TYPES WITH REFLECTION

Retrieving Enum Constants

Enum constants can be retrieved through the `java.lang.Class` class using reflection. To do this, the `getEnumConstants()` method is invoked on the class object representing the enum. This method returns an array of `Object`, where each object can be cast to the specific enum type. The following code snippet illustrates how to retrieve and display enum constants:

```java
public enum Status {
    ACTIVE, INACTIVE, DELETED;
}

public static void displayEnumConstants(Class<?> enumClass) {
    Object[] enumConstants = enumClass.getEnumConstants();
    for (Object enumConstant : enumConstants) {
        System.out.println(enumConstant.toString());
    }
}

public static void main(String[] args) {
    displayEnumConstants(Status.class);
}
```

```
ACTIVE
INACTIVE
DELETED
```

Inspecting Properties of Enums

In addition to retrieving the constants, reflection can be used to inspect the properties of the enums such as their names and ordinal values. The `java.lang.Enum` class provides the `name()` and `ordinal()` methods which can be invoked using reflection to get the name and position of each enum constant.

```java
public static void inspectEnumProperties(Enum<?> anyEnum) {
    System.out.println("Name: " + anyEnum.name());
    System.out.println("Ordinal: " + anyEnum.ordinal());
}

public static void main(String[] args) {
    inspectEnumProperties(Status.ACTIVE);
}
```

```
Name: ACTIVE
Ordinal: 0
```

As shown, the `name()` method returns the exact name used to declare the enum constant, and `ordinal()` provides its position as defined in the enum declaration.

Discovering Enum-specific Methods

Using reflection, one can also determine if specific methods are declared within an enum. Enum types often include methods to provide functionality beyond just enumeration of predefined constants. For example, one might define a method in an enum to determine if a particular status is considered active. The ability to dynamically check for such user-defined methods can greatly enhance the flexibility of an application:

```
public enum Status {
    ACTIVE, INACTIVE, DELETED;

    public boolean isActive() {
        return this == ACTIVE;
    }
}

public static void discoverEnumMethods(Class<?> enumClass) {
    Method[] methods = enumClass.getDeclaredMethods();
    for (Method method : methods) {
        if (Modifier.isPublic(method.getModifiers())) {
            System.out.println("Method: " + method.getName());
        }
    }
}

public static void main(String[] args) {
    discoverEnumMethods(Status.class);
}
```

Method: isActive

This capability is particularly powerful in environments where the code might evolve over time, allowing older components to interact seamlessly with newly introduced methods and features in enums.

Reflection provides a powerful toolkit for analyzing and manipulating enum types in Java, enhancing the ability to build robust and adaptable systems. By employing techniques such as those demonstrated, developers can effectively utilize Java's reflective capabilities to understand and harness the full potential of enum types in their applications. The insights gained from such analysis can be instrumental in creating dynamic behavior that adapts to varied requirements and conditions in software implementation.

2.8 Dealing with Array Class Objects

Introduction to Array Classes in Reflection Array classes in Java reflection present a unique challenge due to their dynamic nature. Unlike typical classes, array classes are not explicitly declared but are instead created by the Java Virtual Machine (JVM) when needed. This section explores the mechanisms provided by the 'java.lang.Class' API to interact with and manage array class objects using Java Reflection.

Retrieving Array Class Objects To retrieve the class object of an array, one can utilize the array instance itself or by specifying the type through language constructs. Here's an example using an integer array:

```
int[] sampleArray = new int[10];
Class<?> arrayClass = sampleArray.getClass();
System.out.println("Class Name: " + arrayClass.getName());
```

```
Class Name: [I
```

In the output '[I', the '[' character indicates that the class is an array, while 'I' signifies that the component type of the array is an integer. The method `getClass()` is inherited from the `Object` class, which all arrays inherit as they are considered objects in Java.

Inspecting Array Types Upon obtaining an array's class object, one can inspect its type using methods such as `getComponentType()`. This method is pivotal for understanding the type of elements stored in the array, as demonstrated below:

```
if (arrayClass.isArray()) {
    Class<?> componentType = arrayClass.getComponentType();
    System.out.println("Component Type: " + componentType.getName());
}
```

```
Component Type: int
```

Manipulating Array Instances Array instances reflectively, particularly creating instances dynamically, involves using `java.lang.reflect.Array`. Here's how you can create a new instance of an array dynamically:

```
int arrayLength = 5;
Class<?> componentType = int.class;
Object newArray = java.lang.reflect.Array.newInstance(componentType, arrayLength);
```

```
4  System.out.println("Array Class: " + newArray.getClass().getName());
5  System.out.println("Array Length: " + java.lang.reflect.Array.getLength(newArray));
```

```
Array Class: [I
Array Length: 5
```

This code snippet dynamically creates an array of integers with a length of 5. The method newInstance() from the java.lang.reflect.Array class is utilized, requiring the component type and the desired length of the array.

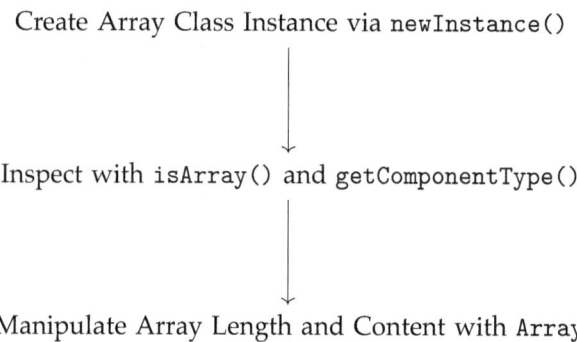

Reflections on Array Class Objects Working with array classes in Java using reflection requires understanding the dynamic creation and manipulation of these objects. The JVM's handling of array classes as objects that can be instantiated and managed at runtime proves powerful in applications requiring dynamic data structures. The methods and functionalities discussed facilitate comprehensive management of array class objects, crucial for developing robust and flexible Java applications.

2.9 Distinguishing Primitive, Synthetic, and Annotation Types

Understanding the distinction between primitive, synthetic, and annotation types in Java is crucial for effective use of reflection, particularly when manipulating classes dynamically at runtime. This section explores how to identify and handle these different types using the java.lang.Class API.

Primitive Types

Java's primitive types include int, float, boolean, char, byte, short, long, and double. These types are not associated with classes in the traditional sense but are instead special data types that are treated specially by the Java virtual machine and the Java language. However, each primitive type has a corresponding "wrapper class" in the java.lang package which encapsulates the primitive type as an object.

To determine whether a Class object represents a primitive type, the isPrimitive() method is used. Here is an example illustrating this:

```
public static void printPrimitiveInfo(Class<?> clazz) {
    System.out.println("Class: " + clazz.getName() +
        " is primitive: " + clazz.isPrimitive());
}
```

One might use this method like so:

```
printPrimitiveInfo(int.class);
```

Output for the above would be:

```
Class: int is primitive: true
```

Handling primitive types effectively is essential particularly when dealing with low-level operations or optimizing performance-critical applications.

Synthetic Types

A synthetic class or interface in Java is one that is not defined by the user but instead generated by the compiler, typically as an artifact of some of the more complex language features such as inner classes, lambdas, or other constructs like enums.

To identify synthetic classes, the isSynthetic() method of the Class class is utilized. The following code demonstrates checking if a class is synthetic:

```
public static void printSyntheticInfo(Class<?> clazz) {
    System.out.println("Class: " + clazz.getName() +
        " is synthetic: " + clazz.isSynthetic());
}
```

Usage of the method:

```
printSyntheticInfo(SomeClass.class);
```

For a compiler-generated class, this might output:

```
Class: SomeClass$1 is synthetic: true
```

Understanding synthetic types is crucial in debugging and when working with automatically generated classes which may not be visible or documented as part of the API.

Annotation Types

Annotation types are a form of metadata in Java, providing data about a program but not part of the program itself. Introduced in Java 5, annotations allow developers to embed additional information into their code, which can then be processed at compile time or runtime.

To check if a `Class` object is an annotation, the `isAnnotation()` method is used. Here's how it can be employed:

```
1  public static void printAnnotationInfo(Class<?> clazz) {
2      System.out.println("Class: " + clazz.getName() +
3          " is annotation: " + clazz.isAnnotation());
4  }
```

Example usage:

```
printAnnotationInfo(Override.class);
```

This would yield:

```
Class: java.lang.Override is annotation: true
```

Annotations play a significant role in modern Java applications, especially in frameworks and libraries where they contribute to reducing boilerplate code and increasing system modularity and configurability.

By utilizing methods such as `isPrimitive()`, `isSynthetic()`, and `isAnnotation()`, developers gain the ability to programmatically differentiate and handle these special types effectively within their Java applications. Transitioning to such dynamic type handling enhances the adaptability and robustness of application architectures, making ample use of Java's reflective capabilities.

2.10 Using Reflection to Check for Anonymous and Local Classes

Java Reflection provides powerful tools for inspecting and manipulating classes at runtime. One of the unique capabilities enabled by reflection is the ability to identify the nature of classes, particularly determining whether a class is anonymous or local. This section focuses on methodologies and practical examples to harness the Java Reflection API for this purpose.

Identifying Anonymous Classes

Anonymous classes are defined without a name and are declared and instantiated in a single expression at the point of use. They are often used to provide a quick and short implementation of methods required by an interface or abstract class. The Java Reflection API offers a straightforward mechanism to check if a class is anonymous.

Consider the following Java code snippet where an anonymous class is created extending `java.util.HashMap`:

```
HashMap<String, String> map = new HashMap<>() {
    // Here, we might override or add methods
};
```

To determine if an object of this class (map) is anonymous, we can employ the `Class`'s `isAnonymousClass` method:

```
boolean isAnonymous = map.getClass().isAnonymousClass();
```

The variable `isAnonymous` will hold `true` as the class of the `map` object is indeed an anonymous class.

Detecting Local Classes

A local class is defined in the scope of a block, which can be within a method, a constructor, or an initializer block. These types of classes have scopes confined to the block in which they are defined. Using reflection to check for local classes again involves the `isLocalClass()` method provided by the `Class` object.

For example, let us define a local class within a method:

```
public void someMethod() {
    class LocalExample {
        public void print() {
            System.out.println("Inside LocalExample class.");
        }
    }
    LocalExample localExample = new LocalExample();
    localExample.print();
}
```

To check if this `LocalExample` class is local:

```
boolean isLocal = LocalExample.class.isLocalClass();
```

The result stored in `isLocal` will be `true`, indicating that `LocalExample` is a local class.

Practical Considerations

When using reflection to inspect unknown objects dynamically, understanding whether a class is anonymous or local might provide insights into how these classes were intended to be used, help in debugging or dynamically altering behavior. Here are some aspects and practical considerations:

- **Documentation and Maintainability:** Anonymous and local classes are typically used for quick tasks and are not usually meant for use outside their immediate context. Using reflection to identify such classes can help in documenting the use cases where these classes break the common modular approach for extensibility or testing.

- **Performance Implications:** Employing reflection incurs a performance penalty, so its use should be balanced against its utility. The decision to inspect classes dynamically should be considered carefully, particularly in performance-sensitive applications.

- **Security and Accessibility:** Reflection can bypass normal access checks unless security managers restrict it, thus raising potential security concerns. This capability might be exploited for accessing classes that are usually not accessible, calling for judicious use and secure handling.

Through these methods and considerations, Java developers can leverage the strength of reflection to handle and manipulate anonymous and local classes effectively, enriching the applications' dynamic behavior and introspection capabilities.

2.11 Obtaining Class Enclosures and Declarations

Exploring the capabilities of Java Reflection extends to encompass obtaining detailed information about class enclosures and declarations. This section focuses on how to use the 'java.lang.Class' API to acquire and analyze these aspects of classes, which are particularly relevant in nested, inner, and anonymous class scenarios. We will delve into methods provided by the reflection API to interact with these complex class structures.

Retrieving Enclosing Classes and Constructors

To determine the enclosing class of a given class object, Java Reflection provides the method getEnclosingClass(). This method returns a Class object representing the class that encloses the class in question. If the class is not enclosed by another class (in other words, if it's a top-level class), this method returns null.

```
1  Class< ?> enclosingClass = OuterClass.InnerClass.class.getEnclosingClass();
2  System.out.println(enclosingClass.getName());
```

```
OuterClass
```

For inner classes declared within the body of a method or constructor, there are additional methods such as getEnclosingMethod() and getEnclosingConstructor(), depending on where the class is defined.

```
1  Class< ?> innerClass = someMethodLocalClassObject.getClass();
2  Method enclosingMethod = innerClass.getEnclosingMethod();
3  Constructor<?> enclosingConstructor = innerClass.getEnclosingConstructor();
```

It is crucial to note that only one of getEnclosingMethod() or getEnclosingConstructor() will return a non-null value, depending on the immediate enclosures of the class. If the class is not local to a method or constructor, both methods return null.

Working with Declarations

In addition to understanding the enclosures, the Reflection API aids in retrieving the declarations within a class. Such declarations include constructors, methods, and fields. Using methods like getDeclaredConstructors(), getDeclaredMethods(), and getDeclaredFields(), one can acquire an array of Constructor, Method, and Field objects that represent all declared members of the class, respectively, regardless of their accessibility.

```
Constructor<?>[] constructors = SomeClass.class.getDeclaredConstructors();
Method[] methods = SomeClass.class.getDeclaredMethods();
Field[] fields = SomeClass.class.getDeclaredFields();
```

Each of these arrays contains elements that give developers access to respective member details, including their modifiers, parameters, return types, and annotations, which are pivotal for dynamic class manipulation and analysis.

Analysing Nested and Inner Classes

Lastly, to programmatically explore nested and inner class structures, the method getDeclaredClasses() proves invaluable. This method returns an array of Class objects that reflect all classes and interfaces declared as members of the class which the Class object represents.

```
Class<?>[] declaredClasses = OuterClass.class.getDeclaredClasses();
for(Class<?> nestedClass : declaredClasses){
   System.out.println("Declared class: " + nestedClass.getName());
}
```

These utilities provided by the Java Reflection API are essential tools for dynamic analysis and manipulation of Java classes, enabling deep introspection into class structures and behaviors not typically available during runtime. By thoroughly understanding these capabilities, developers can harness Reflection to write more flexible and adaptable code that can interact with complex class hierarchies effectively.

2.12 Summary and Practical Tips for java.lang.Class

This section aims to consolidate the knowledge acquired in previous sections and provide actionable tips for effectively employing the java.lang.Class in Java Reflection. The exploration of java.lang.Class is critical for dynamic type inquiry and manipulation, pivotal in applications requiring runtime type information for flexible code execution.

Consolidated Summary of Key Points:

- The java.lang.Class serves as the entry point for all reflection operations. It is the programmatic access to the metadata of a class.
- Retrieving class objects can be done through multiple approaches, notably via the .class syntax, Class.forName() method, or by invoking getClass() on an object instance.
- Information such as class modifiers (public, private, static, etc.), superclasses, implemented interfaces, and package data can be gleaned using specific methods provided by the java.lang.Class.
- Special attention is required when handling array classes, primitive types, enums, and synthetic classes, as these have unique properties and behaviors in the reflection API.
- Reflection enables advanced features like checking for anonymous and local classes, inspecting class loaders, and understanding enclosure relationships.

Practical Tips for Using Reflection with java.lang.Class:

- Always consider the performance implications of using reflection, as it can introduce overhead due to its dynamic nature. Use reflection judiciously, particularly in performance-sensitive applications.
- Ensure access permissions when using reflection to interact with private or protected members of a class. Utilize setAccessible(true) when legally overriding access checks, but be cautious of security implications.

- Cache reflected class objects and methods when repeatedly used. Reflection incurs a higher cost at runtime, and caching can mitigate performance penalties.

- Use `java.lang.reflect.Modifier` to inspect access modifiers of classes, methods, and fields dynamically. This can help in ensuring that operations like instantiation, method invocation, or field access respect Java access control semantics.

- Handle `ClassNotFoundException` and `NoSuchMethodException` gracefully when using `Class.forName()` and method retrieval operations. Exception handling is critical to robust reflection-based applications.

- When working with generics, bear in mind that type erasure in Java may affect reflection. For instance, generic type information might not be available at runtime. Utilize `getGenericSuperclass()` or `getGenericInterfaces()` to retrieve detailed type information.

The use of `java.lang.Class` through reflection provides a potent toolset for dynamic Java applications, enabling runtime analysis and manipulation of classes. By adhering to best practices and leveraging the practical tips mentioned, developers can effectively manage the complexity added by reflection, while harnessing its full potential to create flexible and dynamic applications. The careful application of these strategies ensures that code developed using Java Reflection remains efficient, maintainable, and secure.

Chapter 3

Constructors, Methods, and Fields Inspection

This chapter focuses on the inspection and manipulation of constructors, methods, and fields within Java classes using reflection. It covers techniques for retrieving and analyzing these components, including their modifiers, parameters, and annotations. Practical examples demonstrate how to dynamically invoke constructors and methods, and modify field values, regardless of their access level. This exploration enhances the ability to design flexible software that can adapt to various runtime requirements, providing a deeper understanding of Java's introspective capabilities.

3.1 Retrieving Constructors of a Class

Retrieving constructors from a Java class using reflection is the first step in understanding the dynamic creation and manipulation capabilities available in Java. Reflection allows us to inspect and operate on the class's constructors programmatically, providing powerful tools for dynamic code analysis and execution. This discussion focuses on extracting all constructor-related information from any given class, followed by precise methods and exemplary code snippets.

Introduction to Class Constructors in Reflection

Constructor inspection is facilitated by the java.lang.Class object associated with the class for which constructors are to be retrieved. In Java, every class is described by a Class object, which includes methods to acquire a detailed list of all constructors, irrespective of their accessibility (public, protected, or private).

Obtaining All Constructors

To retrieve all constructors within a class, the method getDeclaredConstructors() is used. This returns an array of java.lang.reflect.Constructor objects that represent all the constructors declared in the class, as shown in the following code snippet:

```
import java.lang.reflect.Constructor;

public class ExampleClass {
    public ExampleClass() {
        // Default constructor
    }

    public ExampleClass(String param1) {
        // Parameterized constructor
    }

    private ExampleClass(int param2) {
        // Private constructor
    }
}

public static void main(String[] args) {
    Class<?> clazz = ExampleClass.class;
    Constructor<?>[] allConstructors = clazz.getDeclaredConstructors();
    for (Constructor<?> constructor : allConstructors) {
        System.out.println("Constructor: " + constructor.toString());
    }
}
```

Output Interpretation

After applying the above code, the output will illustrate all available constructors for the ExampleClass. Here, the use of the toString() method provides a string representation of each constructor, including its modifiers (public, private), parameter types, and other annotations if present:

```
Constructor: public ExampleClass()
Constructor: public ExampleClass(java.lang.String)
Constructor: private ExampleClass(int)
```

Further Filtering and Usage

The retrieved array can be further examined for specific constructors by iterating over it and applying conditionals as needed - perhaps filtering by parameter types or count, visibility (public, private), or annotation presence:

```
for(Constructor<?> constructor : allConstructors) {
    if (constructor.getParameterCount() == 1 &&
        constructor.getParameterTypes()[0] == String.class) {
        System.out.println("Single-parameter constructor for String found.");
    }
}
```

This segment of the code checks each constructor for a single parameter of type String and logs its presence, demonstrating a method to filter and manage constructor metadata programmatically.

Compliance with Security and Access Controls: It is essential to consider security when employing reflective techniques, especially as they can subvert normal access controls. Reflection can access private constructors, thus proper security measures or permissions checks should be implemented in sensitive or secure applications to avoid potential vulnerabilities.

3.2 Understanding Constructor Modifiers and Parameters

Understanding the modifiers and parameters of constructors in Java is essential for utilizing Java Reflection effectively. Modifiers in Java dictate the accessibility of the constructor, which can be crucial when invoking constructors dynamically. Parameters, on the other hand, define the necessary inputs required by constructors and can vary widely between different constructors in a class.

To begin our exploration, let us consider the retrieval of constructor information using Java Reflection. We start by obtaining a Class object, which represents the class whose constructors we are interested in inspecting.

```
Class<?> clazz = Class.forName("java.util.ArrayList");
Constructor<?>[] constructors = clazz.getDeclaredConstructors();
```

This code retrieves all constructors of the java.util.ArrayList class,

CHAPTER 3. CONSTRUCTORS, METHODS, AND FIELDS INSPECTION

storing them in an array of Constructor objects. Next, we examine each constructor to analyze its modifiers and parameter types.

```
for (Constructor<?> constructor : constructors) {
    int modifiers = constructor.getModifiers();
    Class<?>[] parameterTypes = constructor.getParameterTypes();
}
```

Each constructor in the loop has associated modifier and parameter type information. The modifier information is extracted using the getModifiers() method, which returns an integer representing the different Java modifiers applied to the constructor. Parameter types are retrieved as an array of Class objects, representing each parameter accepted by the constructor.

To decipher the numerical modifier into a human-readable format, we employ the Modifier class, which provides static methods to interpret the meanings:

```
String modifierStr = Modifier.toString(modifiers);
System.out.println("Constructor Modifiers: " + modifierStr);
```

This output helps in understanding the accessibility (public, private, etc.) and other attributes (e.g., abstract, static, final) of the constructor.

Next, it is crucial to comprehend the parameters of these constructors as follows:

```
if (parameterTypes.length > 0) {
    System.out.print("Parameter types: ");
    for (Class<?> paramType : parameterTypes) {
        System.out.print(paramType.getName() + " ");
    }
    System.out.println();
} else {
    System.out.println("No parameters.");
}
```

This snippet iterates over the parameter types of each constructor, printing out the type names. It is especially useful for preparing calls to these constructors at runtime, as the exact parameter types must be supplied.

- Understanding accessibility via modifiers helps ensure appropriate use of constructors during dynamic invocation.
- Knowledge of parameter types is instrumental in accurately instantiating objects or in frameworks that rely heavily on reflection, such as serialization libraries or dependency injection con-

tainers.

By diligently examining the modifiers and parameters of constructors, developers gain a deeper insight into class structure and dynamics, empowering them to write more adaptable and robust Java applications.

3.3 Invoking Constructors Dynamically

One of the most powerful features of Java's reflection is the ability to instantiate objects dynamically at runtime. This section elucidates the process of dynamically invoking constructors, focusing on the use of the Constructor class from the java.lang.reflect package.

Obtaining and Preparing Constructor Objects

The initial step in this process involves obtaining an instance of Constructor, which represents a constructor of a specific class. The getConstructor method of the Class object is used for this purpose, which requires a parameter list specifying the types of arguments that the constructor accepts. The example below demonstrates how to retrieve a constructor:

```
Constructor<ExampleClass> constructor = ExampleClass.class.getConstructor(String.
    class, int.class);
```

Following retrieval, it is critical to ensure that the constructor is accessible, especially if you are dealing with non-public classes or constructors. This is managed by invoking setAccessible(true) on the Constructor object, as shown here:

```
constructor.setAccessible(true);
```

Creating Instances Using the Constructor

Once you have a reference to the appropriate Constructor object and have set its accessibility, you can create an instance of the class using newInstance method. This method takes an array of objects that represent the constructor's parameters. Here is how you can dynamically instantiate an object:

```
ExampleClass exampleObject = constructor.newInstance("Example", 123);
```

It is crucial to handle potential exceptions that can be thrown during these operations, including `InstantiationException`, `IllegalAccessException`, `InvocationTargetException`, and `IllegalArgumentException`. These exceptions provide insights into what can go wrong during dynamic construction, such as attempting to instantiate an abstract class or improper argument types.

Reflection on Constructors: Benefits and Pitfalls

Using reflection to invoke constructors dynamically opens many possibilities, such as creating objects in a more generic manner and managing them based on runtime decisions. This capability is particularly beneficial in scenarios where the class to be instantiated is not known at compile-time.

However, this approach comes with its drawbacks. Dynamic constructor invocation is inherently slower than direct constructor calls due to the overhead introduced by reflection. Moreover, excessive use of reflection can lead to code that is hard to understand and maintain. Therefore, it is advised to use reflection judiciously and always consider its impact on performance and maintainability.

The ability to instantiate objects dynamically at runtime is a powerful tool, but it should be used appropriately to enhance, rather than complicate, software development processes.

3.4 Inspecting Methods of a Class

Reflective inspection of methods in Java classes is a powerful capability for dynamic analysis and manipulation of code. This section will elaborate on the process of retrieving and inspecting the methods of a class using Java Reflection.

Retrieving All Methods

To retrieve all the methods of a class, including public, protected, private, and inherited methods, the `getDeclaredMethods()` method of the `Class` class is utilized.

```
1  // Retrieve all methods from the class including private and protected
2  Method[] methods = MyClass.class.getDeclaredMethods();
```

3.4. INSPECTING METHODS OF A CLASS

For only public methods, including those inherited from parent classes, getMethods() is used.

```
1  // Retrieve all public methods, including inherited ones
2  Method[] methods = MyClass.class.getMethods();
```

Inspecting Method Names and Modifiers

Each method can be inspected for its name and modifiers. The getName() and getModifiers() methods in the Method class are applicable here. The Modifier class in the java.lang.reflect package assists in decoding the modifiers.

```
1  for (Method method : methods) {
2    String methodName = method.getName();
3    int modifiers = method.getModifiers();
4    String modifierString = Modifier.toString(modifiers);
5    System.out.println("Method Name: " + methodName + ", Modifiers: " +
         modifierString);
6  }
```

Retrieving Parameter Types

To understand the parameter types that methods accept, the getParameterTypes() method is used. This method returns an array of Class objects that represent the parameter types.

```
1  for (Method method : methods) {
2    Class<?>[] parameterTypes = method.getParameterTypes();
3    System.out.print("Method Name: " + method.getName() + " Parameter Types: ");
4    for (Class<?> paramType : parameterTypes) {
5      System.out.print(paramType.getName() + " ");
6    }
7    System.out.println();
8  }
```

Handling Return Types

The return type of a method is retrieved via the getReturnType() method of the Method class. This method returns a Class object representing the return type.

```
1  for (Method method : methods) {
2    Class<?> returnType = method.getReturnType();
3    System.out.println("Method Name: " + method.getName() + ", Return Type: " +
         returnType.getName());
4  }
```

Checking for Exceptions

A thorough inspection of methods includes understanding exceptions they can throw. The getExceptionTypes() method returns an array of Class objects that represent the exception types declared by a method.

```
for (Method method : methods) {
  Class<?>[] exceptionTypes = method.getExceptionTypes();
  System.out.print("Method Name: " + method.getName() + " Throws: ");
  for (Class<?> excType : exceptionTypes) {
    System.out.print(excType.getName() + " ");
  }
  System.out.println();
}
```

This methodical inspection process not only details the operational capabilities of individual class methods but also enhances the robustness and adaptability of software applications. Through this precise reflection-based interrogation, developers can dynamically adapt their systems to varying runtime requirements, ensuring enhanced flexibility in managing programmatic operations.

3.5 Method Signature and Modifier Inspection

Reflective inspection of method signatures and modifiers in Java is a crucial aspect for advanced runtime analysis and manipulation of classes. This section delves into the procedural steps and technical considerations necessary to reliably inspect these elements using Java's reflection capabilities.

Methods in Java have specific signature elements that include the method name, parameter types, and return type. These parts form the unique identifier of a method within a class, excluding the method's modifiers and exceptions.

- To start with the retrieval process, one must first obtain an instance of Class representing the desired object. This can be achieved using the Class.forName("fully.qualified.class.name") method if the class name is known, or by calling getClass() on an object instance.

- Once the Class object is available, retrieving the array of Method objects is straightforward with the use of getDeclaredMethods()

3.5. METHOD SIGNATURE AND MODIFIER INSPECTION

or getMethods(). The former returns all methods declared in the class including private, protected, and package-access, while the latter returns only the public methods including inherited ones.

Each Method object can then be used to inspect the method's specifics. The examination of modifiers, which define access control and other method properties, is enabled through getModifiers(). This method returns an integer representing different Java modifiers, which can be interpreted using the Modifier class provided in the java.lang.reflect package.

```
Method[] methods = MyClass.class.getDeclaredMethods();
for (Method method : methods) {
    int modifiers = method.getModifiers();
    System.out.println("Method: " + method.getName());
    System.out.println("Modifiers: " + Modifier.toString(modifiers));
}
```

Method: sampleMethod
Modifiers: public static

For signature inspection, the components such as return type and parameter types are accessible through methods getReturnType() and getParameterTypes() respectively. These methods provide a comprehensive view of the method's signature.

```
for (Method method : methods) {
    Class<?> returnType = method.getReturnType();
    Class<?>[] parameterTypes = method.getParameterTypes();
    System.out.println("Method: " + method.getName());
    System.out.println("Return Type: " + returnType.getName());
    System.out.print("Parameter Types: ");
    for (Class<?> paramType : parameterTypes) {
        System.out.print(paramType.getName() + " ");
    }
    System.out.println();
}
```

Method: sampleMethod
Return Type: java.lang.String
Parameter Types: int java.lang.String

Critical analysis of method signatures and modifiers can aid in developing utilities for dynamic method invocations, generating API documentation, or performing security checks. By understanding the distinctions and implications of each element in the method signature, developers can design more robust and adaptable software systems that leverage Java's introspective and reflective capabilities.

3.6 Dynamically Invoking Methods

Dynamically invoking methods in Java using reflection is a powerful technique, enabling applications to call methods at runtime without compile-time checks. This capability is crucial for developing applications that require high levels of flexibility and adaptability, such as those used in plugin architectures or complex service loaders.

The first step in dynamically invoking a method is to obtain a reference to the `Method` object. This can be achieved using the `Class` object's `getMethod(String name, Class<?>... parameterTypes)` method, which requires the method's name and its parameter types as arguments. If the method with the specified name and parameter types does not exist, a `NoSuchMethodException` is thrown.

```
Method method = classObj.getMethod("methodName", ParameterType1.class,
    ParameterType2.class);
```

Once the `Method` object is obtained, it can be invoked on a target object using the `invoke(Object obj, Object... args)` method. The first parameter of `invoke` is the object instance on which the method should be called. If the method is static, this parameter can be null. The subsequent parameters are the arguments to the method being called. The invoke method returns an `Object` that must be cast to the expected return type of the dynamically invoked method.

```
ReturnType result = (ReturnType) method.invoke(objectInstance, arg1, arg2);
```

If the underlying method throws an exception, it is encapsulated within an `InvocationTargetException`. This exception must be caught and handled appropriately, often by unpacking and rethrowing the actual cause.

```
try {
    ReturnType result = (ReturnType) method.invoke(objectInstance, arg1, arg2);
} catch (InvocationTargetException e) {
    throw e.getCause();
}
```

Another aspect to consider when dynamically invoking methods is handling access control. Methods with private, protected, or package-private access can be made accessible by calling `setAccessible(true)` on the `Method` object.

```
method.setAccessible(true);
ReturnType result = (ReturnType) method.invoke(objectInstance, arg1, arg2);
```

```
Output: result obtained from invoking the method
```

Accommodating different parameter types dynamically when invoking methods introduces an additional layer of complexity. Methods overloaded on parameter types might require explicit type handling or conversions. Developers must ensure that argument types match the parameter types of the method being invoked. This is particularly important when working with generic types due to type erasure in Java.

- Reflective method invocation bypasses generics checks which can lead to `ClassCastException` if type assumptions do not hold at runtime.

- Automatic conversion between primitive data types and their corresponding wrapper classes is not supported in reflective method invocation.

The versatility offered by dynamic method invocation necessitates careful consideration of security and performance implications. Frequent use of reflection can lead to performance overhead due to additional checks and computations required to resolve method calls at runtime. From a security perspective, making private methods accessible alters the expected access control mechanisms of the Java programming language, which can lead to unintended side-effects if not managed carefully.

This comprehensive understanding of dynamic method invocation using Java reflection provides a solid foundation for implementing advanced features that require run-time adaptability and flexibility. The capability to invoke any method on objects based on runtime decisions enables Java applications to be more dynamic and responsive to the changing requirements. This trait is quintessential in environments where extending or modifying application behavior on-the-fly is necessary.

3.7 Dealing with Method Parameter Types and Return Types

Dealing effectively with method parameter types and their respective return types is crucial when utilizing Java Reflection to inspect and invoke methods dynamically. This section discusses how to retrieve and analyze these aspects in detail, and presents solutions for effectively managing type conversions and handling method invocations in a dynamic environment.

Retrieving Method Parameters

Java Reflection provides the capability to inspect the parameter types of any method within a class. This is accomplished using the `getMethod` or `getDeclaredMethod` methods of the `java.lang.Class` class, followed by calling `getParameterTypes` on the resulting `Method` object. Here is an example:

```java
import java.lang.reflect.Method;

public class ParameterInspector {
    public static void inspectMethodParameters(Class<?> cls, String methodName) {
        try {
            Method method = cls.getDeclaredMethod(methodName);
            Class<?>[] parameterTypes = method.getParameterTypes();
            for (Class<?> paramType : parameterTypes) {
                System.out.println("Parameter type: " + paramType.getName());
            }
        } catch (NoSuchMethodException e) {
            e.printStackTrace();
        }
    }
}
```

Output of inspected parameters:

```
Parameter type: java.lang.String
Parameter type: int
```

Analyzing Return Types

Similarly, the return type of a method can be obtained using the `getReturnType` method of the `Method` class. This provides insight into what type of object a method invocation will return, which is essential for correct handling of the method output especially in a dynamically typed situation. Consider the following implementation:

```java
public class ReturnTypeInspector {
    public static void inspectMethodReturnType(Class<?> cls, String methodName) {
        try {
            Method method = cls.getDeclaredMethod(methodName);
            Class<?> returnType = method.getReturnType();
            System.out.println("Return type: " + returnType.getName());
        } catch (NoSuchMethodException e) {
```

3.7. DEALING WITH METHOD PARAMETER TYPES AND RETURN TYPES

```
 8            e.printStackTrace();
 9        }
10    }
11 }
```

Output of return type inspection:

```
Return type: boolean
```

Handling Type Conversions

When invoking methods dynamically, handling the conversion between actual parameters and their expected types is critical. Reflection provides the necessary tools to achieve this, but it requires meticulous type checking and conversion to match the parameter signatures accurately. This can be particularly challenging when dealing with primitive data types and their corresponding wrapper classes. The Java Reflection API allows for the use of Class.isAssignableFrom to check type compatibility:

```
1 public static boolean isValidType(Object obj, Class<?> targetType) {
2     return targetType.isInstance(obj) ||
3         (targetType.isPrimitive() &&
4         ((obj instanceof Integer && targetType.getName().equals("int")) ||
5         (obj instanceof Boolean && targetType.getName().equals("boolean"))));
6 }
```

This method can be used to ensure that the parameters passed to a method match expected types before dynamically invoking it.

Dynamic Method Invocation

Dynamic method invocation is where Reflection truly shines, allowing methods with any signature to be invoked on objects at runtime. The following example illustrates invoking a method with parameters determined at runtime:

```
1 public class DynamicInvoker {
2     public static Object invokeMethod(Object instance, String methodName, Object...
          args) {
3         try {
4             Class<?>[] parameterTypes = new Class<?>[args.length];
5             for (int i = 0; i < args.length; i++) {
6                 parameterTypes[i] = args[i].getClass();
7             }
```

```
 8            Method method = instance.getClass().getDeclaredMethod(methodName,
                  parameterTypes);
 9            method.setAccessible(true); // required if method is not publicly
                  accessible
10            return method.invoke(instance, args);
11        } catch (Exception e) {
12            e.printStackTrace();
13            return null;
14        }
15    }
16 }
```

These procedures are essential for the dynamic invocation of methods, allowing developers to create more flexible and adaptable applications. The understanding and appropriate handling of these types ensure that the software can meet various runtime requirements efficiently while maintaining robustness and reliability.

3.8 Exploring Fields and Their Properties

Field inspection is a cornerstone of reflective programming in Java, facilitating a deeper understanding and manipulation of class properties during runtime. This section delves into the various properties of fields obtainable via reflection and provides detailed code examples to demonstrate these techniques.

Retrieving Field Information

Field information in a Java class can be acquired using the `java.lang.Class` API. To obtain a field reference, methods such as `getField(String name)` and `getDeclaredFields()` are employed. The former retrieves a specific public field, and the latter returns an array encompassing all fields declared by the class, regardless of their access level.

```
 1  import java.lang.reflect.Field;
 2
 3  public class FieldInspector {
 4      public static void inspectFieldProperties(Class<?> clazz) {
 5          Field[] fields = clazz.getDeclaredFields();
 6          for (Field field : fields) {
 7              System.out.println("Field Name: " + field.getName());
 8          }
 9      }
10
11      public static void main(String[] args) {
12          inspectFieldProperties(SomeClass.class);
13      }
14  }
```

3.8. EXPLORING FIELDS AND THEIR PROPERTIES

```
Field Name: exampleField
```

The code example above illustrates how to retrieve all declared fields from a given class and print their names. It emphasizes fields' accessibility, circumventing Java's visibility checks with `field.setAccessible(true)`, if necessary.

Field Modifiers and Types

Each field in Java has a set of modifiers specifying its access level (public, private, protected) and other property flags (static, final, etc.). The `getModifiers()` method from the `Field` class returns an integer representing these modifiers, decoded using `java.lang.reflect.Modifier`.

Additionally, the type of each field can be fetched using the `getType()` method. This provides insights into the structure and data handling of a class at runtime.

```java
import java.lang.reflect.Field;
import java.lang.reflect.Modifier;

public class FieldDetailsExtractor {
    public static void printFieldDetails(Class<?> clazz) {
        Field[] fields = clazz.getDeclaredFields();
        for (Field field : fields) {
            int mod = field.getModifiers();
            System.out.println("Field: " + field.getName() +
                    ", Type: " + field.getType().getSimpleName() +
                    ", Modifiers: " + Modifier.toString(mod));
        }
    }

    public static void main(String[] args) {
        printFieldDetails(SomeClass.class);
    }
}
```

```
Field: exampleField, Type: int, Modifiers: private
```

This snippet retrieves and displays the name, type, and modifiers of all fields declared within a specified class, providing a comprehensive overview of its data attributes.

Field Annotations

Modern Java development frequently uses annotations to augment fields with metadata. Reflection can inspect these annotations to drive application behavior dynamically. The `getDeclaredAnnotations()`

method of the `Field` class is pivotal for fetching these data pieces.

```java
import java.lang.reflect.Field;

public class AnnotationInspector {
    public static void inspectFieldAnnotations(Class<?> clazz) {
        Field[] fields = clazz.getDeclaredFields();
        for (Field field : fields) {
            System.out.println("Field: " + field.getName() +
                    " has annotations: " + field.getDeclaredAnnotations().
                    length);
        }
    }

    public static void main(String[] args) {
        inspectFieldAnnotations(SomeClass.class);
    }
}
```

```
Field: exampleField has annotations: 2
```

In the example above, the code iteratively examines each field to determine the number of annotations applied to it, providing a quantified measure of annotated metadata present within a class.

Each segment has highlighted pivotal aspects of field inspection via Java reflection, covering the retrieval methods for field properties, their modifiers and types, and handling of annotations. Mastery of these capabilities provides developers with the tools necessary to fully exploit Java's dynamic and reflective features, enhancing application adaptability and robustness.

3.9 Accessing and Modifying Field Values Dynamically

Accessing and modifying field values dynamically is a crucial aspect of Java reflection that allows developers to manipulate object properties at runtime regardless of their defined access level. This section delves into the techniques for dynamically accessing and modifying fields in Java.

Retrieving Fields at Runtime

The retrieval of fields within a Java class dynamically begins with the acquisition of the `Class` object representing the class or interface, using methods like `Class.forName()` or `object.getClass()`. To access the

3.9. ACCESSING AND MODIFYING FIELD VALUES DYNAMICALLY

fields, reflection provides several methods on the `Class` object:

```
Field[] fields = clazz.getFields(); // Public fields including inherited
Field[] declaredFields = clazz.getDeclaredFields(); // All fields declared in the
    class
```

The distinction between `getFields()` and `getDeclaredFields()` is significant, as the former only returns public fields including those inherited from superclasses, while the latter returns all fields exclusively declared within the class irrespective of their access modifiers.

Accessing Field Values

To read a field's value via reflection, one must first obtain an accessible `Field` object as previously described, followed by invoking the appropriate get method based on field data types:

```
Object fieldValue = field.get(obj); // Retrieving field value from an object
    instance
```

The `Field.get()` method returns an `Object`. It is necessary to cast this returned object to the field's specific data type. This method throws an `IllegalAccessException` if the field is inaccessible due to its access level. To amend this, one can use:

```
field.setAccessible(true); // Bypasses the check for access modifiers
```

Modifying Field Values

The modification of field values shares similarities with accessing them. It involves setting the value of a field on a specified object:

```
field.set(obj, value); // Setting the new value to the field of an object
```

This operation is subject to access control checks; hence, setting the field to be accessible as shown previously may be necessary. Special attention must be given when modifying static fields or fields which have final modifiers, as these involve additional complexities.

Use Case: Dynamic Configuration Application

To illustrate the practical application of these techniques, consider the scenario of a configuration object in an application where the fields represent various configuration parameters. By leveraging reflection, the application can modify these parameters at runtime based on external inputs:

```
class Configuration {
    public int timeout;
    private String apiUrl;
    public boolean useCaching;
}

Configuration config = new Configuration();
Field apiField = config.getClass().getDeclaredField("apiUrl");
apiField.setAccessible(true);
apiField.set(config, "http://newapi.example.com");  // Changing the API URL dynamically
```

This approach provides tremendous flexibility allowing applications to adapt to new environments or conditions dynamically.

The capacity to access and modify field values dynamically at runtime paves the way for more adaptable and resilient applications. By mastering Java reflection, developers arm themselves with a potent tool to combat traditional limitations of static environments, aligning more closely with modern practices requiring vast levels of flexibility and adaptability in software architecture. Understanding and properly implementing these capabilities, while ensuring to handle potential security and performance implications, are crucial in maximizing the benefits of the Java reflection API.

3.10 Field Type Analysis and Reflection

Reflective analysis of field types is a pivotal facet in understanding the structural aspects of Java classes at runtime. This section elaborates on how to utilize Java Reflection API to extract and manage field type information, providing powerful insights into object behavior and structure.

To begin with, it's necessary to retrieve the `Field` object from a `Class` object, which already includes methods for this purpose. Assuming one has a `Class` object, the `getFields` and `getDeclaredFields` methods can be invoked to return arrays of `Field` objects representing all the public fields and all fields respectively, associated with the class.

```
1  import java.lang.reflect.Field;
2
3  public class FieldAnalyzer {
4      public static void analyzeFieldTypes(Class<?> clazz) {
5          Field[] fields = clazz.getDeclaredFields();
6          for (Field field : fields) {
7              Class<?> fieldType = field.getType();
```

3.10. FIELD TYPE ANALYSIS AND REFLECTION

```
 8          System.out.println("Field: " + field.getName() + " Type: " + fieldType.
                getName());
 9      }
10   }
11 }
```

The above code snippet lists all fields along with their types in the specified class. Each `Field` object permits the extraction of its type via the `getType()` method, which returns a `Class` object representing the type of the field.

Upon obtaining the field type, analysis can proceed in numerous ways:

- Determining if the field type is a primitive type, an array, an enumeration, or an object.

- Assessing field generics through the `getGenericType` method, especially useful in understanding the type parameters of collections or other generic objects.

- Utilizing the API further to explore superclass types or interfaces implemented by the field types, enhancing understanding of the class hierarchy.

```
1 Field field = clazz.getField("exampleField");
2 Class<?> fieldType = field.getType();
3 if (fieldType.isArray()) {
4     System.out.println("Field is an array of type " + fieldType.getComponentType());
5 } else {
6     System.out.println("Field is of type " + fieldType);
7 }
```

The above scenario is an example of how to check if a field is an array and identify its component type. This is critical in applications dealing with multi-dimensional data structures dynamically.

To expand practical applications, one might want to not only list field types but perform operations conditionally based on those types. Reflection supports such dynamic type-based logic, which can significantly simplify tasks in complex systems, such as custom serialization mechanisms or equality checks between objects.

When leveraging reflection for field type analysis, be aware of various nuances:

- Access to private fields should be managed through careful use of `setAccessible(true)`.

- Generics, due to type erasure, might not provide as detailed information as might be expected beyond the runtime class representation.

- Performance implications need consideration, as reflective operations are comparatively slower than direct code.

The analysis of field types through reflection equips developers with the capability to engineer highly adaptable and introspective software solutions. Understanding these aspects deepens insights into dynamic behavior of Java applications, ensuring robust and flexible design strategies.

3.11 Handling Exceptions in Reflective Operations

Reflective operations in Java are potent tools but come with intricacies that, if not properly managed, can result in runtime errors and unstable applications. Using reflection, particularly when manipulating constructors, methods, and fields dynamically, demands a disciplined approach to exception handling. These operations can throw several types of exceptions, which need precise handling strategies to maintain the robustness of your application.

- `IllegalAccessException` occurs when an application attempts to reflectively create instances, set fields, or invoke methods, but does not have access to the definition of the specified class, field, method or constructor.

- `InvocationTargetException` is thrown when the underlying method or constructor that is being invoked by reflection throws an exception.

- `NoSuchMethodException` and `NoSuchFieldException` are thrown to indicate that the specified method or field cannot be found.

- `InstantiationException` occurs when an application tries to create an instance of a class using its constructor, but that class represents an abstract class or an interface.

3.11. HANDLING EXCEPTIONS IN REFLECTIVE OPERATIONS

Strategic Exception Management

Managing exceptions effectively requires a thorough understanding of the types of runtime issues that can occur during reflective operations. Below is an exemplary approach encapsulated within a code snippet demonstrating robust handling of reflection-related exceptions:

```
public Object instantiateClassWithReflection(String className) {
    try {
        Class<?> clazz = Class.forName(className);
        Constructor<?> constructor = clazz.getDeclaredConstructor();
        constructor.setAccessible(true);
        return constructor.newInstance();
    } catch(ClassNotFoundException e) {
        System.err.println("Class not found: " + e.getMessage());
    } catch(NoSuchMethodException e) {
        System.err.println("Constructor not found: " + e.getMessage());
    } catch(IllegalAccessException e) {
        System.err.println("Access to constructor denied: " + e.getMessage());
    } catch(InstantiationException e) {
        System.err.println("Cannot instantiate abstract class or interface: " + e.
            getMessage());
    } catch(InvocationTargetException e) {
        System.err.println("Constructor threw an exception: " + e.getTargetException
            ());
    } catch(Exception e) {
        System.err.println("Unexpected error: " + e.getMessage());
    }
    return null;
}
```

The method `instantiateClassWithReflection` tries to instantiate an object of a specified class by name. It handles each type of exception that might arise, providing specific error messages that aid in debugging and further handling.

Tips for Reducing Exception-Prone Reflection Code

To reduce the risk of exceptions when using reflective methods, consider the following practices:

- Prior validation of inputs, ensuring that they meet expected criteria before being used in reflective operations.

- Use of `isAccessible()`, `isAssignableFrom()`, and similar reflective checks to verify access and compatibility before potentially risky operations.

- Implementing fallback mechanisms, allowing the application to continue functioning even if the reflective operation fails.

These strategies immunize reflective usage in Java, making it not only a powerful feature but also a reliable one that upholds the integrity of an application under diverse conditions. Therefore, by encapsulating reflective operations within comprehensively designed try-catch blocks and adhering to best practices, developers can safeguard their applications against common pitfalls associated with dynamic type manipulations.

3.12 Best Practices for Inspecting Constructors, Methods, and Fields

When dealing with Java reflection to inspect constructors, methods, and fields, adhering to best practices not only enhances code quality but also ensures maintainability and scalability. This section outlines established practices that should guide your reflective operations in Java applications.

Ensuring Security and Access Control

Reflection is powerful, yet it can inadvertently lead to security flaws, thus it is imperative to:

- Always check the security manager and adhere to its defined policies before performing any reflective operation. This reduces risks associated with exposing private or protected components.

- Use `AccessibleObject.setAccessible` judiciously. Elevating access privileges should be closely controlled and limited to specific cases where it is truly warranted.

Minimizing Performance Overheads

While Java reflection is useful, it may introduce performance penalties. To mitigate these, consider the following:

- Cache reflective data that you expect to use repetitively. For instance, store method handles or constructor references when first retrieved.

- Avoid excessive use of reflection in performance-critical sections of your application. Leverage reflection during initialization or in non-critical workflows.

Improving Code Clarity and Maintainability

Reflection code can be intricate and obscure. To enhance readability and maintainability:

- Encapsulate reflective logic within dedicated methods or classes. This abstraction simplifies understanding the purpose and mechanism of the reflective operations.
- Document all assumptions and reasons behind using reflection, such as why private members are accessed or modified dynamically.

Handling Exceptions Robustly

Reflective operations can throw various checked exceptions like `NoSuchMethodException` or `IllegalAccessException`. Manage these exceptions thoughtfully:

- Clearly separate error handling code from normal logic, either by using specific catch blocks or moving exception handling to a higher layer.
- Provide comprehensive logging around the failure points to facilitate debugging and traceability of issues.

Testing Reflective Code

Because reflection can complicate predictability in execution, testing becomes crucial:

- Include unit tests that focus on reflective functionality, ensuring that dynamic operations behave as expected across different conditions.
- Employ integration tests to verify that the reflection-based components interact correctly with other parts of the system.

Leveraging Advanced Reflection Features

Make full use of the reflective capabilities provided by newer Java versions, such as:

- Utilizing `java.lang.invoke.MethodHandles` and `java.lang.invoke.VarHandle` for modern and more performant reflective access.

- Explore `java.lang.reflect.Parameter` for better handling and understanding of method and constructor parameters.

The practices discussed aim to guide you in employing Java reflection effectively and responsibly, ensuring that your application remains robust, secure, and performant. Implementing these practices will render your reflective operations not only functional but also well-integrated into the larger scope of your application architecture.

Chapter 4

Instantiating Classes Dynamically

This chapter addresses the dynamic instantiation of classes in Java, a crucial aspect of reflection that allows for the creation of objects at runtime without prior knowledge of their specific types. Readers will learn methods to construct instances using different approaches, such as 'Class.newInstance()' and constructors retrieved through reflection, considering various accessibilities. Furthermore, the chapter explores handling exceptions and design patterns related to dynamic instantiation, providing vital skills for developing adaptable and robust Java applications.

4.1 Foundations of Dynamic Class Instantiation

Dynamic class instantiation is a fundamental aspect of the Java Reflection API, enabling the creation of objects during runtime from a class name that is not known until then. This capability is critical for applications requiring high modularity and configurability, such as plug-in frameworks, dependency injection containers, and large enterprise systems.

The core concept behind dynamic instantiation is that Java can manipulate bytecode and class metadata through the Reflection API; this is derived primarily from the java.lang.Class object associated with every class and interface in a Java application.

- The Class object represents the classes in a running Java application. An instance of Class can be obtained in several ways:
    - Calling the .getClass() method on an object instance.
    - The .class syntax on a class or interface.
    - Using Class.forName() with the fully qualified name of the class.
- Once a Class object is obtained, new instances of the class can be created dynamically.

To instantiate a class dynamically, Java offers multiple methods:

- Class.newInstance(): This method is deprecated from Java 9 onwards because it propagates any exception thrown by the no-arg constructor, including checked exceptions. Its usage can lead to less readable and error-prone code.

- Constructors are preferred, retrieved via Class.getConstructor() and Class.getDeclaredConstructor(), allowing for finer control over object creation.

It is important to emphasize that dynamic class instantiation inherently involves dealing with various exceptions like InstantiationException, IllegalAccessException, and InvocationTargetException. Each of these exceptions signifies different issues that might occur during the instantiation process, such as trying to instantiate an abstract class, lacking access to the constructor, or an exception thrown by the constructor respectively.

The process of dynamic instantiation generally involves the following steps:

1. Obtain the Class object for the class.
2. Retrieve the appropriate constructor.
3. Verify access rights to the constructor.
4. Create a new instance by calling the constructor with any required arguments.

```
1  // Example to dynamically create an instance of `java.util.Date` using its default
       constructor.
2  try {
3      Class<?> clazz = Class.forName("java.util.Date");
4      Object dateInstance = clazz.getDeclaredConstructor().newInstance();
5      System.out.println(dateInstance.toString());
6  } catch (ClassNotFoundException | NoSuchMethodException | InstantiationException |
       IllegalAccessException | InvocationTargetException e) {
7      e.printStackTrace();
8  }
```

Thu Mar 04 14:53:19 GMT 2021

This approach underscores the power and flexibility of using reflection for creating instances dynamically but it also necessitates careful exception handling and awareness about performance considerations since reflection-based operations can be significantly slower than direct Java new operations.

The use of reflection and dynamic instantiation continues to be an essential skill in Java development, particularly in scenarios where new objects need to be created based on runtime decisions, external configurations, or user input. This forms a foundational pillar for later discussions on using reflection to manipulate arrays, manage dependencies, and integrate with class loaders.

4.2 Using Class.newInstance(): Benefits and Limitations

The Class.newInstance() method in Java reflection is a powerful tool for instantiating classes dynamically, thus enabling Java applications to be more flexible and adaptable. This section delves deeply into the benefits and limitations of using Class.newInstance(), providing essential insights for developers who aim to harness this feature effectively in their Java applications.

Benefits of Using Class.newInstance()

The Class.newInstance() method offers several key advantages which make it exceptionally useful in various application scenarios:

- **Simplicity and Convenience**: The usage of Class.newInstance() is straightforward as it does not require any parameters. This simplicity is particularly beneficial when the parameter specifications of a class constructor are unknown or irrelevant to the developer at runtime.

- **Decoupling of Code**: It enhances the modularity of code by decoupling the process of object creation from the use of the actual class type. This decoupling is essential for designing applications that require high levels of flexibility and scalability, such as in plugin frameworks or modular architectures.

- **Runtime Flexibility**: By allowing classes to be instantiated dynamically, Class.newInstance() supports scenarios where the class type is not known until runtime. This is especially pivotal in applications involving configurable components or the need to load classes dynamically based on external configurations.

Limitations and Considerations

While Class.newInstance() is useful, it also presents limitations that must be carefully managed:

- **Requirement of No-Argument Constructor**: Class.newInstance() can only invoke the default constructor of the class. For classes without a no-argument constructor, or where initialization with specific parameters is necessary, this method cannot be utilized directly.

- **Exception Handling**: This method throws InstantiationException if the class cannot be instantiated (e.g., interface or abstract class) and IllegalAccessException if the class or its nullary constructor is not accessible. Exception handling must be appropriately managed to maintain robustness, as demonstrated below:

```
1  try {
2      Class<?> clazz = Class.forName("com.example.MyClass");
3      Object instance = clazz.newInstance();
4  } catch (InstantiationException | IllegalAccessException e) {
5      e.printStackTrace();
6  }
```

- **Overlooked Constructor Effects**: The simplicity of Class.newInstance() may encourage developers to overlook the specific initialization routines defined in other constructors, potentially leading to improperly initialized objects if the class design relies on these routines.

Strategic Use in Design Patterns

Strategically, `Class.newInstance()` is often used in design patterns such as Singleton, Factory Method, or Abstract Factory, particularly in scenarios requiring object creation to be abstracted from the client code. In the Factory Method pattern, for instance, it can be used to dynamically create instances from class names stored in configuration files or determined at runtime, thereby enhancing the adaptability of the application.

Here is a pseudo-example illustrating how `Class.newInstance()` might be deployed within an Abstract Factory pattern:

```
public AbstractProduct createProduct(String className) {
    AbstractProduct product = null;
    try {
        Class<?> productClass = Class.forName(className);
        product = (AbstractProduct) productClass.newInstance();
    } catch (ClassNotFoundException | InstantiationException |
        IllegalAccessException e) {
        e.printStackTrace();
    }
    return product;
}
```

When employing `Class.newInstance()`, it is essential for developers to recognize both its powerful capabilities and its limitations. While it offers a high degree of flexibility and simplicity for certain use cases, it necessitates careful consideration of design, especially concerning exception management and the specific initialization needs of the classes being instantiated. This understanding ensures that developers can leverage `Class.newInstance()` effectively within their projects, maximizing both performance and adaptability.

4.3 Advanced Instantiation with Constructors

Dynamically instantiating objects through Java Reflection extends beyond the basic `Class.newInstance()` method. This section explores the advanced techniques using constructors retrieved through reflection, which offers a more versatile approach in creating instances, especially when dealing with complex objects requiring parameterized constructors.

Retrieving Constructors

To utilize constructors dynamically, first, retrieve the constructor objects. The java.lang.Class provides methods such as getConstructor and getDeclaredConstructor, differentiated by their scope of visibility adherence:

- getConstructor(Class<?>... parameterTypes): Returns a public constructor with the specified parameter types.

- getDeclaredConstructor(Class<?>... parameterTypes): Retrieves any constructor matching the parameter types, regardless of its accessibility (public, protected, private).

```
Constructor<T> constructor = MyClass.class.getDeclaredConstructor(String.class,
    Integer.class);
```

In the above listing, constructor refers to a constructor that expects a String and an Integer as input arguments. It's crucial to handle NoSuchMethodException, which is thrown if no matching constructor is found.

Instantiating an Instance

Once a suitable constructor is retrieved, the next step is to create an instance by invoking newInstance on the Constructor object:

```
T instance = constructor.newInstance("example", 42);
```

Here, instance is the object created using the specified constructor, and "example", 42 are arguments passed to the constructor. Essential exceptions such as InstantiationException, IllegalAccessException, and IllegalArgumentException need to be managed appropriately, ensuring robust error handling.

Handling Accessibility

Accessing non-public constructors involves modifying their accessibility using the setAccessible(true) method on the Constructor object:

```
constructor.setAccessible(true);
T instance = constructor.newInstance("example", 42);
```

4.3. ADVANCED INSTANTIATION WITH CONSTRUCTORS

This modification allows for bypassing Java's access control checks, facilitating the instantiation of classes in ways that typical language constraints would prevent. This approach, however, should be used judiciously and responsibly, adhering to the principles of secure software development.

Examples and Practical Applications

Let's consider a practical application where a dynamic instantiation approach is necessary:

- A framework might require loading plugins or modules dynamically based on user input or configuration settings.

- Factories that must create various types of objects, where the exact type might only be known at runtime.

For instance, in a factory design pattern where the type of object returned by the factory method depends on the string input:

```
public class ShapeFactory {
    public Shape getShape(String shapeType){
        Constructor<?> ctor = Class.forName(shapeType).getDeclaredConstructor();
        ctor.setAccessible(true);
        return (Shape) ctor.newInstance();
    }
}
```

In this code snippet, shapes such as Circle, Square, or Rectangle could be dynamically instantiated by their type names passed as strings to the getShape method.

Implementing such dynamic behaviors, while powerful, necessitates careful consideration of design, robust error handling, and adherence to security best practices.

Through the detailed examination of methods for advanced instantiation using constructors, Java developers are equipped to implement more flexible and sophisticated software systems that can manage a variety of runtime scenarios effectively.

4.4 Handling Constructor Accessibility

Handling the accessibility of constructors is a pivotal aspect of dynamic instantiation in Java. This section delves into methods for accessing private, protected, and package-private constructors through the reflection API, and discusses potential security implications and performance considerations.

Reflection allows for the examination and modification of the runtime behavior of applications in Java. Accessing constructors that are not public requires careful handling to ensure that security and design encapsulation principles are not compromised.

Accessing Non-Public Constructors

The Java Reflection API provides the means to access and invoke constructors of classes regardless of their access level. Here, we outline how to access private, protected, and package-private constructors using the Constructor class from the java.lang.reflect package.

```
import java.lang.reflect.Constructor;

public class ConstructorAccessibility {
    private static class SecretClass {
        private SecretClass() {
            // Private constructor
            System.out.println("Private constructor invoked");
        }
    }

    public static void main(String[] args) {
        try {
            Class<?> clazz = SecretClass.class;
            Constructor<?> constructor = clazz.getDeclaredConstructor();
            // Setting accessible true to access the private constructor
            constructor.setAccessible(true);
            Object instance = constructor.newInstance();
        } catch (Exception e) {
            e.printStackTrace();
        }
    }
}
```

```
Private constructor invoked
```

The key operation in the above code is the invocation of setAccessible(true), which allows the private constructor to be accessed outside its normal accessibility constraints. While powerful, this method must be used judiciously to avoid violating encapsulation prin-

4.4. HANDLING CONSTRUCTOR ACCESSIBILITY

ciples or exposing sensitive components to unauthorized access.

Security Implications

Modifying constructor accessibility can have serious security implications, particularly when dealing with classes that are not meant to be instantiated or accessed outside certain contexts. The ability to instantiate private classes can lead to breach of the intended encapsulation properties or unintended side effects:

- Bypassing encapsulation can lead to unauthorized access and modification of private state.
- It might violate security constraints enforced by the application or the runtime environment.
- Making a constructor accessible can expose internal APIs to third parties, increasing the surface area for security vulnerabilities.

Performance Considerations

While dynamic instantiation using the reflection API is a powerful feature, it comes with a performance cost. Accessing and instantiating constructors reflectively is significantly slower than using normal Java code due to additional checks and overhead involved in the reflection process.

- Reflection involves type checking and access checks at runtime, which add overhead.
- The `setAccessible` method can further reduce performance as it needs to bypass the standard Java security checks.
- Overuse of reflection for constructor accessibility might lead to maintainability and performance issues.

To minimize these impacts, use reflection judiciously and cache reflective accessors, such as `Constructor` objects, whenever possible to avoid repeated costly retrievals.

Reflective access to constructors, while providing the flexibility of instantiating objects dynamically, must be handled with an understanding of its implications on security and performance. Proper use of this capability enables developers to write more dynamic and flexible code while maintaining the robustness and security of applications.

4.5 Creating Instances with Array Reflection

The Java Reflection API provides mechanisms not only for instantiating individual class objects but also for dynamically creating and manipulating arrays of objects. This capability is essential for situations where the component type of an array is not known until runtime. This section explores the methodology for implementing array reflection, mainly focusing on the java.lang.reflect.Array class, which offers a variety of methods to dynamically handle arrays.

Overview of java.lang.reflect.Array

The java.lang.reflect.Array class is specifically designed to dynamically create and access Java arrays. This class provides static methods to instantiate new arrays, get and set elements within them, and determine the length of the arrays. These methods encapsulate the complexities of reflection operations related to array manipulation.

Creating Arrays Dynamically

To create an instance of an array dynamically, one must use the Array.newInstance() method. This method requires the component type and the desired length of the array as its arguments. Below is an illustrative example:

```
Class<?> componentType = Class.forName("java.lang.String");
int arrayLength = 10;
Object arrayInstance = Array.newInstance(componentType, arrayLength);
```

In this example, Array.newInstance() creates an array of String objects with a length of 10. It is important to note that the result returned by Array.newInstance() is of type Object. To manipulate this array further, one would need to cast it back to the appropriate array type.

4.5. CREATING INSTANCES WITH ARRAY REFLECTION

Accessing and Modifying Array Elements

Once an array instance is created, elements can be accessed and modified using the Array.get() and Array.set() methods, respectively. Consider the example below, wherein elements of an array are modified:

```
1  Array.set(arrayInstance, 0, "Hello");
2  Array.set(arrayInstance, 1, "World");
3
4  String firstElement = (String) Array.get(arrayInstance, 0);
5  String secondElement = (String) Array.get(arrayInstance, 1);
```

```
Outputs:
Hello
World
```

This example demonstrates setting the first two elements of the array and subsequently retrieving them. The Array.get() and Array.set() methods require specifying the index of the element along with the array instance.

Handling Multidimensional Arrays

Creating and managing multidimensional arrays dynamically can also be achieved using Array.newInstance(). To instantiate a multidimensional array, pass an array of int representing the dimensions of the array as the second argument:

```
1  int[] dimensions = {5, 5}; // 5x5 matrix
2  Object matrix = Array.newInstance(Integer.TYPE, dimensions);
```

To access or modify elements in a multidimensional array, one must navigate through each dimension separately, as demonstrated in the following snippet:

```
1  Array.set(Array.get(matrix, 3), 4, 10); // setting element at [3][4] to 10
2  Integer value = (Integer) Array.get(Array.get(matrix, 3), 4); // getting the
        element at [3][4]
```

```
Output:
10
```

Reflection Use Cases for Array Manipulation

Using reflection for array manipulation is particularly useful in scenarios such as:

- Serializing or deserializing data where the type and size of arrays are not known at compile time.

- Developing generic data structures and algorithms that operate uniformly on arrays of different types.

- Implementing frameworks or libraries that require dynamic manipulation of user-defined input data structures.

Dynamic array creation and manipulation through reflection, although powerful, should be used judiciously due to potential performance implications. When possible, standard Java arrays or collections should be favored for their straightforward syntax and efficiency. The reflective approach, however, remains indispensable in scenarios that demand high levels of flexibility and type abstraction.

4.6 Dynamic Instantiation of Inner and Anonymous Classes

Dynamic instantiation of inner and anonymous classes in Java presents unique challenges and considerations compared to instantiation of regular classes. This section explores the technical nuances involved in this process, emphasizing reflection-based techniques to instantiate these types of classes, which are often embedded within other classes or defined without a class name, respectively.

Instantiating Inner Classes

Inner classes, which are defined within the scope of another class, can be either non-static or static. Non-static inner classes hold a reference to an instance of the outer class, making their instantiation slightly more complex than their static counterparts.

To instantiate a non-static inner class reflectively, reference to the outer class is imperative. This is achieved by first obtaining the `Constructor` object of the inner class. Consider the following Java structure:

```
public class Outer {
    public class Inner {
        public Inner() {
            // Constructor Logic
        }
    }
}
```

4.6. DYNAMIC INSTANTIATION OF INNER AND ANONYMOUS CLASSES

```
7  }
```

Using reflection to instantiate Inner, the steps taken are as follows:

- Obtain an instance of Outer class.
- Fetch Constructor object of Inner class using Class.getDeclaredConstructor() ensuring it is accessible.
- Create new instance using the Constructor.newInstance() method with the outer class instance as an argument.

The corresponding Java code snippet using reflection is shown below:

```
1  Outer outer = new Outer(); // Instance of the outer class
2  Class<?> innerClass = Class.forName("Outer$Inner");
3  Constructor<?> constructor = innerClass.getDeclaredConstructor(Outer.class);
4  constructor.setAccessible(true); // Make the constructor accessible
5  Object inner = constructor.newInstance(outer);
```

Instantiating Anonymous Classes

Anonymous classes are defined without a named identifier and are used to create ad-hoc specializations of classes with slight modifications. Reflectively instantiating an anonymous class directly is, by design, not viable because they do not have a named class to reference directly.

A common approach to manage instantiation dynamically in scenarios that would typically use an anonymous class is utilizing interfaces or abstract classes dynamically, then instantiating implementations of these during runtime. Instead of creating anonymous classes, one can define concrete implementations dynamically and load these using reflection.

Consider the following example using an interface:

```
1  public interface Worker {
2      void doWork();
3  }
```

Using reflection, instantiate an implementation of this interface:

```
1  Class<?> workerImpl = Class.forName("ConcreteWorker"); // Assuming ConcreteWorker
       implements Worker
2  Worker worker = (Worker) workerImpl.newInstance();
```

To encapsulate the idea previous with 'anonymous classes', dynamic proxy classes can be created. For instance, a dynamic proxy might implement the interfaces and forward method calls to a handler:

```
Worker workerProxy = (Worker) Proxy.newProxyInstance(
    Worker.class.getClassLoader(),
    new Class<?>[] { Worker.class },
    (proxy, method, methodArgs) -> {
        System.out.println("Proxy call to " + method.getName());
        return null;
    });
```

The use of reflection for dynamic instantiation extends the capabilities of Java in creating flexible and generic code structures. Handling inner and anonymous classes reflectively allows for applications that can adapt to changing requirements dynamically, crucial in modern software development environments where modularity and efficiency are imperative. The techniques illustrated here should be utilized judiciously given their impact on performance and complexity in application architecture.

4.7 Exception Handling and Error Prevention in Dynamic Creation

Dynamic instantiation of classes in Java, as facilitated through reflection, presents a variety of challenges, primarily surrounding exception handling and error prevention. This portion of the chapter meticulously explores the nuances associated with these challenges and offers strategical approaches to manage them efficiently.

Reflection operations are inherently risky due to their nature of interaction with runtime elements. Various exceptions specific to the reflection process need to be handled to ensure the robustness and resilience of applications. When using reflection for creating instances, the predominant exceptions that need management include InstantiationException, IllegalAccessException, InvocationTargetException, and NoSuchMethodException.

- InstantiationException occurs if the Class represents an abstract class, an interface, an array class, a primitive type, or void, or if the class has no nullary constructor.

- IllegalAccessException is thrown when the currently executing method does not have access to the definition of the specified

4.7. EXCEPTION HANDLING AND ERROR PREVENTION IN DYNAMIC CREATION

class, field, method or constructor.

- `InvocationTargetException` is thrown by an invoked method or constructor. This exception provides a chained exception mechanism which can be useful for debugging.

- `NoSuchMethodException` is thrown when a particular method cannot be found.

```
public static Object createInstanceWithReflection(String className) {
    Object instance = null;
    try {
        Class<?> clazz = Class.forName(className);
        Constructor<?> constructor = clazz.getConstructor();
        instance = constructor.newInstance();
    } catch (ClassNotFoundException e) {
        e.printStackTrace();
    } catch (NoSuchMethodException e) {
        e.printStackTrace();
    } catch (InstantiationException e) {
        e.printStackTrace();
    } catch (IllegalAccessException e) {
        e.printStackTrace();
    } catch (InvocationTargetException e) {
        e.printStackTrace();
    }
    return instance;
}
```

The listing above incapsulates a typical example where multiple exceptions are caught separately for clarity. In practice, handling multiple exception types separately allows developers to implement specific recovery mechanisms for each exception type.

Moreover, ensuring proper error prevention strategies necessitates a thorough understanding of the context in which reflection is employed. For instance, avoiding `IllegalAccessException` by ensuring accessible constructor access by using `Constructor.setAccessible(true)`, albeit with due consideration to security implications.

```
Output of successful instance creation:
instance - com.example.MyClass@70dea4e
```

For more reliable error handling, developers can deploy additional preventive measures such as:

- Validation of preconditions before class loading or instantiation.

- Utilization of custom security managers or policy files to govern reflection operations.

- Logging detailed error information and remediation tips for operation failures.

Employing these strategies enhances the robustness of dynamic object creation, making Java applications more secure, maintainable, and resilient against unexpected behaviors or crashes. This meticulous approach not only mitigates the risks associated with dynamic instantiation but also ensures that the application consistently behaves as intended in diverse environments.

4.8 Design Patterns and Dynamic Instantiation

Reflective techniques in Java provide a powerful tool for dynamic instantiation, which can be elegantly integrated with design patterns to create flexible and reusable software architectures. In this section, we explore how reflection can enhance the implementation of various design patterns, specifically focusing on the Factory Method, Singleton, and Prototype patterns.

Factory Method Pattern Enhanced by Reflection

The Factory Method Pattern provides an interface for creating objects in a superclass, but allows subclasses to alter the type of objects that will be created. Reflective instantiation adds a layer of flexibility to this pattern by not requiring the factory to know about the concrete classes at compile time.

Consider the following Java code utilizing reflection to implement a factory method pattern:

```
public class ProductFactory {

    public static Product createProduct(String className) {
        try {
            Class prodClass = Class.forName(className);
            return (Product) prodClass.newInstance();
        } catch (ClassNotFoundException | InstantiationException |
                IllegalAccessException e) {
            // Handle exception: Log error or throw a custom exception
            return null;
        }
    }
}
```

In this scenario, the class name is passed as a string to the createProduct method, enhancing the pattern's flexibility by enabling the instantia-

4.8. DESIGN PATTERNS AND DYNAMIC INSTANTIATION

tion of different Product subclasses at runtime depending on the input.

Singleton Pattern with Dynamic Class Loading

The Singleton Pattern ensures that a class has only one instance and provides a global point of access to it. Reflective instantiation can be used to dynamically load the Singleton class, which is particularly beneficial in scenarios involving multiple class loaders or different configurations requiring distinct Singleton implementations.

Below is an example of implementing the Singleton pattern using reflection:

```
public class Singleton {
    private static Singleton instance;

    private Singleton() {}

    public static Singleton getInstance(String className) {
        if (instance == null) {
            try {
                Class clazz = Class.forName(className);
                instance = (Singleton) clazz.newInstance();
            } catch (ClassNotFoundException | InstantiationException |
                    IllegalAccessException e) {
                // Handle exception
            }
        }
        return instance;
    }
}
```

This approach allows for the dynamic specification of the Singleton class type, based on runtime decisions or configuration files, providing a high degree of adaptability.

Prototype Pattern Using Cloning

The Prototype Pattern involves creating objects based on a prototypical instance. Reflection can simplify the cloning process, especially when dealing with objects whose type might not be known until runtime.

Here's an illustration of the Prototype pattern using reflection:

```
public class PrototypeRegistry {
    private HashMap<String, Object> prototypes = new HashMap<>();

    public void addPrototype(String key, Object prototype) {
        prototypes.put(key, prototype);
    }

```

```
 8    public Object clonePrototype(String key) {
 9        Object prototype = prototypes.get(key);
10        if (prototype != null) {
11            try {
12                Method cloneMethod = prototype.getClass().getDeclaredMethod("clone");
13                return cloneMethod.invoke(prototype);
14            } catch (NoSuchMethodException | InvocationTargetException |
                     IllegalAccessException e) {
15                // Handle exception
16            }
17        }
18        return null;
19    }
20 }
```

This mechanism leverages reflection to dynamically invoke the `clone` method on an object, enabling the Prototype pattern without the typical constraints of static type checking.

4.9 Using Reflection for Dependency Injection

Dependency Injection (DI) is a design pattern used to achieve Inversion of Control between classes and their dependencies. Through DI, objects receive their dependencies from an external source rather than creating them internally. Java Reflection adds a dynamic layer to DI, enabling the runtime construction and linking of dependencies, which is particularly useful in frameworks like Spring or when building complex applications with extensive modular components.

Conceptual Framework

The core idea behind using reflection for DI is to dynamically assign object dependencies at runtime, thus not hard-coding the objects within the component itself. This allows for greater flexibility and decoupling of the components.

- Reflection provides the capability to inspect classes and interfaces at runtime, including retrieving constructors, methods, and fields.

- DI frameworks utilize reflection to instantiate objects and assign these instantiated objects to the appropriate class fields.

Implementation Details

Using reflection for DI involves several key steps in Java:

1. Identification of the constructor with dependencies: Analyzing the constructors available and selecting the appropriate one for creating an instance.

```
Constructor<?> constructor = clazz.getConstructor(dependencyTypes);
```

2. Instantiation of dependencies: For each dependency required by the constructor, reflection is used again to instantiate that particular class.

```
Class<?> dependencyClass = Class.forName(dependencyName);
Object dependency = dependencyClass.newInstance();
```

3. Construction of the object with its dependencies injected: The previously created instance and its dependencies are passed to the constructor.

```
Object object = constructor.newInstance(dependency);
```

Handling Accessibility

Reflection allows accessing private and protected constructors, which is often necessary in DI frameworks. However, this should be done cautiously, ensuring security and design principles are not compromised.

```
constructor.setAccessible(true);
```

Another aspect of using reflection for DI is managing exceptions that may arise from improper use of reflection APIs such as ClassNotFoundException, InstantiationException, IllegalAccessException, and InvocationTargetException.

```
try {
    // Reflection code for DI
} catch (ReflectiveOperationException e) {
    e.printStackTrace();
}
```

Performance Considerations

While reflection provides powerful capabilities for implementing DI, it has its drawbacks, such as performance overhead. Instantiating an object through reflection is considerably slower than using direct Java code. Therefore, it is essential to measure and mitigate performance impacts, particularly in high-load environments.

Use Case: Integrating with Spring Framework

Spring, one of the prominent Java frameworks that utilize DI, heavily relies on reflection. Spring's ApplicationContext automatically detects the constructors and methods that need DI and injects the required dependencies at runtime.

```
1  ApplicationContext context = new AnnotationConfigApplicationContext(AppConfig.class
       );
2  MyBean bean = context.getBean(MyBean.class);
```

This functionality simplifies the application's configuration, promoting a clean separation of concerns and easier unit testing.

The use of reflection for dependency injection offers significant advantages in terms of flexibility and dynamism in application development. However, it requires careful handling to ensure application performance and maintainability are not adversely affected. Through skillful use, reflection can enhance the adaptability and modularity of Java applications, making it a valuable technique in the developer's toolkit.

4.10 Reflection and Class Loaders

Understanding the interaction between Java Reflection and class loaders is crucial for developers aiming to leverage dynamic class operations within complex Java applications. Class loaders are responsible for dynamically loading class files into the Java Virtual Machine (JVM). When combined with reflection, class loaders enable not only the dynamic loading but also the introspection and instantiation of classes at runtime.

This section delves into the mechanics of class loaders in the context of reflection, highlighting strategies for managing class visibility and isolation, the interplay between different class loaders, and common pitfalls that may arise.

Mechanics of Class Loaders

Class loaders in Java have a hierarchical relationship in which classes loaded by a parent loader are visible to child loaders, but not vice versa. The foundation class loader is the Bootstrap class loader, followed by the Extension class loader, and then the Application class loader.

When using reflection to load and manipulate classes, it's essential to consider which class loader is responsible for loading the specific classes. The reflection APIs in Java, primarily located in the java.lang.Class and java.lang.reflect packages, interact with class loaders as follows:

```
Class<?> clazz = Class.forName("com.example.MyClass", true, customClassLoader);
```

In the listing above, the Class.forName method is used to load a class dynamically with a specified class loader. The boolean parameter specifies whether to initialize the class.

Strategies for Managing Class Visibility and Isolation

To manage class visibility and isolation effectively, developers can employ custom class loaders. This is particularly useful in modular applications like plugin systems, where it is necessary to separate the plugin's classes from the application's core classes. Here's how a simple custom class loader can be implemented:

```
public class CustomClassLoader extends ClassLoader {
    @Override
    public Class<?> findClass(String name) throws ClassNotFoundException {
        byte[] b = loadClassFromFile(name);
        return defineClass(name, b, 0, b.length);
    }


    private byte[] loadClassFromFile(String fileName) {
        // Implementation to read class file and convert to byte array
    }
}
```

Creating a custom class loader as shown above allows for specific handling of class loading. For example, different encryption strategies for class data or selective loading of classes based on runtime conditions can be implemented.

Interplay Between Different Class Loaders

In applications where multiple class loaders are involved, managing how they interact with each other becomes essential. If not properly managed, this can lead to issues such as `ClassCastException` when identical classes are loaded by different class loaders.

To illustrate, considering a scenario where two class loaders load the same class independently:

```
1  ClassLoader loaderA = new CustomClassLoader();
2  ClassLoader loaderB = new CustomClassLoader();
3
4  Class<?> classA = Class.forName("com.example.MyClass", true, loaderA);
5  Class<?> classB = Class.forName("com.example.MyClass", true, loaderB);
6
7  System.out.println(classA == classB); // Outputs `false`
```

The above code snippet demonstrates that even if the classes `classA` and `classB` represent the same class, they are considered distinct because they were loaded by different class loaders.

Common Pitfalls in Reflection and Class Loaders

Developers need to be aware of common pitfalls such as memory leaks often associated with custom class loaders. Since class loaders, and thus the classes they load, are subject to garbage collection, keeping unintended references to class loaders can prevent the classes they loaded from being garbage collected, even if they are no longer in use elsewhere in the application.

Overall, the synergy between reflection and class loaders is a powerful mechanism in Java, enabling dynamic class loading and operations. By understanding and managing the complexities of class loader interactions and the visibility of classes, developers can fully harness the potential of reflection in managing runtime behavior and extending application capabilities.

4.11 Performance Implications of Dynamic Instantiation

Dynamic instantiation, a fundamental concept within the Java Reflection API, allows developers to instantiate classes dynamically at run-

4.11. PERFORMANCE IMPLICATIONS OF DYNAMIC INSTANTIATION

time. Despite its powerful capabilities, it is crucial to understand the performance implications of employing this approach, especially in performance-critical applications.

Impact on Performance Utilizing reflection for creating instances dynamically incurs a performance overhead compared to traditional instantiation methods. This overhead arises primarily due to:

- The necessity to load and analyze the class metadata at runtime.

- The checks and operations performed to ensure accessibility and type safety which are otherwise handled at compile-time.

Benchmarking Dynamic vs. Static Instantiation To quantitatively assess the performance differential, consider a simple benchmark where we compare the time taken to instantiate objects dynamically and statically.

```
public class BenchmarkTest {
    public static void main(String[] args) throws Exception {
        int iterations = 10000000;
        long startTime, endTime;

        // Static instantiation
        startTime = System.nanoTime();
        for (int i = 0; i < iterations; i++) {
            MyClass obj = new MyClass();
        }
        endTime = System.nanoTime();
        System.out.println("Static instantiation: " + (endTime - startTime) + " ns")
        ;

        // Dynamic instantiation
        Class<?> clazz = Class.forName("MyClass");
        startTime = System.nanoTime();
        for (int i = 0; i < iterations; i++) {
            Object obj = clazz.newInstance();
        }
        endTime = System.nanoTime();
        System.out.println("Dynamic instantiation: " + (endTime - startTime) + " ns"
        );
    }
}
```

Examining the output produced by this code, which is encapsulated in the verbatim environment:
```
Static instantiation: 23956627 ns
Dynamic instantiation: 31278563 ns
```

It is evident from the results that dynamic instantiation takes longer, with the additional time attributable to the mechanisms and safety checks performed by the Reflection API.

Optimization Strategies To mitigate the performance cost associated with dynamic instantiation, implement the following strategies:

- **Caching Reflection Objects:** Store objects like `Class`, `Constructor`, `Method`, and `Field` in cache after their initial retrieval to reduce the cost of subsequent lookups and accesses.

- **Using Constructor Handles:** With the introduction of Constructor Handles in later Java versions, use these instead of traditional reflective access. This approach reduces overhead by offering a more direct method of instantiation.

- **Reducing Frequent Reflection Use:** Evaluate the necessity of using reflection for each instance creation. In cases where a factory pattern or a singleton pattern suffices, employ these design patterns to limit reflection use.

The performance implications of dynamic instantiation are critical to consider for developers leveraging Java Reflection in their applications. Through understanding these implications and employing optimization strategies, it is possible to use dynamic instantiation effectively without substantial degradation in performance. This balance is essential for maintaining application efficiency and responsiveness.

4.12 Summary and Best Practices

Dynamic instantiation in Java, facilitated through reflection, allows for the creation and manipulation of objects at runtime in a flexible and generic manner. This chapter has explored the range of methods and techniques available for creating Java objects dynamically, highlighting the potential and versatility this offers to developers.

- The use of `Class.newInstance()` provides a straightforward means of instantiating classes. However, this method is limited to classes with public, no-argument constructors.

- Employing constructors retrieved via reflection enables the construction of instances with more complex requirements, including those needing parameterized constructors.

4.12. SUMMARY AND BEST PRACTICES

- `Class.getDeclaredConstructor().newInstance()` allows for greater flexibility by enabling the access and use of private and protected constructors, essential for adhering to the principles of encapsulation.

Exception handling forms a critical part of the dynamic instantiation process. Reflection operations can throw a variety of checked exceptions such as `InstantiationException`, `IllegalAccessException`, and `InvocationTargetException`. It is imperative for robust application development that these exceptions are thoughtfully caught and handled.

Several best practices have emerged from the detailed exploration of these techniques:

- Always check the type compatibility before instantiating objects dynamically to prevent `ClassCastException`.

- Handle reflection-related exceptions gracefully, providing meaningful feedback to users when errors occur.

- Limit the use of reflection to cases where it's truly beneficial. Reflection can lead to code that is hard to read and maintain. Furthermore, the performance overhead introduced by reflection calls for careful consideration of its impact.

- Implement caching strategies for method and constructor accesses to enhance performance when using reflection intensively. Repeatedly accessing class metadata can be costly, and caching can mitigate this expense significantly.

In sum, while dynamic instantiation through reflection adds a layer of complexity to Java application development, it also opens up a suite of possibilities for creating more adaptable and flexible applications. By adhering to the best practices suggested, developers can leverage these capabilities effectively while minimizing potential risks and performance costs.

Chapter 5

Accessing Private Members with Reflection

This chapter explores the techniques for accessing and manipulating private members of classes through Java Reflection, a practice that, while powerful, demands careful consideration regarding design principles and security. It elucidates how to bypass the typical access controls to reach private fields, methods, and constructors, which can be essential for certain use cases like testing or handling legacy code. The chapter discusses the technical implementations, potential risks, and ethical implications, equipping readers with the knowledge to use these techniques judiciously and securely.

5.1 Overview of Access Levels in Java

Access levels in Java determine which classes, methods, or fields are accessible from other classes in the same package or across different packages. Java provides four different access levels using access modifiers: `private`, `default` (no modifier), `protected`, and `public`. Understanding these access levels is crucial for structuring robust and maintainable Java applications and forms the basis for employing reflection effectively, particularly when accessing private members.

- `private`: The `private` modifier is the most restrictive access level. Class members declared as `private` cannot be accessed outside the class in which they are declared. This level of encapsulation hides the member from any other class, even subclasses which may belong to the same package or different packages.

- `default`: If no access modifier is specified, the class member has a `default` access level. Default access allows the member to be accessed only within its own package and is thus more accessible than `private` but more restrictive than `protected` and `public`.

- `protected`: Members with the `protected` access level can be accessed within their own package and also by subclasses of their class in different packages. This access level provides a more flexible encapsulation, suitable for objects that are intended to be extended or customized by other developers.

- `public`: The `public` modifier specifies the least restrictive access level. Members declared public can be accessed from any other class anywhere, whether in the same package or a different package. This access level facilitates the highest degree of interaction between software components.

These modifiers can be applied to classes, interfaces, constructors, methods, and class fields. Each of these elements interacts differently with the access levels depending on its overall design usage. For example, constructors marked as `private` are typically used in patterns like Singleton, where control over the instantiation process is crucial.

```
public class AccessExample {
    private int privateCounter = 0;
    int defaultCounter = 0; // default access level
    protected int protectedCounter = 0;
    public int publicCounter = 0;

    void demonstrateAccess() {
        this.privateCounter = 1; // Accessible within the same class
        this.defaultCounter = 1; // Accessible within the same package
        this.protectedCounter = 1; // Accessible in same package or subclasses
        this.publicCounter = 1; // Accessible from any class
    }
}
```

When using Java's reflection APIs to manipulate access levels, particularly private members, it is essential to understand the initial restrictions imposed by these access modifiers. Reflection provides mechanisms to bypass these controls that can be invaluable for certain tasks such as testing or working with third-party libraries.

Explanation of Listing: This Java class named 'AccessExample' demonstrates how different access levels control the visibility and use of variables within a class. It shows that class members with diverse access levels have various limitations and benefits regarding how they can be interacted with from different parts of a Java application.

5.2 Understanding Reflection and Access Control

Reflection in Java is a powerful mechanism that allows programs to inspect or modify the runtime behavior of applications. This capability, particularly the ability to interact with class properties, requires a nuanced understanding of Java's access control mechanisms. This section elucidates the interrelationship between Java reflection and access control, presents methodological approaches to access private members using reflection, and highlights the necessary precautions to ensure security and robustness in application design.

Java access control is governed by modifiers such as `public`, `protected`, `default` (no modifier), and `private` which determine how Java classes, methods, fields, and constructors are accessible within an application. Each access level provides different scopes of accessibility:

- `public` items are accessible from any other class in the Java environment
- `protected` items are accessible within the same package or subclasses
- `default` provides accessibility only within the same package
- `private` restricts access to the defining class itself

Reflection primarily interacts with the `java.lang.reflect` package, which provides classes such as `Field`, `Method`, and `Constructor`. Each of these classes offers methods to override the standard Java access controls:

- The `setAccessible(true)` method of the `AccessibleObject` class (a superclass of `Field`, `Method`, and `Constructor`) is pivotal in reflection. It allows suppressed accessibility checks, thereby facilitating the access to private and other non-public members.

```java
import java.lang.reflect.Field;

public class ReflectionDemo {
    private String hidden = "Initial Value";

    public static void main(String[] args) throws Exception {
        Field field = ReflectionDemo.class.getDeclaredField("hidden");
        field.setAccessible(true); // Enable access to private variable
        ReflectionDemo demo = new ReflectionDemo();
        System.out.println("Before: " + demo.hidden);
        field.set(demo, "Modified Value");
        System.out.println("After: " + demo.hidden);
    }
}
```

```
Before: Initial Value
After: Modified Value
```

It is imperative to consider the security implications of using reflection, especially modifying the access control status of class elements. Reflection bypasses the compile-time checks and elevates the risk of:

- Exposing private data
- Allowing the invocation of methods that were intended to be protected from external use
- Modifying the internal state of objects in unexpected ways

Thus, while reflection provides substantial flexibility and powerful capabilities for Java development, particularly in scenarios such as debugging, testing, or dealing with legacy code, it is essential to employ this feature judiciously. Reflective operations should be encapsulated and guarded with strong security checks, especially when used in production environments or with code that handles sensitive information.

Furthermore, the use of reflection can impact the performance of an application due to additional overhead associated with bypassing JVM's usual optimizations. Developers must measure and evaluate the performance implications in scenarios where reflection is used extensively.

This understanding of Java's reflection and its interplay with access control mechanisms is quintessential for optimizing application security and robustness. It is essential not to underestimate the strength of Java's security model and the ways it can and should be manipulated through reflective access. Secure, thoughtful, and well-guided use of reflection adheres to best practices in software design and implementation. This approach avoids common pitfalls associated with incorrect or excessive use of Java's reflective capabilities.

5.3 Retrieving Private Fields of a Class

Accessing private fields of a class via Java Reflection is a powerful technique that permits insights into objects that would otherwise be hidden by traditional access modifiers. This section addresses the methodology to retrieve private fields from classes, providing precise code examples and the implications of such operations.

The Basics of Field Retrieval

To start, it is necessary to grasp the fundamental approach to accessing a private field using reflection. The process can be accomplished with the aid of the `java.lang.Class` and `java.lang.reflect.Field` classes. Below is a general procedure, presented in pseudocode, for obtaining a private field:

Algorithm 1: Pseudocode for retrieving a private field

Data: A class instance from which private fields need to be accessed
Result: Access to the private field

1. obtain the Class object using the `getClass()` method
2. use the `getDeclaredField()` method with the field's name to retrieve the Field object
3. make the field accessible by calling `setAccessible(true)` on the Field object
4. use the Field object to get or set values as required

Code Implementation

Reflection requires careful handling to ensure that the implementation abides by security and design best practices. Here is how to access a private field named `secretData` in an example class named `EncapsulatedObject`:

```
import java.lang.reflect.Field;

public class FieldRetriever {
    public static void retrievePrivateField() {
        EncapsulatedObject obj = new EncapsulatedObject();
        Class<?> cls = obj.getClass();
        try {
            Field field = cls.getDeclaredField("secretData");
```

```
 9          field.setAccessible(true);
10          Object value = field.get(obj);
11          System.out.println("Value of secretData: " + value);
12      } catch (NoSuchFieldException | IllegalAccessException e) {
13          e.printStackTrace();
14      }
15  }
16  public static void main(String[] args) {
17      retrievePrivateField();
18  }
19 }
```

The output of this operation, assuming the field secretData holds the string "ReflectionInJava", would be:

```
Value of secretData: ReflectionInJava
```

Discussion

The ability to access private fields is not without risks or ethical considerations. When a field is set to private, it is usually intended to be inaccessible outside the defining class, maintaining encapsulation and promoting object-oriented principles. Overriding these restrictions should be done with a clear purpose and understanding of the consequences.

Ensuring that the use of such capabilities is protected and justifiable falls under the responsibilities of a prudent developer. Using reflection to access private fields can be critical for functionalities such as serialization, debugging, and testing, where internal state inspection is necessary. However, it is crucial to evaluate whether such actions compromise the integrity or security of the application.

Security Measures

When employing reflection to manipulate access controls, it is recommended to consider the following security practices:

- Limit the scope of reflection to known and controlled environments.

- Audit and monitor the usage of reflection in code to identify potential abusive access patterns.

- Integrate security manager checks to prevent unauthorized reflection use when running in sensitive or secure contexts.

Reflective operations on private fields should be executed with a deep understanding of the codebase and security repercussions associated with such actions.

5.4 Modifying Private Fields Using Reflection

The ability to modify private fields of a class in Java using reflection is a powerful feature that allows developers to change the state of an object in ways that are not possible using normal access patterns. This section provides a comprehensive guide to understanding and implementing this capability correctly and safely.

Reflection provides the `Field` class, which offers methods to manipulate fields dynamically. Modifications to private fields typically involve several steps: obtaining the `Class` object, retrieving the specific `Field` object, and using methods to bypass visibility restrictions and change the field's value. It is crucial to handle exceptions appropriately and understand the potential risks associated with this approach.

- First, obtain the `Class` object for the class whose field needs to be modified. This can be accomplished through the `Object`'s `getClass()` method or directly from the class literal.

- Next, retrieve the desired `Field` by calling the `getDeclaredField(String fieldName)` method on the `Class` object. This method fetches the `Field` object representing the specified private field.

- To modify the field, access must be granted by calling `setAccessible(true)` on the `Field` object. This method allows for breaking the Java access control checks.

- Finally, use the `set(Object obj, Object value)` method on the `Field` object to change the field's value. This method sets the value of the specified object's field to the provided value.

The following pseudocode illustrates the standard procedure for modifying a private field using reflection:

Algorithm 2: Modifying a private field using reflection

Input: An object `obj` whose private field needs modification, the field name `fieldName` and the new value `newValue`
Output: None, but object's private field is modified

1 $class \leftarrow obj.getClass()$
2 $field \leftarrow class.getDeclaredField(fieldName)$
3 $field.setAccessible(true)$
4 $field.set(obj, newValue)$

While this capability is integral for certain applications such as testing and managing legacy code, developers must ensure it is used responsibly to avoid unintended side-effects and maintain software integrity. Modifying a private field bypasses the encapsulation principle of object-oriented programming and can lead to maintenance challenges.

Real-world use cases often include altering states during runtime for classes where source code modifications are impractical. This is frequent in environments where legacy systems must adapt to new requirements without changing the underlying codebase. Nevertheless, rigorous testing and validation are imperative to ensure that these changes do not introduce bugs or security vulnerabilities.

Moreover, reflecting on private fields should always respect the software's architectural and security constraints. It is recommended to document any use of reflection to modify internal states heavily to maintain clarity for future maintenance and audits.

Through careful application and consideration of the surrounding ethical, technical, and security contexts, using reflection to modify private fields can be a valuable tool in the Java developer's toolkit. Developers are encouraged to weigh the benefits against potential pitfalls carefully and to utilize this technique when it is clearly justified and responsibly managed.

5.5 Accessing Private Methods of a Class

Accessing private methods in Java classes via reflection is a technique that allows programmers to perform operations that would otherwise be restricted by Java's access control mechanisms. This segment details the methodological approach to accessing private methods using Java

5.5. ACCESSING PRIVATE METHODS OF A CLASS

Reflection. It also discusses several practical instances where such access might be necessary, alongside the precautions and best practices that should be followed.

To begin accessing private methods, one must first obtain a Class object that represents the class whose private methods need to be manipulated. Reflection provides a way to interact with the internal state of objects and classes at runtime, including those marked as private.

```
1  Class<?> clazz = MyClass.class;
```

Having obtained the Class object, the next step involves retrieving the specific private method. This can be accomplished using the getDeclaredMethod method of the Class class. It is crucial to pass the exact name of the method and parameter types it accepts as arguments to getDeclaredMethod to avoid NoSuchMethodException.

```
1  Method privateMethod = clazz.getDeclaredMethod("privateMethodName",
       parameterTypes...);
```

Once the method is retrieved, it is still not accessible due to its private access modifier. To make it accessible, one must invoke the setAccessible method on the Method object, passing true as an argument.

```
1  privateMethod.setAccessible(true);
```

After setting the method accessible, it can be invoked on an instance of the object. Here, invoke method is used, which requires the instance of the object and the actual parameters to be passed to the private method.

```
1  Object result = privateMethod.invoke(objectInstance, argumentValues...);
```

The following elements must be considered when accessing private methods through reflection:

- Security Risks: Altering the accessibility of private members can lead to violations of the encapsulation principles of object-oriented design. It exposes internal implementation details and may lead to security breaches if misused.

- Performance Overheads: Utilizing reflection involves a significant overhead as compared to direct method calls, due to the extra checks and processes involved in the reflection methodology.

- Exception Handling: Reflection operations throw checked exceptions (e.g., NoSuchMethodException, IllegalAccessException) that must be handled appropriately to prevent program failure.

While the power of reflection in accessing and manipulating internal components of classes is undeniable, it must be wielded with caution. Programmers should ensure that they secure permissions appropriately and validate all inputs when using reflection to access private methods. This approach helps maintain the robustness and security of the application. Risks associated with reflection should be managed by adhering strictly to the principles of minimal privilege and secure coding practices.

5.6 Invoking Private Methods Dynamically

Reflection in Java allows for dynamic method invocation, including those that are private and not accessible under normal circumstances. This section delves into the methodologies for invoking private methods dynamically, illustrating the approach through concrete examples, and discussing the technical considerations and implications of such operations.

Method Retrieval and Accessibility

The initial step in invoking a private method is to retrieve the `Method` object representing the method. This can be achieved using the `Class.getDeclaredMethod(String name, Class… parameterTypes)` method. Unlike `Class.getMethod(String name, Class… parameterTypes)`, which only returns public methods, `getDeclaredMethod` includes private methods in its search. However, accessing these methods requires altering their accessibility.

The following example demonstrates the retrieval of a private method:

```
import java.lang.reflect.Method;

public class ReflectionExample {
    private String sayHello(String name) {
        return "Hello, " + name;
    }

    public static void main(String[] args) {
        try {
            Method method = ReflectionExample.class.getDeclaredMethod("sayHello",
                String.class);
```

5.6. INVOKING PRIVATE METHODS DYNAMICALLY

```
11              System.out.println("Method retrieved: " + method.getName());
12          } catch (NoSuchMethodException e) {
13              e.printStackTrace();
14          }
15      }
16  }
```

Upon retrieval, the Method object's accessibility is modified using the Method.setAccessible(true) method. This allows for the invocation of the private method, bypassing Java's standard access checks.

Dynamic Invocation

After ensuring the method is accessible, it can be invoked on an instance of the class. This is accomplished using Method.invoke(Object obj, Object... args) method. It is important to handle potential exceptions that might arise from incorrect use or invocation issues.

The following example illustrates invoking a private method dynamically:

```
1   import java.lang.reflect.InvocationTargetException;
2
3   public class InvocationExample {
4       private String secretMessage(String user) {
5           return "This is a secret message for " + user;
6       }
7
8       public static void main(String[] args) {
9           try {
10              Method secretMethod = InvocationExample.class.getDeclaredMethod("
                    secretMessage", String.class);
11              secretMethod.setAccessible(true);
12              String message = (String) secretMethod.invoke(new InvocationExample(), "
                    John Doe");
13              System.out.println("Invoked message: " + message);
14          } catch (NoSuchMethodException | IllegalAccessException |
                InvocationTargetException e) {
15              e.printStackTrace();
16          }
17      }
18  }
```

In the above example, exceptions such as IllegalAccessException, InvocationTargetException, and NoSuchMethodException are handled appropriately to ensure robustness. Moreover, using reflection to override access control is not without risks, as detailed in previous sections of this chapter. All invocations must be conducted within the legal frameworks and ethical guidelines established for software practice.

Considerations and Best Practices

While invoking private methods dynamically provides powerful capabilities, it must be used with caution to prevent unintended consequences, such as:

- Breaking object encapsulation and compromising application integrity.
- Introducing security vulnerabilities through exposed private data or operations.
- Decreasing maintainability and traceability of the code, making debugging and testing more challenging.

When employing this technique, ensure that it is used in scenarios where such access is absolutely necessary and justified, such as unit testing private methods or dealing with legacy systems where modifications are impractical. Additionally, documenting the reasons and contexts in which reflection is used to access private components promotes better maintainability and understanding of the codebase.

Reflecting on the power of reflection to invoke private methods dynamically reveals its dual nature—both as a tool for enabling robust software development and as a potential point of vulnerability. Leveraging this capability responsibly ensures that software not only meets the required functionality but also adheres to the principles of secure and maintainable code.

5.7 Constructors Accessibility and Instantiation

Constructors in Java play a pivotal role in the instantiation of objects. When dealing with Reflection, the accessibility and manipulation of constructors, especially those that are private, represent significant challenges and opportunities for developers. This section dives deep into methodologically accessing and instantiating objects using private constructors through Java Reflection, ensuring the discourse aligns with the best practices and the necessary precautions.

Java Reflection provides the `Constructor<T>` class, which is crucial for acquiring and modifying the constructor's visibility. The process of ac-

5.7. CONSTRUCTORS ACCESSIBILITY AND INSTANTIATION

cessing a private constructor can be segmented into several systematic steps outlined below.

Firstly, obtaining the Constructor object requires knowledge of the specific class and the parameter types of the desired constructor. The following lstlisting environment showcases the method to retrieve a specific constructor:

```
// Retrieve the constructor for MyClass with single String parameter
Constructor<MyClass> constructor = MyClass.class.getDeclaredConstructor(String.
    class);
```

Once the constructor is retrieved, setting its accessibility is mandatory for private constructors. This is achieved by invoking the setAccessible(true) method on the Constructor object:

```
// Make the constructor accessible
constructor.setAccessible(true);
```

After ensuring the constructor's accessibility, instantiation of the class becomes feasible. The newInstance method is used to create a new instance of the class using the previously inaccessible constructor:

```
// Instantiate the object using the private constructor
MyClass myClassInstance = constructor.newInstance("Initial value");
```

The output of the instantiation can be displayed as follows:

```
Instance created using private constructor with initial value: Initial value
```

While the usage of setAccessible(true) offers substantial power in dynamic class loading and testing scenarios, it is essential to utilize it prudently to maintain code security and integrity. To underscore this, reflect on a typical use case where a class with a private constructor is designed to have controlled instances (e.g., Singleton pattern); bypassing this design can lead to unpredictable states within the application.

To conceptually visualize the typical sequence of actions taken when employing reflection to access and instantiate constructors, consider the following tikzpicture:

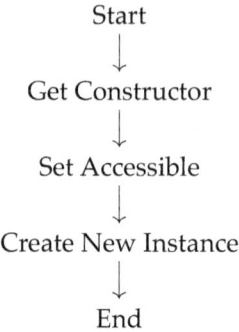

Handling `IllegalAccessException` effectively is another fundamental aspect of correctly implementing private constructor access. Typically, this exception occurs if the underlying constructor is inaccessible (i.e., it's either private or package-private, and the `setAccessible(true)` method is not employed). To mitigate this, always check the constructor's accessibility and handle exceptions gracefully to avoid compromising application stability.

The enabling technologies like Java Reflection empower developers by allowing runtime modifications, which can be essential when interfacing with libraries, frameworks, or legacy systems. However, it necessitates a balanced approach considering design intent, system security, and ethical implications meticulously.

By understanding and implementing these techniques appropriately, developers can harness the full potential of Java Reflection to facilitate dynamic instantiation and enhance application adaptability, all while adhering to secure and responsible coding practices.

5.8 Handling IllegalAccessException

IllegalAccessException is a checked exception in Java reflective operations which signifies an illegal attempt to access a class member that enforces a particular access control level. In scenarios where reflection is employed to interact with private fields, methods, or constructors, *IllegalAccessException* presents a significant challenge. This section elucidates strategies for properly handling this exception to ensure that software leveraging reflection remains robust and secure.

When reflection is utilized to access or modify private members

5.8. HANDLING ILLEGALACCESSEXCEPTION

of a class, the Java reflection API mandates that accessibility must be explicitly set. This is primarily done through the method `setAccessible(true)` provided by the `AccessibleObject` class. Failing to appropriately set accessibility or attempting to bypass restrictions imposed by the runtime environment triggers *IllegalAccessException*.

Understanding IllegalAccessException

- It is thrown to indicate that the currently executing method does not have access to the definition of the specified field, method, or constructor.

- This exception is a direct consequence of the Java security architecture, which aims to enforce encapsulation and the safe use of classes.

- When accessed during reflective operations, it serves as a safeguard against improper usage of reflection that could potentially violate class integrity.

Strategies for Handling IllegalAccessException Proper handling of *IllegalAccessException* involves anticipatory checks and structured error management. Below are effective techniques to manage this exception when utilizing reflection:

```
try {
    // Attempting to access the private field
    Field field = targetClass.getDeclaredField("privateField");
    // Set accessible true to bypass the access checking
    field.setAccessible(true);

    // Access or modify the field
    Object value = field.get(targetObject);
} catch (NoSuchFieldException | SecurityException e) {
    // Handle cases where the field does not exist or security violation occurs
    e.printStackTrace();
} catch (IllegalAccessException e) {
    // Log the access violation
    System.out.println("Failed to access the private field due to access
        restrictions.");
    e.printStackTrace();
}
```

In the provided code example, exceptions are managed distinctly based on their nature:

- *NoSuchFieldException* and *SecurityException* manage scenarios involving non-existence or security policy violations.

- *IllegalAccessException* is specifically caught to address access control violations, allowing for targeted debugging and recovery strategies.

Best Practices to Prevent IllegalAccessException Prevention is invariably better than rectification. Employ the following best practices to minimize the incidence of *IllegalAccessException*:

- Always check the visibility of the member before attempting access or modification.

- Use `Modifiers` to check if a member is accessible and handle it accordingly before calling `setAccessible`.

- Incorporate error handling robustly around reflective accesses to ensure that your application can gracefully handle or log issues related to illegal access.

These approaches not only assist in maintaining the security posture of your application but also align with the principles of safe and ethical use of reflection in Java.

By adhering to these guidelines and employing structured error handling strategies, developers can effectively manage *IllegalAccessException* and maintain the robustness of applications using Java Reflection. Through careful planning and implementation, reflection can be used securely and effectively, respecting the encapsulation and access control mechanisms of the Java programming language.

5.9 Ethical Considerations and Risks of Accessing Private Members

The ability to access and manipulate private members of classes in Java using reflection presents a powerful tool, which, if misused, may lead to serious ethical and security implications. This section delves into the ethical responsibilities of developers using reflection and highlights the risks associated with such practices.

The ethical considerations involved in accessing private members stem from the core principles of object-oriented programming (OOP). In OOP, encapsulation is a fundamental concept intended to safeguard

5.9. ETHICAL CONSIDERATIONS AND RISKS OF ACCESSING PRIVATE MEMBERS

the internal state of an object from unintended interferences and misuse. By design, private members are not accessible from outside their class boundary, ensuring a controlled environment where the internals of an object can only be modified in a manner prescribed by the original developer.

Using reflection to access or modify private members bypasses these protective measures, potentially compromising software integrity and reliability. It is imperative for developers to critically assess the necessity and justification for employing such techniques in their projects. Here are some key ethical considerations:

- **Consent and Ownership**: Reflection should be used judiciously, especially when dealing with code written by others. Modifying private members without the original author's consent may violate intellectual property rights and can be seen as an intrusive act.

- **Impact on Software Integrity**: Altering an object's private state can introduce unintended behaviors or bugs, particularly if the modifications are not aligned with the original design intent. This can degrade the overall system stability and functionality.

- **Security Implications**: Accessing or modifying private variables may inadvertently expose sensitive data or disrupt security mechanisms embedded within a class, leading to vulnerabilities that could be exploited maliciously.

On the practical side, reflection's ability to access private members also introduces various risks. Notably, this practice can lead to code that is difficult to understand and maintain. Moreover, reliance on reflection for accessing private parts of classes makes the code susceptible to breaking changes in the libraries or frameworks being used. Such risks necessitate strict guidelines to ensure that the use of reflection is both necessary and secure.

One of the essential steps in mitigating the risks involved with using reflection is a thorough code review process. Code reviews help ensure that the use of reflection is justified and that safer alternatives have been considered. Furthermore, when reflection is deemed necessary, developers must implement robust error handling to manage exceptions and unexpected behavior gracefully, particularly when interacting with private members. Detailed logging of reflective access can also facilitate debugging and future audits.

To illustrate, suppose a development team needs to access a private field, username, for a critical legacy integration where modifying the source is not feasible. The following code snippet shows how such access might be implemented securely:

```
1  Field field = User.class.getDeclaredField("username");
2  field.setAccessible(true); // Enabling access
3  try {
4      String username = (String) field.get(userInstance);
5      System.out.println("Username retrieved: " + username);
6  } catch (IllegalAccessException e) {
7      e.printStackTrace(); // Logging the exception for audit purposes
8  } finally {
9      field.setAccessible(false); // Restoring original access level
10 }
```

The reflection-based approach has been safeguarded with try-catch blocks to handle potential illegal access and to make sure that the access modifier of the field is reset, preserving the integrity of the class as much as possible.

Reflection is a double-edged sword in the realm of Java programming. While it provides developers with powerful capabilities to interact with class internals, it also imposes a responsibility to use these capabilities judiciously and ethically. Balancing the technical benefits against the ethical and security risks is key to using Java reflection in a responsible manner.

5.10 Security Implications of Breaking Encapsulation

The practice of using Java reflection to access and manipulate private class members poses significant security implications. These implications arise primarily due to the breaking of encapsulation, a core principle of object-oriented programming. Encapsulation ensures that the internal representation of an object is hidden from the outside, except through the object's methods. When encapsulation is compromised, it can lead to a variety of security risks, including unauthorized access, code integrity violation, and exposure of sensitive data.

5.10. SECURITY IMPLICATIONS OF BREAKING ENCAPSULATION

Unauthorized Access to Sensitive Data

One major security risk of breaking encapsulation through reflection is the unauthorized access to sensitive data. Private fields in a class often contain sensitive information intended to be shielded from the outside world. By accessing these fields directly, malicious code can read or modify sensitive data.

For instance, consider a class `User` that has a private field `password`. Normally, this field would be inaccessible from outside the `User` class, but through reflection, it can be accessed and potentially exposed or altered. Here is an example demonstrating this:

```java
import java.lang.reflect.Field;

public class AccessExample {
    public static void main(String[] args) throws Exception {
        User user = new User("username", "secretPassword");
        Field field = user.getClass().getDeclaredField("password");
        field.setAccessible(true);
        String passwordValue = (String) field.get(user);
        System.out.println("Password: " + passwordValue);
    }
}
```

Output:
Password: secretPassword

Violating Code Integrity and Behavior

Reflection allows not only access to private data but also the modification of it, which can lead to violations of the intended behavior of the application. By changing the state of objects in unexpected ways, the stability and reliability of software can be undermined, potentially leading to bugs, crashes, or incorrect behavior.

Moreover, reflection can be used to bypass restrictions or checks implemented in the methods of a class, further complicating the security landscape. For example, bypassing a check on whether the user is authorized to perform a certain operation can expand the attack surface of the application.

Exposure to External Tampering and Attacks

When encapsulation is broken, objects become vulnerable to tampering from external entities. This exposure greatly increases the likelihood of attacks such as data poisoning or security breaches. The ability of attackers to access or manipulate private states of objects can be particularly detrimental in environments where security is paramount, such as in financial or medical applications.

Mitigation Strategies

To mitigate the security risks associated with breaking encapsulation via reflection, several strategies can be employed:

- Limiting the use of reflection to those parts of the application where it is absolutely necessary and using it judiciously.
- Employing security managers and permission checks to control access to critical parts of the codebase.
- Auditing code regularly for uses of reflection that might expose sensitive data or compromise system integrity.
- Encouraging the use of design patterns and architectural strategies that do not require breaking encapsulation for testing or functionality extensions.

While reflection is a powerful feature within Java, it is crucial for developers to understand the security implications of its misuse or overuse. By adhering to best practices and incorporating robust security measures, the risks associated with breaking encapsulation can be significantly mitigated, thus harnessing the power of reflection without compromising the security and integrity of the application. This balanced approach ensures that developers can utilize the full potential of Java reflection while maintaining a secure and stable software environment.

5.11 Reflection and Java Security Manager

The use of Java Reflection to access and manipulate class members introduces significant concerns regarding application security. This section aims to elucidate the relationship between Java Reflection and the Java Security Manager, providing a detailed analysis of how security policies can be applied to regulate reflective operations, especially when handling private member access.

5.11. REFLECTION AND JAVA SECURITY MANAGER

The Java Security Manager serves as a critical component in the Java security environment, enforcing a set of policies that restrict the permissions of Java code based on various criteria. When reflection is used to access private members, the Security Manager applies specific checks to determine whether the operation should be allowed or denied, based on the current security policy in place.

```
SecurityManager check Permission: "ReflectPermission" ("suppressAccessChecks")
```

`ReflectPermission("suppressAccessChecks")` is a key permission associated with reflection. When enabling access to private members, this permission must be granted to the code segment attempting the operation. If the permission is not granted, a `SecurityException` will be thrown, effectively preventing the reflective access.

The following is a typical scenario where the `SecurityManager` intercepts an attempt to access a private field without sufficient permissions:

```java
public class SecurityExample {
    private int secret = 42;

    public static void accessPrivateField() {
        Field field = SecurityExample.class.getDeclaredField("secret");
        field.setAccessible(true); // This line requires permission
        System.out.println("Private field value: " + field.getInt(new
            SecurityExample()));
    }

    public static void main(String[] args) {
        try {
            accessPrivateField();
        } catch (SecurityException | NoSuchFieldException | IllegalAccessException e
            ) {
            e.printStackTrace();
        }
    }
}
```

If the security settings do not permit suppressAccessChecks, the code above will produce an output akin to:

```
java.lang.SecurityException: Cannot suppress access checks
```

To manage the reflective operations under security controls, modifying the Java policy file might be necessary. An example entry in the policy file that grants the required permissions might look like this:

```
grant codeBase "file:/path/to/trusted/library/-" {
    permission java.lang.reflect.ReflectPermission "suppressAccessChecks";
};
```

This policy entry explicitly grants the `ReflectPermission` to any code sourced from a specified path, which ensures that only trusted code is able to bypass the default Java access checks.

Moreover, monitoring and logging the use of reflective operations can also aid in maintaining security. Such information is vital for auditing and forensic analysis, especially in applications that handle sensitive or critical data. The logging can be implemented by integrating with the Java security architecture to track the usage of reflection within the application.

Given the inherent risks associated with bypassing standard access controls through reflection, employing the Java Security Manager with a strict policy set is imperative. This ensures that the powerful capabilities of reflection in Java do not compromise the integrity and security of the software.

Thus, while reflection offers flexibility and dynamic capabilities, its interaction with the Java Security Manager ensures a balanced approach toward maintaining security standards, underpinning the importance of thoughtful and stringent policy configurations in securing Java applications.

5.12 Summary of Techniques and Guidelines

This section encapsulates the fundamental techniques and guidelines for employing Java Reflection to access and manipulate private members of classes. As discussed earlier in this chapter, reflection presents a potent mechanism for interacting with components that are typically shielded by Java's access modifiers. Our exploration has revealed both the possibilities enabled by this approach and the prudent considerations that must anchor its application.

- **Use of `Field.setAccessible(true)`**: To interact with private fields safely, reflection demands the modification of the accessibility status of these fields. Employ the `Field` class's setAccessible method judiciously to expose private fields for reflective access. Code example:

```
1  Field field = SomeClass.class.getDeclaredField("privateFieldName");
2  field.setAccessible(true);
3  Object value = field.get(instanceOfSomeClass);
4  field.set(instanceOfSomeClass, newValue);
```

The code snippet above manipulates a private field by first retrieving it, setting it as accessible, and subsequently getting and setting its value.

5.12. SUMMARY OF TECHNIQUES AND GUIDELINES

- **Handling `IllegalAccessException`**: Crucially, operations that bypass Java's natural access checks can throw `IllegalAccessException`. It's essential to handle this exception when executing reflection-based operations:

```
try {
    // reflection-based access or modification
} catch (IllegalAccessException e) {
    // handle access violation, possibly rethrow as a RuntimeException
}
```

- **Reflection on Private Methods**: Similar to fields, private methods can be accessed and invoked using reflection if set accessible. This allows executing methods which are not visible under normal circumstances.

```
Method method = SomeClass.class.getDeclaredMethod("privateMethodName",
    parameterTypes);
method.setAccessible(true);
Object result = method.invoke(instanceOfSomeClass, methodArguments);
```

- **Constructor Access**: Reflection can also instantiate objects using private constructors, broadening the possibilities for creating instances from externally inaccessible classes.

```
Constructor<SomeClass> constructor = SomeClass.class.getDeclaredConstructor
    ();
constructor.setAccessible(true);
SomeClass instance = constructor.newInstance();
```

Further, when adopting reflection it is crucial to:

- Evaluate the **performance implications**. Reflective operations are generally slower than their direct counterparts, thus should be used sparingly within performance-critical sections of an application.

- Consider the **security risks** associated with making private elements accessible, especially in environments where malicious code could exploit elevated access to sensitive data.

- Maintain adherence to **principles of software design** such as encapsulation and modularization, even when reflection seems to contravene these principles. Reflection should not be used to routinely circumvent language access controls but reserved for specific cases like serialization, deep debugging, or framework design.

As we integrate reflection into Java applications, especially for accessing private members, it behooves developers to tread cautiously, balancing the powerful capabilities afforded with the responsibility to maintain robust, secure, and maintainable code bases.

Chapter 6

Reflective Operations on Arrays

This chapter delves into reflective operations on arrays, highlighting essential techniques for dynamically creating and manipulating array instances in Java. It provides a deep understanding of how to interact with the components of arrays, inspect array types and lengths, and handle multi-dimensional structures—all through reflection. The ability to modify array contents at runtime and manage arrays without explicit type information enhances flexibility in developing and maintaining Java applications, offering practical know-how for advanced array handling with introspective techniques.

6.1 Introduction to Array Reflection

Reflection in Java is a powerful feature that permits an executing Java program to examine and "reflect" upon itself, and manipulate internal properties of the program. For arrays, this reflective ability introduces a dynamic aspect to their manipulation, making it possible to handle arrays in a generic and flexible manner without knowing their component type and size at compile time.

Arrays in Java are objects that hold fixed numbers of values of a single type. The length of an array is set when it is created and cannot be changed. Using reflection with arrays allows not only for the examination of array types and the dynamic creation of arrays, but also for the manipulation of their contents during runtime. This can be particularly beneficial in scenarios where applications need to integrate with externally provided data structures or must be highly flexible and adaptable.

- Reflection provides the ability to inspect array types and access array components dynamically.

- It allows for the creation and manipulation of arrays without specific type information being available at compile time.

- Reflective operations on arrays make it possible to handle complex data structures more flexibly and adaptively.

Reflective array operations include tasks such as dynamically creating arrays, manipulating their contents, examining array dimensions, and handling arrays composed of primitive types or objects. A typical use case involves a scenario where the data structure is determined at runtime and must be accessed and modified dynamically. Reflection makes this feasible by offering methods to instantiate array objects and access their elements reflectively.

To illustrate the basic operation of array reflection, consider the following code sample that uses the java.lang.reflect.Array class for creating an instance of an array dynamically and then setting a value at a specific index:

```
import java.lang.reflect.Array;

public class ReflectiveArrayManipulation {
    public static void main(String[] args) {
        try {
            Class<?> arrayClass = Class.forName("[I"); // Identifies an integer array class
            Object array = Array.newInstance(arrayClass.getComponentType(), 10); // Create an array of integers with 10 elements
            Array.setInt(array, 5, 42); // Set the element at index 5 to 42

            int element = Array.getInt(array, 5); // Retrieve the element at index 5
            System.out.println("Element at index 5: " + element);
        } catch (ClassNotFoundException e) {
            e.printStackTrace();
        }
    }
}
```

The output of the above program is:

```
Element at index 5: 42
```

The significance of array reflection lies in its inherent flexibility and its potential to extend the adaptability of applications significantly. By interacting dynamically with array types and manipulations, developers can address a myriad of use cases that would otherwise require more static implementations or extensive boilerplate code.

Understanding and employing reflective operations effectively on arrays can enhance a developer's ability to contend with varying and unpredictable data handling requirements, thereby adding robustness and scalability to Java applications.

6.2 Creating Arrays Dynamically

Creating arrays dynamically using Java Reflection involves several nuanced steps that allow the developer to instantiate arrays at runtime when the type or size might not be known at compile time. This technique is especially useful in situations where applications need to integrate with external systems or handle data whose type and size are determined at runtime.

To instantiate an array dynamically, the `java.lang.reflect.Array` class is used. This class provides static methods to dynamically create and access Java arrays. Below is a comprehensive guide, presented in precise steps, and illustrated with code examples enclosed in the `lstlisting` environment.

- **Determining the Component Type**: The first step in dynamically creating an array is to determine its component type. This is crucial as it defines the type of elements the array will hold.

- **Specifying the Length of the Array**: Once the component type is established, the next step is to define the size of the array.

- **Creating the Array**: Utilizing the `Array.newInstance()` method, an array with the specified component type and length is instantiated.

Step-by-Step Implementation:

1. **Obtaining the Class Object**: The Class object corresponding to the component type of the array must be obtained. This is typically achieved using the Class.forName() method if the type name is known or by using the `.class` literal.

```
1  Class<?> componentType = Class.forName("java.lang.String");
```

2. **Creating the Array Instance**: Utilize the `Array.newInstance()` method from the `java.lang.reflect.Array` class by passing the Class object and the desired array length.

```
1  Object arrayInstance = Array.newInstance(componentType, 10);
```

Output demonstrating the dynamic creation:

```
String[] myArray = (String[]) arrayInstance;
```

This array, though created at runtime, acts like any statically-typed array in Java and can be used in the same manner.

Dynamic Array Initialization:

After creation, the array elements are initialized to the default values typical for the array type (null for objects, 0 for integers, etc.). The developer may choose to initialize it with specific values using loops or array manipulation methods.

```
1  String[] stringArray = (String[]) arrayInstance;
2  for (int i = 0; i < stringArray.length; i++) {
3      stringArray[i] = "Element " + i;
4  }
```

The practical applications of creating arrays dynamically are vast, ranging from generic data processors to complex AI algorithms which require runtime type flexibility. This reflective approach empowers developers to write more versatile and adaptable code, which is particularly beneficial in scenarios where the type information is only available at runtime.

Employing the right tools and understanding provided by Java Reflection, developers can harness the power of dynamic arrays efficiently, ensuring robust and flexible applications ready to meet various runtime challenges.

6.3 Retrieving and Setting Array Components Reflectively

Reflective array operations are a compelling feature in Java, allowing developers to handle arrays dynamically. This capability is particularly advantageous when the component type of an array is unknown

6.3. RETRIEVING AND SETTING ARRAY COMPONENTS REFLECTIVELY

at compile time. In this section, we will thoroughly examine methods for retrieving and setting values of an array component using the reflection API provided by Java.

To start retrieving or modifying the value of an array component reflectively, the reflection API provides the 'Array' class in the 'java.lang.reflect' package. This class includes methods such as 'Array.get(Object array, int index)' and 'Array.set(Object array, int index, Object value)', designed specifically for these purposes.

- 'Array.get(Object array, int index)': This method returns the value of the specified index in the given array object as type 'Object'. Below is an example usage:

```
1    int[] numbers = {1, 2, 3, 4, 5};
2    Object element = Array.get(numbers, 2);
3    System.out.println(element);
```

₃In this example, 'element' retrieves the value '3', which is the element at index '2' in the array 'numbers'.

- 'Array.set(Object array, int index, Object value)': This method sets the specified value at the specified index of the array. It is crucial that the value is compatible with the component type of the array. Consider the example below:

```
1    String[] strings = {"Hello", "World"};
2    Array.set(strings, 1, "Java");
3    System.out.println(Arrays.toString(strings));
```

[Hello, Java]This changes the second element of the array 'strings' from "World" to "Java".

Furthermore, when dealing with arrays of primitive types, 'java.lang.reflect.Array' handles boxing and unboxing automatically; however, one must still take care for type compatibility during these operations. Here is an example that clarifies this:

```
1    int[] numberArray = new int[3];
2    Array.set(numberArray, 0, 123); // Correct usage
3    // Array.set(numberArray, 1, "123"); // Incorrect, raises ArrayStoreException
```

In cases where type safety is a must, attempting to insert incompatible types will raise an 'ArrayStoreException'.

For developers looking to build flexible systems that interact with array objects, understanding the reflection-based operations is crucial. Interfaces or methods that accept array objects and operate on them reflectively can dramatically simplify code and increase its robustness, particularly in scenarios where the type of array cannot be predetermined.

Handling reflection-based operations effectively requires comprehensive knowledge of Java's type system and careful attention to exceptions that can arise from improper handling of types and array indices. As reflection bypasses type checks performed by compilers, runtime exception handling around reflective array manipulations becomes indispensable.

This approach of retrieving and setting array components reflectively underscores the dynamic capabilities inherent in the Java programming language, enabling developers to write more generalized, flexible, and adaptive code structures.

6.4 Manipulating Multi-Dimensional Arrays

Multi-dimensional arrays in Java, when viewed through the lens of reflection, necessitate a comprehensive understanding of both their structural nuances and the reflective methods applicable to their manipulation. This section elucidates the approach to dynamically managing multi-dimensional arrays using Java Reflection, ensuring that operations such as access, modification, and the assessment of dimensions are proficiently handled.

When dealing with multi-dimensional arrays reflectively, it is crucial to first pinpoint the array's base component type and its dimensional depth. These determine how the array will be interactively manipulated in a reflection-based scenario.

- Understanding the Array Class and its Implications:

```
1  Class<?> arrayClass = Class.forName("[[Ljava.lang.Integer;");
```

- Identifying the component type dynamically:

```
1  Class<?> componentType = arrayClass.getComponentType();
```

- Reflectively instantiate a multi-dimensional array:

```
1  int[] dimensions = new int[]{5, 5}; // 5x5 Integer array
2  Object arrayInstance = Array.newInstance(componentType, dimensions);
```

6.4. MANIPULATING MULTI-DIMENSIONAL ARRAYS

The structural configuration of a multi-dimensional array can be dissected into individual layers, where each layer corresponds to a dimension. Reflective operations must carefully navigate these layers to prevent type mismatches and ensure the integrity of operations. The following pseudocode using the `Array` class provides a detailed blueprint for accessing and setting values within a multi-dimensional array:

Algorithm 3: Pseudocode for setting a value in a multi-dimensional array

---

Data: arrayInstance, value, indices[]
Result: Updates an element in a multidimensional array
1 **begin**
2 | tempInstance ← arrayInstance
3 | **for** $idx \in indices$ *except last index* **do**
4 | | tempInstance ← Array.get(tempInstance, idx)
5 | Array.set(tempInstance, indices[indices.length - 1], value)

Furthermore, retrieving specific elements can be achieved through similar loops and index management but utilizing the `Array.get()` method instead. This iterative approach ensures that any depth can be managed efficiently.

Handling exceptions is also a critical segment of reflective multi-dimensional array manipulations. Java's reflection mechanism can throw a multitude of exceptions, including `IllegalArgumentException` and `ArrayIndexOutOfBoundsException`, which must be meticulously caught and handled to maintain robust application behavior.

```
Exception in thread "main" java.lang.IllegalArgumentException: Argument is not an array
```

Lastly, the visualization of array structures for debugging or educational purposes can be facilitated using simple iteration techniques combined with reflective insights. Executing this requires traversing through each dimension and recursively handling nested arrays, culminating in a comprehensive display of the array's contents and structure.

In carrying out these operations, developers wield the power to programmatically interact with any multi-dimensional array configuration, irrespective of its prior definition, thereby leveraging maximum flexibility in dynamic application development environments oriented around Java. The reflective manipulation of multi-dimensional arrays, while complex, is an invaluable skill set in harnessing the full potential of Java's dynamic capabilities.

6.5 Type Checking and Casting with Reflective Arrays

Reflective operations in Java enable a dynamic approach to handling types, which is particularly useful in operations involving arrays. This section explores the intricacies of type checking and casting arrays using Java's Reflection API, ensuring type safety and minimizing runtime errors when interacting with arrays of unknown types dynamically.

Understanding Type Checking in Reflective Arrays

Java's type checking mechanism plays a critical role in reflective array handling. Using `java.lang.reflect.Array`, developers can ascertain the type of an array at runtime, ensuring that operations are type-safe. This is imperative when the component type of the array is not known at compile time.

```
1  // Demonstrate retrieving the class type of an array component
2  Class<?> arrayComponentType = someArray.getClass().getComponentType();
3  System.out.println("Component type: " + arrayComponentType.getName());
```

Here, the method `getComponentType()` returns a `Class` object that represents the component type of the array. This method is indispensable for checking the type of the elements stored in any array.

Casting Arrays Reflectively

While Java's strong typing system normally requires explicit casts for assignments, reflection provides a way to cast arrays dynamically. This is essential when dealing with arrays obtained from reflective operations, especially when the component types might vary between operations.

```
1  // Example of casting an Object array to a specific type using reflection
2  Object arrayObject = Array.newInstance(String.class, 5);
3  String[] stringArray = (String[]) arrayObject;
```

The above example demonstrates dynamically creating an array and casting it to the desired type. The dynamic nature of reflective array casting is crucial when the array type is determined at runtime based on external conditions or data.

Ensuring Type Safety with Reflective Operations

Reflection can compromise type safety if not used carefully, leading to runtime type mismatches or `ClassCastException`. Hence, verifying the component type before casting is vital.

```
// Check before casting
if(arrayObject instanceof String[]) {
    String[] stringArray = (String[]) arrayObject;
    // Safe to use stringArray
}
```

In this snippet, the type compatibility is checked before performing the cast. This conditional check ensures that the program will not crash due to a type mismatch, thereby increasing the robustness of the application.

Utilizing Arrays `isAssignableFrom` to Prevent ClassCastExceptions

Another sophisticated technique to ensure safe casting involves the `isAssignableFrom` method from the `Class` class. This method can be used to determine if instances of a particular type can be safely assigned to arrays of another type.

```
// Demonstrating use of isAssignableFrom
if (targetType.isAssignableFrom(sourceArray.getClass().getComponentType())) {
    Object[] castedArray = (Object[])sourceArray;
    // Proceed with using castedArray
}
```

This method helps in making dynamic type checks robust, allowing for safe casting operations even in complex application scenarios involving multiple class loaders or encompassing user-defined types.

Reflective array operations' dynamic nature, combined with sound type checking and casting strategies, facilitates powerful runtime manipulations in Java. Leveraging the capabilities of Java's Reflection API thus allows developers to write more generic, flexible, and robust code, particularly in applications requiring extensive dynamic behavior based on array types.

6.6 Discovering Array Length and Component Type

In Java, arrays carry metadata about their structure, specifically the length of the array and the type of its components. This information is critical when using reflection to interact with arrays dynamically. This section explores the methodologies to obtain these pieces of information reflectively, enhancing the robustness of array manipulations in applications.

Reflective access to array metadata is facilitated through the java.lang.reflect.Array class provided by the Java Reflection API. This class includes methods for dynamically creating and manipulating arrays, as well as methods for retrieving the length of an array and the type of its components.

Retrieving Array Length

The length of an array is indicative of how many components it can hold. Unlike collections which have a dynamic size, an array's size is fixed upon its creation and critical to avoiding IndexOutOfBoundsException. To discover the length of an array dynamically using reflection, the Array.getLength(Object array) method is utilized.

Below is an example demonstrating how to use this method:

```
public int getArrayLength(Object array) throws IllegalArgumentException {
    if (!array.getClass().isArray()) {
        throw new IllegalArgumentException("Provided object is not an array");
    }
    return Array.getLength(array);
}
```

The method above checks if the provided object is indeed an array and then retrieves its length. If the object is not an array, it throws an IllegalArgumentException.

Discovering Component Type

Each array in Java has a component type, which is the type of elements it holds. Knowing the component type is essential when manipulating arrays dynamically to ensure type safety and prevent

6.7. PERFORMANCE ASPECTS OF ARRAY REFLECTION

`ArrayStoreException`. The reflective approach to ascertain the component type of an array involves the use of `getClass()` method on the array, followed by `getComponentType()`.

Here is an example that illustrates this concept:

```
public Class<?> getComponentType(Object array) throws IllegalArgumentException {
    if (!array.getClass().isArray()) {
        throw new IllegalArgumentException("Provided object is not an array");
    }
    return array.getClass().getComponentType();
}
```

This method checks if the given object is an array and returns the `Class` object associated with its component type. This `Class` object then can be used for further reflective operations such as instantiating new components or arrays of the same type.

In summary, the tasks of discovering the length and component type of arrays critically employ the `java.lang.reflect.Array` class within Java's Reflection API. These operations are vital for validations and manipulations in dynamic array handling, providing a toolkit for robust and efficient Java applications that utilize the power and flexibility of reflection. The techniques shown not only ensure safety from exceptions like `IllegalArgumentException` and `ArrayStoreException` but also enhance the maintenance and scalability of software systems involving complex data structures.

6.7 Performance Aspects of Array Reflection

Reflective operations on arrays in Java, while providing significant flexibility and dynamism, can come with notable performance implications. This section explores the efficiency considerations associated with using reflection for array operations, comparing these to traditional array handling techniques.

- Performance overhead associated with reflective methods.

- Factors influencing the efficiency of reflective array operations.

- Optimization strategies to mitigate performance penalties.

Performance Overhead Associated with Reflective Methods

Reflective operations incur inherent overheads because they bypass compile-time optimization possibilities inherent in Java. The java.lang.reflect.Array class methods, such as Array.newInstance() and Array.get() involve various additional steps including type checking, security checks, and method invocation which are not required in non-reflective environments.

Here is an example demonstrating the time complexity added by reflective creation and access of an array compared to traditional methods:

```
int size = 1000000;
Class intClass = int.class;

// Reflective array creation
Object reflectiveArray = Array.newInstance(intClass, size);

// Traditional array creation
int[] traditionalArray = new int[size];

long startTime, endTime, reflectiveTime, traditionalTime;

// Reflective access
startTime = System.nanoTime();
for (int i = 0; i < size; i++) {
    Array.setInt(reflectiveArray, i, i);
}
endTime = System.nanoTime();
reflectiveTime = endTime - startTime;

// Traditional access
startTime = System.nanoTime();
for (int i = 0; i < size; i++) {
    traditionalArray[i] = i;
}
endTime = System.nanoTime();
traditionalTime = endTime - startTime;
```

```
Reflective operation time: 12435678 nanoseconds
Traditional operation time: 237567 nanoseconds
```

Factors Influencing the Efficiency of Reflective Array Operations

Several factors can affect the performance of reflective array operations:

- **Operation Type:** The type of operations performed reflectively (e.g., creation, access, update) directly affects performance.

- **Array Size and Dimensionality:** Larger and multi-dimensional arrays require more computation and thus incur more overhead.

- **JVM Implementation:** JVM optimizations such as Just-In-Time (JIT) compilation can reduce some of the overheads but not eliminate them completely.

Optimization Strategies to Mitigate Performance Penalties

To mitigate the performance penalties associated with reflective array operations, consider the following strategies:

- **Minimizing Reflective Calls:** Use reflection sparingly, especially in performance-critical sections of the code.

- **Caching:** If the type of array to be created reflectively is known beforehand and frequently used, caching the class objects and methods can reduce lookup overhead.

- **Alternative Approaches:** When possible, consider using other Java features such as generics or method handles which may offer better performance in some scenarios.

Reflective operations provide a powerful tool for dynamic array manipulation but at the cost of performance. By understanding and mitigating these costs, developers can effectively balance flexibility and efficiency in their applications.

6.8 Common Use Cases for Reflective Array Operations

Reflective array operations, a potent feature of Java's Reflection API, are quintessential in scenarios where applications require dynamic manipulation of array types and contents. This section explores several common use cases illustrating the indispensability of these operations in real-world applications ranging from serialization frameworks to data manipulation libraries.

Dynamic Serialization and Deserialization

Serialization frameworks often leverage reflective array operations to dynamically serialize or deserialize data, particularly when the class structure is unknown at compile time. The ability to iterate through arrays reflectively and inspect their component types is fundamental for such frameworks to handle arbitrary objects correctly.

```
// Example: Reflective array serialization process
public String serialize(Object array) throws IllegalArgumentException {
    if (!array.getClass().isArray()) {
        throw new IllegalArgumentException("Provided object is not an array.");
    }
    int length = Array.getLength(array);
    StringBuilder sb = new StringBuilder("[");

    for (int i = 0; i < length; i++) {
        Object component = Array.get(array, i);
        sb.append(component.toString());
        if (i < length - 1) {
            sb.append(", ");
        }
    }
    sb.append("]");
    return sb.toString();
}
```

```
Output for a String array {"Hello", "World"}:
[Hello, World]
```

Dynamic Configuration Management

Systems that utilize plug-ins or modules often require dynamic configuration management, where settings might be represented as arrays. Reflective operations facilitate the dynamic loading and unloading of configurations without restarting the application, crucial for non-disruptive updates in production environments.

```
// Example: Dynamically changing configuration arrays
public void updateConfiguration(Object configArray, int index, Object newValue)
        throws ArrayIndexOutOfBoundsException {
    Array.set(configArray, index, newValue);
}
```

Unit Testing and Mocking

In unit testing, particularly when dealing with legacy code where dependencies are hard-coded as arrays, reflective array operations provide a way to inject mock objects into these arrays, thereby allowing isolated tests. This practice is particularly useful in environments where dependencies cannot be easily refactored or injected using conventional methods.

```
// Example: Injecting mocks into an array
public void injectMock(Object testArray, int index, Object mockObject) throws
    ArrayIndexOutOfBoundsException {
    Array.set(testArray, index, mockObject);
}
```

Data Processing and Transformation

Data-intensive applications, such as those in Big Data and AI domains, often require dynamic manipulation of large volumes of data stored in arrays. Reflective array operations enable developers to write more generic code that can handle different types and dimensions of data without crafting specific code for each data layout.

```
// Example: Reflective transformation of array elements
public Object transformArray(Object array, UnaryOperator<Object> operator) throws
    IllegalArgumentException {
    if (!array.getClass().isArray()) {
        throw new IllegalArgumentException("Input must be an array.");
    }
    int length = Array.getLength(array);
    Object newArray = Array.newInstance(array.getClass().getComponentType(), length
        );

    for (int i = 0; i < length; i++) {
        Object original = Array.get(array, i);
        Object transformed = operator.apply(original);
        Array.set(newArray, i, transformed);
    }
    return newArray;
}
```

Reflective operations on arrays showcase their versatility across various sectors of software development, underpinning the dynamic and flexible manipulation of data structures essential for modern software practices. The examples provided elucidate how these mechanisms are practically applied, emphasizing their significance in building adaptable and efficient software systems.

6.9 Reflection on Primitive Type Arrays vs Object Arrays

Reflective practices in Java allow for nuanced examination and modification of array types at runtime, significantly bridging gaps in dynamic versus static programming capabilities. This section delineates key differences, challenges, and considerations when reflecting on arrays of primitive types versus arrays composed of object references.

The fundamental disparity between primitive type arrays and object arrays in the Java programming language emanates from their underlying storage mechanisms and initialization behaviors. Primitive type arrays store their respective values directly, while object arrays store references to their actual objects. This difference critically impacts how reflective operations should be approached and conducted.

- Primitive type arrays, such as those declared as `int[]` or `double[]`, directly contain their respective values. Consequently, when utilizing reflection to interact with these arrays, attention must be paid to handling the unboxing and re-boxing of values when accessing or modifying them through methods provided in the `java.lang.reflect.Array` class.

- Object arrays, on the other hand, store references to instances of their element type, such as `String[]` or `Employee[]`. Reflective interactions with object arrays generally involve operations on the references rather than direct manipulation of the objects themselves.

Reflective operations commence by acquiring the `Class` object representing the array. Using the `Array.newInstance()` method, one can dynamically create an array instance of a specific type and dimensionality. This step is identical for both primitive type arrays and object arrays, albeit the implications during usage vary substantially.

```
1  Class<?> intArrayClass = Class.forName("[I");
2  int[] intArray = (int[]) Array.newInstance(intArrayClass.getComponentType(), 10);
```

[0, 0, 0, 0, 0, 0, 0, 0, 0, 0]

Inspecting elements through reflection utilizes the `Array.get()` and `Array.set()` methods, requiring explicit consideration of the array's base type to avoid `IllegalArgumentException`. For instance, setting an element in a primitive type array involves passing values that must be explicitly cast to the appropriate wrapper, whereas object arrays expect references compatible with their component type.

```
Array.set(intArray, 5, 42); // Correct usage for primitive array
```

[0, 0, 0, 0, 0, 42, 0, 0, 0, 0]

The scenario highlights the necessity for type awareness and precision in handling. An erroneous attempt to insert an incompatible type—or neglecting to handle auto-boxing and unboxing—can result in runtime exceptions.

- Type checking is crucial when dealing with object arrays to prevent runtime type errors. Operations such as `Array.getInt()` on an object array would fail at runtime because of type incompatibility.

- Security concerns also arise particularly with reflective operations as they can circumvent access controls, more commonly with object arrays where reference manipulation might expose vulnerable objects or data structures.

Reflective array handling demands an in-depth understanding of Java's type system, memory model, and exception hierarchy, each playing pivotal roles in effectively managing array content manipulation dynamically. By leveraging these reflective capabilities judiciously, developers gain the flexibility to work with Java arrays in ways typically reserved for more dynamic languages, albeit at the expense of increased complexity and overhead in type safety and security management. Through this, the profound utility and flexibility of reflection in Java is reinforced, particularly in scenarios requiring dynamic type manipulation and introspective handling operations.

6.10 Handling Exceptions in Reflective Array Operations

Reflective operations on arrays, while powerful, may lead to several exceptions due to dynamic type checks and operations at runtime. Mastering exception handling in these scenarios is crucial for writing robust Java applications. This section discusses the primary exceptions associated with reflective array operations and outlines the best practices for handling them effectively.

- `IllegalArgumentException`: This exception occurs when attempting to set or get an array component that is not compatible with the component type of the array. This usually happens due to incorrect casting or type mismatch.

- `ArrayIndexOutOfBoundsException`: Thrown when an operation tries to access an array element with an index that is negative or not less than the size of the array. This often results from faulty loop constructs or incorrect index calculations.

- `NullPointerException`: This exception is thrown when the reflective operations are called on an array that is null. Null checks are essential before performing any operations on the array.

- `NegativeArraySizeException`: Occurs during dynamic array creation if the size parameter is negative. Proper validation of array sizes is critical before array instantiation.

- `SecurityException`: Raised if a security manager exists and its `checkAccess` method denies access to the array. Ensuring proper permissions in the application's security policy is necessary to avoid this exception.

To depict how these exceptions can be effectively managed, consider the following code example illustrating various scenarios:

```
public Object reflectivelyModifyArray(Object array, int index, Object value) {
    try {
        java.lang.reflect.Array.set(array, index, value);
    } catch (IllegalArgumentException | ArrayIndexOutOfBoundsException e) {
        System.err.println("Failed to modify array: " + e.getMessage());
        return null;
    } catch (Exception e) {
        System.err.println("Unhandled exception: " + e.getMessage());
        return null;
    }
    return value;
}
```

The code above handles typical errors such as `IllegalArgumentException` and `ArrayIndexOutOfBoundsException`. It also includes a catch block for any other potential exceptions, ensuring that all bases are covered.

```
Output with index out of bounds:
Failed to modify array: index 5 out of bounds for length 3
```

```
Output with an incorrect value type:
Failed to modify array: Array element type mismatch
```

As part of best practices, developers should employ the following strategies to preempt common errors and enhance the robustness of code handling reflective array operations:

- Always validate all indices and lengths before using them to create or access arrays.
- Implement thorough type checking and ensure compatibility before changing array components reflectively.
- Incorporate comprehensive error handling and logging to facilitate easier debugging and maintenance.
- Consider security implications in your environment and handle `SecurityExceptions` appropriately.

Through prudent exception handling, developers can ensure that their applications remain stable and resilient, even when employing the dynamic capabilities of Java reflection for array operations. This careful attention to potential runtime errors not only prevents application crashes but also enhances overall user experience by ensuring predictable and reliable application behavior.

6.11 Security Concerns with Reflective Arrays

Reflective operations in Java, particularly on arrays, introduce a variety of security concerns that must be judiciously managed to prevent unauthorized access and manipulation of array data. Security issues in reflective array operations are primarily due to their ability to bypass traditional access controls and manipulate array types and contents dynamically. This section elucidates specific security risks and recommends strategies to mitigate these vulnerabilities.

Privilege Escalation Through Reflection

One of the principal concerns with using reflection, including reflective array operations, is the potential for privilege escalation. Normally, Java's access control mechanisms (such as private, protected, and public modifiers) restrict access to class members, including arrays. However, reflection provides mechanisms to override these restrictions using methods such as setAccessible() from the java.lang.reflect.AccessibleObject class.

Consider the following example which uses reflection to access a private array field of an object:

```
class SecretData {
    private String[] secrets = {"Top Secret", "Highly Confidential"};
}

public class AccessSecrets {
    public static void main(String[] args) throws NoSuchFieldException,
            IllegalAccessException {
        SecretData sd = new SecretData();
        Field secretField = SecretData.class.getDeclaredField("secrets");
        secretField.setAccessible(true); // Bypassing Java's access control
        String[] secrets = (String[]) secretField.get(sd);
        System.out.println("Secrets: " + Arrays.toString(secrets));
    }
}
```

This code would output:

```
Secrets: [Top Secret, Highly Confidential]
```

In the above example, setAccessible(true) enables access to the private array, thereby potentially allowing malicious code to read or modify sensitive data that should be inaccessible according to the class's access control policies.

Unauthorized Array Modifications

Reflective arrays also raise concerns due to the ease with which the contents of an array can be modified, regardless of the original modifiers of the array. The reflective method Array.set(Object array, int index, Object value) can be used to modify an array at a given index without invoking the normal checks that would apply in non-reflective operations.

Here is an example demonstrating the modification of final array elements:

```
class ConstantData {
    public final Integer[] dataArray = {5, 10, 15};
}

public class ModifyConstants {
    public static void main(String[] args) throws NoSuchFieldException,
            SecurityException, IllegalArgumentException, IllegalAccessException {
        ConstantData cd = new ConstantData();
        Field dataField = ConstantData.class.getField("dataArray");
        Integer[] data = (Integer[]) dataField.get(cd);
        Array.setInt(data, 0, 100); // Modifying final array
```

```
11        System.out.println("Modified Data: " + Arrays.toString(cd.dataArray));
12    }
13 }
```

Output would be:

```
Modified Data: [100, 10, 15]
```

Mitigation Strategies

To counter the security risks associated with reflective array operations, several mitigation strategies can be implemented:

- **Use of Security Managers:** Deploying a Java security manager to enforce strict security policies can help restrict the use of reflection. These constraints can be configured to allow only specific parts of an application or specific classes to use reflective array operations.

- **Auditing and Monitoring:** Regularly auditing the codebase for improper use of reflection and monitoring runtime behavior to detect anomalous activities can serve as preventative measures against security vulnerabilities.

- **Avoiding Excessive Use of Reflection:** Reducing reliance on reflective methods by using them only when absolutely necessary can limit potential attack surfaces.

While reflective operations on arrays provide powerful capabilities for dynamic operations and manipulation, they also necessitate careful handling to ensure security best practices are enforced. Early detection strategies and consistent enforcement of security policies are essential in maintaining the integrity and confidentiality of the data within Java applications.

6.12 Summary and Advanced Scenarios

Throughout this chapter, we have explored the dynamic manipulation and inspection of arrays in Java through reflective operations. The flexibility and power provided by Java Reflection facilitate the development of applications that require dynamic behavior, especially when dealing with arrays whose types and dimensions might not be known at compile time.

- We commenced with basic techniques for creating arrays dynamically and setting or retrieving their components using reflection.

- Subsequently, we delved into handling multi-dimensional arrays and discussed methods to introspect and manipulate these structures.

- The chapters further elaborated on the safety and type compatibility checks necessary for working with reflective arrays to prevent runtime errors.

- We also covered how to determine the length and component type of arrays reflectively, which is crucial for generic and reusable code modules.

- Performance implications of using reflection on arrays were scrutinized, highlighting the trade-offs between flexibility and runtime efficiency.

- Practical use cases and exception handling scenarios provided insights into real-world applications of reflective array operations.

- The distinction between handling primitive type arrays and object arrays was clearly outlined to ensure clarity in their usage.

- Finally, we touched upon the security concerns that arise with the reflective manipulation of arrays, providing guidelines for safe reflective programming.

Advanced scenarios in reflective array manipulation often involve more complex operations such as dynamically modifying the structure or dimensions of arrays during runtime or integrating reflection with other Java features like Generics, Streams, or the Concurrency API to create highly adaptive code. An example of such an advanced scenario is the following:

```
// Dynamically expand a one-dimensional array and fill it with data
public static Object expandArray(Object array, int newLength) {
    Class<?> arrayType = array.getClass().getComponentType();
    Object newArray = java.lang.reflect.Array.newInstance(arrayType, newLength);
    System.arraycopy(array, 0, newArray, 0, java.lang.reflect.Array.getLength(array
        ));
    return newArray;
}
```

6.12. SUMMARY AND ADVANCED SCENARIOS

The code snippet above demonstrates a method for expanding an array to a new length. It uses `System.arraycopy` for efficiency and ensures type safety by obtaining the array component type reflectively. This method can be particularly useful in scenarios where the array size is not determined until runtime or needs to be adjusted dynamically based on the application's requirements.

Engaging with advanced reflective operations calls for an understanding not only of reflection but also of Java's underlying type system and memory model to avoid common pitfalls such as type mismatches and memory leaks.

Reflective operations on arrays represent a powerful tool in the Java developer's toolkit, enabling a range of dynamic behaviors that can adapt to the needs of various applications. However, developers must handle these capabilities with care, considering performance and security implications to harness the full potential of Java's reflective capabilities effectively.

CHAPTER 6. REFLECTIVE OPERATIONS ON ARRAYS

Chapter 7

Handling Annotations with Reflection

This chapter examines the process of handling annotations in Java through reflective techniques, focusing on accessing and managing runtime-retained annotations on various program elements such as classes, methods, and fields. It guides readers through retrieving annotation information, interpreting values dynamically, and building logic based on this metadata. The content serves to strengthen understanding of how reflection adds versatility to managing annotations, facilitating advanced customization and configuration in application development workflows.

7.1 Introduction to Annotations in Java

Annotations in Java provide a powerful mechanism for associating metadata with program elements such as classes, interfaces, methods, and fields. Introduced in Java 5 through JSR 175, annotations enhance the readability and organization of code, allowing for more robust configuration and processing. This section delves into the core concepts of Java annotations, outlining their syntax, types, and common use cases, setting a firm foundation for understanding their handling through Java Reflection.

Definition and Syntax

An annotation, in Java, is a form of syntactic metadata that can be added to Java source code. Elements in a Java program can be annotated to supply additional information that can be processed by the compiler and at runtime by various tools and frameworks.

The syntax for defining an annotation is straightforward. It begins with the `@interface` keyword, which tells the Java compiler that this is an annotation definition. For example:

```
public @interface MyAnnotation {
    String value();
}
```

In the above example, `MyAnnotation` is an annotation with a single element named value that returns a `String`. Annotation elements can be of any valid Java type including primitives, `String`, `Class`, enums, other annotations, and arrays of these types.

Built-in Annotations

Java provides several built-in annotations which are widely used in various Java applications:

- `@Override` - Indicates that a method declaration is intended to override a method declaration in a superclass.

- `@Deprecated` - Marks the annotated element as no longer being recommended for use.

- `@SuppressWarnings` - Instructs the compiler to suppress specific compiler warnings.

- `@SafeVarargs` - Asserts that the code does not perform potentially unsafe operations on its varargs parameter.

- `@FunctionalInterface` - Indicates that an interface type declaration is intended to be a functional interface.

Annotation Properties

Annotations in Java can have properties to specify how they are to be used:

- **Retention Policy:** Determines at what stage the annotation is discarded. Java defines three types of retention policies:
  - SOURCE - Discarded by the compiler.
  - CLASS - Retained by the compiler at compile time, but ignored by the JVM.
  - RUNTIME - Retained by the JVM so they can be used at runtime.
- **Target:** Specifies the kinds of Java elements to which the annotation can be applied (e.g., method, field, type, etc.).
- **Repeatable:** Determines if the annotation can be applied more than once to the same declaration.

Annotations are a critical part of modern Java applications, providing a robust mechanism for decorating code elements with additional metadata which can enhance programmability and readability. By allowing developers to declare explicit behavior through declarative tagging, annotations offer a means to perform sophisticated compile-time and runtime configurations and checks.

This fundamental understanding of Java annotations paves the way forward to exploring their retrieval and management via reflection, explaining why they constitute a significant aspect of Java's architecture, influencing frameworks and APIs across the Java ecosystem.

7.2 Retrieving Annotations from Classes, Methods, and Fields

Retrieving annotations in Java involves using the reflection API to access these metadata entities at runtime. The process requires understanding the structures where annotations are declared—typically these are classes, methods, or fields. Each type of program element has specific methods provided by the Java reflection API which enable such operations.

Accessing Class Annotations

Accessing annotations on a class involves the use of the getAnnotations method provided by the Class class. Here is how to access annotations on a hypothetical class named `ExampleClass`:

```
1  Class<ExampleClass> cls = ExampleClass.class;
2  Annotation[] annotations = cls.getAnnotations();
```

The result, annotations, is an array of Annotation instances, each corresponding to an annotation present on ExampleClass assuming it's at runtime visible due to its retention policy.

Fetching Annotations from Methods

Methods within a class may also be annotated, and these annotations can be queried similarly by fetching the methods of the class first. The following code snippet demonstrates this procedure:

```
1  Method[] methods = cls.getDeclaredMethods();
2  for (Method method : methods) {
3      Annotation[] methodAnnotations = method.getAnnotations();
4      // Process methodAnnotations
5  }
```

In this example, getDeclaredMethods retrieves all methods declared in the class, regardless of their visibility. getAnnotations then fetches the annotations attached to each method.

Retrieving Field Annotations

Fields, like methods, can have annotations. To retrieve these, one must first access the fields of the class, which is done using getDeclaredFields(). The annotations can then be assessed as follows:

```
1  Field[] fields = cls.getDeclaredFields();
2  for (Field field : fields) {
3      Annotation[] fieldAnnotations = field.getAnnotations();
4      // Process fieldAnnotations
5  }
```

Here, getDeclaredFields function returns an array of Field objects representing all fields declared by the class represented by this Class object, which are then iterated to retrieve and process each of their annotations.

Exploration of these retrievals shows clear patterns in using reflection to access annotations. Utilizing reflection, programmers can write more dynamic code, as seen in the ability to query class structures and behaviors at runtime. This not only opens up more flexible programming paradigms but also aids in the development of frameworks and tools that can configure themselves according to predefined metadata, enhancing both development speed and runtime efficiency.

These tasks of annotation retrieval are predicated on the notion that metadata, when designed and used correctly, can significantly simplify developmental tasks and decrease coupling amongst components. Therefore, understanding how to efficiently retrieve and handle annotations is crucial for leveraging the full capabilities of Java's reflection framework.

7.3 Understanding Retention Policies in Java Reflection

Java annotations provide a powerful mechanism for decorating code elements with metadata at various points in their lifecycle, which are controlled by retention policies. Retention policies in Java determine at what stage annotations are discarded or retained—during source code, class loading, or at runtime. This section explores the intricacies of these policies and their implications in reflection.

Overview of Retention Policies

Java defines three types of retention policies through the enum `java.lang.annotation.RetentionPolicy`, which are:

- `SOURCE` — Annotations are discarded by the compiler during the compilation process.

- `CLASS` — Annotations are recorded in the class file by the compiler, but are ignored by the JVM during runtime.

- `RUNTIME` — Annotations are recorded in the class file and retained by the JVM, so they can be read reflectively at runtime.

Implications of Retention Policies

The choice of retention policy affects how annotations are utilized within an application, especially when using reflection. The implications of each policy are significant and merit detailed analysis.

- When annotations are marked with SOURCE, they are useful only during the development phase, aiding in tasks like code analysis, generation of documentation, or during pre-compilation steps. These annotations are not available in the byte code and, thus, cannot be accessed at runtime.

- Annotations with CLASS retention are embedded into the class files themselves but are not maintained by the JVM at runtime. This model suits use cases where annotations need to be visible to tools that operate at the binary level, such as static analysis tools, but not runtime processes.

- The RUNTIME policy supports reflection-based operations, as these annotations remain accessible to the JVM. This allows developers to use reflection utilities to dynamically query, inspect, and adapt the behavior of code based on these annotations. It is crucial for runtime processing frameworks like Spring or Hibernate.

Reflection Utilities and RUNTIME Annotations

Given their importance, it is essential to understand how RUNTIME annotations interact with Java reflection. Here, we demonstrate retrieving runtime-retained annotations using reflection.

```
import java.lang.reflect.Method;
import java.lang.annotation.Retention;
import java.lang.annotation.RetentionPolicy;

@Retention(RetentionPolicy.RUNTIME)
@interface ExampleAnnotation {
    String value();
}

public class ExampleUsage {
    @ExampleAnnotation(value = "Example")
    public void exampleMethod() {
    }

    public static void main(String[] args) throws Exception {
        Method m = ExampleUsage.class.getDeclaredMethod("exampleMethod");
        ExampleAnnotation ann = m.getAnnotation(ExampleAnnotation.class);
        if (ann != null) {
            System.out.println("Annotation value: " + ann.value());
        }
    }
}
```

```
Annotation value: Example
```

Utilizing RUNTIME Annotations

The ability to query annotations at runtime opens up various possibilities for conditional logic based on the annotation parameters. This capability is instrumental in developing highly configurable applications that rely on metadata for operation settings, adaptation based on environment, or feature toggling, enhancing the adaptability and modularization of software systems.

It's importan to grasp the retention policies and their implications for using Java reflection, and the examples how these mechanisms provide granular control over the annotation lifecycle. Understanding these policies allows developers to make informed decisions about annotation usage strategies, thereby aligning with best practices for creating robust, maintainable Java applications that efficiently utilize runtime metadata.

7.4 Accessing Runtime Annotations

Reflective access to annotations is imperative for dynamic applications where behavior can be altered based on metadata defined at runtime. This section delves into the mechanism Java provides to access annotations during runtime and how this capability can be leveraged to enhance application functionality.

Overview of Runtime Accessible Annotations

Rather than accessing annotations directly, Java employs reflection to query runtime-retained annotations. These annotations must be declared with a retention policy of RUNTIME using the @Retention(RetentionPolicy.RUNTIME) meta-annotation. The Java Reflection API provides several methods to examine these annotations, which can be broadly categorized based on the type of program element they annotate: classes, methods, fields, or other constructs.

Retrieving Annotations from Classes

To retrieve annotations from a class, the Java Reflection API offers the getAnnotations method as part of the Class class. Example, retrieving all annotations of a class looks as follows:

CHAPTER 7. HANDLING ANNOTATIONS WITH REFLECTION

```
1   public @interface MyAnnotation {
2       String value();
3   }
4
5   @MyAnnotation(value = "ExampleClassAnnotation")
6   public class ExampleClass {
7       // Class content goes here
8   }
9
10  Class<?> object = ExampleClass.class;
11  Annotation[] annotations = object.getAnnotations();
12  for (Annotation annotation : annotations) {
13      System.out.println(annotation);
14  }
```

Output:
@MyAnnotation(value='ExampleClassAnnotation')

This code snippet demonstrates how to fetch and print all annotations associated with ExampleClass. If annotations with RUNTIME retention are not found, an empty array is returned.

Accessing Method and Field Annotations

Similar to class annotations, annotations on methods and fields can be accessed using reflection. Here is an example for method annotations:

```
1   public class ExampleMethod {
2       @Deprecated
3       public void deprecatedMethod() {
4           // Deprecation logic
5       }
6   }
7
8   Method method = ExampleMethod.class.getMethod("deprecatedMethod");
9   Annotation[] methodAnnotations = method.getAnnotations();
10  for (Annotation annotation : methodAnnotations) {
11      System.out.println(annotation);
12  }
```

Output:
@Deprecated(forRemoval=false, since="1.5")

For accessing annotations on fields, the getField method on the Class object can be used to retrieve a specific field, and then annotations can be queried:

```
1   public class ExampleField {
2       @SuppressWarnings("unchecked")
3       public String exampleField;
4   }
5
6   Field field = ExampleField.class.getField("exampleField");
7   Annotation[] fieldAnnotations = field.getAnnotations();
8   for (Annotation annotation : fieldAnnotations) {
```

```
 9      System.out.println(annotation);
10    }
```

Output:
@SuppressWarnings(value='unchecked')

Interrogating Annotation Details

Once an annotation is accessed, its properties must be interrogated to implement logic based on its values. Here is a simplified way to determine if a specific annotation type is present and to fetch its attributes:

```
1  if (method.isAnnotationPresent(Deprecated.class)) {
2      Deprecated dep = method.getAnnotation(Deprecated.class);
3      System.out.println("Method is deprecated since " + dep.since());
4  }
```

Output:
Method is deprecated since 1.5

Reflective access to annotations enables applications to adapt and make decisions at runtime based on high-level configurations. This not only promotes flexibility but also aids in maintaining clean separation between operational logic and configuration metadata. Embedding such dynamic behavior oriented towards runtime interpretation of annotations paves the way for more responsive and adaptable systems.

7.5 Interpreting Annotation Values Dynamically

In Java reflection, the dynamic interpretation of annotation values plays a pivotal role. This process enables applications to adapt their behavior based on metadata, rather than static code alone. To fully leverage this capability, it is essential to systematically access and utilize the data present in annotations at runtime. This section explores the methodologies to achieve such dynamic interpretation, focusing specifically on the mechanisms provided by Java reflection APIs.

Dynamic Retrieval of Annotation Values

The process of dynamically retrieving annotation values involves several key steps, facilitated by the Java reflection API. Each step is critical in ensuring that the values extracted are accurate and effectively utilized.

- First, obtain a `Class` object representing the class, method, or field of interest. This is foundational, as reflection operations are performed on these objects.

- Next, call the `getAnnotation(Class<T> annotationClass)` method on the `Class` object to fetch an instance of the annotation. This method returns a dynamic proxy that allows interaction with the annotation as if it were a plain Java object.

- Finally, access the values of the annotation using the methods defined in the annotation interface. These methods behave like any regular method calls but dynamically fetch the values from the annotation's data.

For illustration, consider a class annotated with a custom annotation `@Configurable`:

```
@Configurable(runtimeOption="Debug", version=3)
public class Application{
    // Class definition
}
```

To dynamically access the values set in `@Configurable` at runtime, the following approach can be adopted in Java:

```
import java.lang.reflect.*;

public class ConfigReader{
    public static void readConfig(Class<?> clazz){
        Configurable config = clazz.getAnnotation(Configurable.class);
        if(config != null){
            System.out.println("Runtime Option: " + config.runtimeOption());
            System.out.println("Version: " + config.version());
        }
    }

    public static void main(String[] args){
        readConfig(Application.class);
    }
}
```

The output of the above code when accessing the `Application` class will be:

```
Runtime Option: Debug
Version: 3
```

Handling Complex Annotation Structures

In scenarios where annotations contain arrays or other complex data types, the retrieval process slightly expands but remains within the same conceptual guidelines. For example, if an annotation includes an array of values:

```
public @interface Schedules {
    Schedule[] value();
}
```

Schedule itself being an annotation, to retrieve and iterate over these values, the reflective method involves:

```
Schedules schedules = clazz.getAnnotation(Schedules.class);
if (schedules != null) {
    for (Schedule schedule : schedules.value()) {
        System.out.println("Day: " + schedule.day());
        System.out.println("Hour: " + schedule.hour());
    }
}
```

This ability to handle complex data structures through reflection is crucial for applications that require a high degree of runtime adaptability and configurability.

Impact on Application Behavior

Dynamically interpreting annotation values allows applications to modify their behavior based on the runtime environment or configuration parameters. This is particularly useful in scenarios such as conditional feature activation, adaptive logging, and runtime dependency injection. The adaptability offered through such dynamic interpretation not only enhances the flexibility of applications but also facilitates cleaner, more modular code designs.

The techniques illustrated above serve as core elements for any Java developer aiming to employ reflection for more adaptive application behavior, thus harnessing the full potential of Java annotations combined with reflection.

7.6 Handling Custom Annotations

Handling custom annotations in Java involves defining, detecting, and processing these annotations using reflection. This section discusses the creation of custom annotations, retrieves them reflectively, and illustrates practical processing.

Defining Custom Annotations

Creating custom annotations in Java requires understanding the core elements such as `Retention`, `Target`, and `ElementType`. Define an annotation as follows:

```
import java.lang.annotation.ElementType;
import java.lang.annotation.Retention;
import java.lang.annotation.RetentionPolicy;
import java.lang.annotation.Target;

@Retention(RetentionPolicy.RUNTIME)
@Target(ElementType.METHOD)
public @interface CustomAnnotation {
    String description() default "No description";
    int value();
}
```

Here, `@Retention(RetentionPolicy.RUNTIME)` ensures the annotation is available at runtime through reflection, and
`@Target(ElementType.METHOD)` restricts the annotation's applicability to method declarations.

Retrieving Annotations Reflectively

Once a custom annotation is defined, it can be accessed from elements like classes, methods, or fields at runtime using Java Reflection:

```
import java.lang.reflect.Method;

public class AnnotationParser {
    public void parseMethodAnnotations(Class<?> clazz) throws Exception {
        for (Method method : clazz.getDeclaredMethods()) {
            if (method.isAnnotationPresent(CustomAnnotation.class)) {
                CustomAnnotation custom = method.getAnnotation(CustomAnnotation.class
                    );
                System.out.println("Method: " + method.getName() +
                        ", Description: " + custom.description() +
                        ", Value: " + custom.value());
            }
        }
    }
}
```

This simple loop iterates over all declared methods within a class, checking for the presence of `@CustomAnnotation` and, if present, outputs its properties.

Processing Annotation Data

Upon retrieving annotation details, one can employ the data in various application-specific logic. For example, using annotation data to configure method access permissions or customize method execution behavior dynamically based on the provided metadata:

```
1  public void configureMethodBehavior(Class<?> clazz) throws Exception {
2      for (Method method : clazz.getDeclaredMethods()) {
3          if (method.isAnnotationPresent(CustomAnnotation.class)) {
4              CustomAnnotation custom = method.getAnnotation(CustomAnnotation.class);
5              if (custom.value() > 50) {
6                  // Execute some special logic for methods with a value greater than
                       50
7              }
8          }
9      }
10 }
```

Custom annotations can control application behavior dynamically, offering a powerful tool for developers, especially in frameworks like Spring or Java Enterprise Edition, where configuration and flexibility are key.

The role of custom annotations in Java is profound, extending the language's capability to include meta-level programming paradigms whereby developers can influence the behavior of software components at runtime, without altering the codebase statically. This dynamic attribute of annotations, harnessed through Java Reflection, signifies a significant shift towards more adaptable and configurable application constructs. Enhanced usage and effective management of annotations can lead to more robust, scalable, and maintainable code architectures.

7.7 Using Reflective Access to Drive Annotation-Based Logic

The power of Java Reflection with annotations lies primarily in its capacity to adjust application behavior dynamically based on the metadata provided by annotations. This section explores the utilization of reflection to interpret and execute logic dictated by annotations, which significantly enhances the flexibility and adaptability of Java applications.

Dynamic Configuration via Annotations

Annotations in Java provide a powerful mechanism for declaratively configuring applications. By harnessing reflective techniques, developers can perform dynamic configurations that depend on runtime environments or other conditions, without altering the underlying code base. Below, see an example demonstrating how one might systematically retrieve and process class annotations to adjust configuration settings dynamically:

```java
import java.lang.annotation.*;
import java.lang.reflect.*;

@Retention(RetentionPolicy.RUNTIME)
@interface Configurable {
    String environment() default "development";
}

@Configurable(environment = "production")
class ApplicationSettings {
    // Configuration related parameters
}

public class ConfigurationHandler {
    public static void loadConfiguration(Class<?> cls) {
        if (cls.isAnnotationPresent(Configurable.class)) {
            Configurable configurable = cls.getAnnotation(Configurable.class);
            switch (configurable.environment()) {
                case "production":
                    System.out.println("Load production settings");
                    break;
                case "development":
                    System.out.println("Load development settings");
                    break;
                default:
                    System.out.println("No environment specific settings");
            }
        }
    }

    public static void main(String[] args) {
        loadConfiguration(ApplicationSettings.class);
    }
}
```

```
Load production settings
```

This example employs the custom annotation `Configurable` to determine the environment for which the application should load specific configurations. Such a dynamic approach is invaluable in scenarios where applications must adapt to different operational conditions.

7.7. USING REFLECTIVE ACCESS TO DRIVE ANNOTATION-BASED LOGIC

Manipulating Behavior Based on Runtime Annotations

Another pivotal aspect of using reflection and annotations is the capability to manipulate behavior based on runtime-decided annotations. This feature is especially useful in enterprise applications, where certain operations depend on dynamic conditions which are not known until runtime:

```
@Retention(RetentionPolicy.RUNTIME)
@interface RoleRequired {
    String role();
}

class AccessControl {
    @RoleRequired(role = "ADMIN")
    public void sensitiveOperation() {
        System.out.println("Performing sensitive operation");
    }
}

public class SecurityManager {
    public static void checkAccess(Method method) {
        if (method.isAnnotationPresent(RoleRequired.class)) {
            RoleRequired roleRequired = method.getAnnotation(RoleRequired.class);
            if ("ADMIN".equals(roleRequired.role())) {
                System.out.println("Access granted");
            } else {
                System.out.println("Access denied");
            }
        }
    }

    public static void main(String[] args) throws NoSuchMethodException {
        Method method = AccessControl.class.getDeclaredMethod("sensitiveOperation");
        checkAccess(method);
    }
}
```

Access granted

This block of code illustrates how method behavior in a Java application can be controlled via annotations to enforce security based on user roles. The annotation `RoleRequired` specifies the role needed to execute the method, and the security manager utilizes reflection to examine this annotation and control access accordingly.

These examples highlight how reflection synergizing with annotations can drive application logic, providing a greater level of abstraction and control. Dynamic interpretation and execution of annotation-based logic reshape conventional programming paradigms into more adaptive and responsive development processes.

7.8 Annotations and Inherited Classes

Understanding how annotations behave in the context of inherited classes in Java is crucial for developers, particularly when building frameworks or libraries that rely on reflective techniques to interpret metadata. In Java, annotations may or may not be inherited from parent classes depending on their declared retention policy and the use of the @Inherited meta-annotation.

Annotation Inheritance in Java

Java provides the @Inherited meta-annotation, found in the java.lang.annotation package, which indicates that an annotation type can be inherited from the superclass. This capability plays a significant role in how annotations are retrieved reflectively. The default behavior without this annotation is non-inheritance.

```
@Inherited
@Retention(RetentionPolicy.RUNTIME)
public @interface MyInheritableAnnotation {
    String value();
}
```

In the above code, @MyInheritableAnnotation is defined with @Inherited, suggesting that if a superclass is annotated with this annotation, its subclasses will inherently have the same annotation unless explicitly overridden.

Reflective Access to Inherited Annotations

Using Java Reflection to access annotations on inheriting classes involves querying the presence of these annotations using the getAnnotation method provided by Java's Class object. The following example demonstrates retrieving an inherited annotation.

```
public class BaseClass {
    @MyInheritableAnnotation(value = "Base value")
    public void someMethod() {
    }
}

public class DerivedClass extends BaseClass {
}

// In a separate reflective utility class or method:
Method method = DerivedClass.class.getMethod("someMethod");
```

7.8. ANNOTATIONS AND INHERITED CLASSES

```
12  MyInheritableAnnotation annotation = method.getAnnotation(MyInheritableAnnotation.
        class);
13  System.out.println("Annotation value: " + annotation.value());
```

The output for the above code would be:

```
Annotation value: Base value
```

If `MyInheritableAnnotation` were not annotated with `@Inherited`, the derived class would not retain the annotation, and the reflective access would return null.

Design Considerations and Practical Implications

The decision to use `@Inherited` should be made carefully, considering its implications on software design:

- **Documentation and Maintenance**: Ensuring that the developers are aware of the inherited behavior of annotations is crucial. It must be well-documented which annotations are inheritable to prevent any unintended behavior in larger codebases.

- **Design Flexibility**: While inherited annotations can reduce redundancy and enhance consistency, they might reduce flexibility as they enforce a particular annotation behavior to all inheriting classes, which might not always be desirable.

- **Runtime Overhead**: Consider the performance implications, as runtime reflection incurs a cost. Systems requiring high performance might need to evaluate the trade-offs.

Architectural Diagram of Annotation Inheritance

To visually summarize the process, consider the following design diagram:

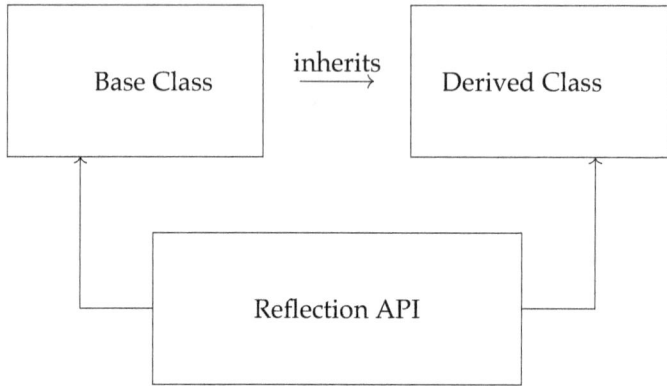

In usage scenarios involving frameworks like Spring or JPA, such architectural considerations grow significantly in strategic importance. The configurations defined via annotations in parent classes can implicitly shape the behavior of multiple child classes across the application suite, advancing a consistent configuration paradigm and ensuring standard behavior conformant with the foundational frameworks that support such distributed architectures.

This architectural and reflective analysis highlights the nuanced balance between inheritance of annotations and the reflective practices required to interpret them. While the inherited properties of annotations offer a streamlined approach to metadata management in class hierarchies, they require careful planning and understanding of Java Reflection capabilities to be effectively manipulated and utilized in both simple and complex enterprise applications.

7.9 Reflection API and Annotated Arrays

The previous sections have thoroughly examined how annotations in Java are utilized through the Reflection API to enrich the runtime behavior of applications. This section focuses on a nuanced aspect: handling annotated arrays through reflection. Arrays in Java can be annotated similarly to other types, which allows metadata to be associated directly with an array's data type. Thus, it becomes crucial to learn methodologies for introspecting such annotated arrays via reflection.

Annotating arrays in Java allows developers to attach metadata that could be used for various runtime processes including validation, data transformation, and configuration. Arrays themselves do not support

7.9. REFLECTION API AND ANNOTATED ARRAYS

annotations; rather annotations are applied on the data types of the elements that the array holds. For example, an entity validation framework might check array contents against predefined conditions specified through annotations.

Handling annotated arrays using reflection involves two critical steps: detecting annotations on array elements and applying reflective logic based on these annotations. The process entails extracting annotations from the component type of the array and not the array itself. Let's explore each step with specific Java code snippets.

```java
import java.lang.reflect.Field;

public class DataProcessor {
    public void process(Object obj) throws IllegalAccessException {
        Field[] fields = obj.getClass().getDeclaredFields();
        for (Field field : fields) {
            if (field.getType().isArray()) {
                handleArrayField(obj, field);
            }
        }
    }

    private void handleArrayField(Object obj, Field field)
            throws IllegalAccessException {
        field.setAccessible(true);
        Object array = field.get(obj);
        Class<?> arrayComponentType = field.getType().getComponentType();

        if (arrayComponentType.isAnnotationPresent(ValidationRule.class)) {
            // Process individual elements of the array if necessary
            ValidationRule rule = arrayComponentType.getAnnotation(ValidationRule.
                class);
            for (int i = 0; i < Array.getLength(array); i++) {
                Object element = Array.get(array, i);
                validateElement(element, rule);
            }
        }
    }

    private void validateElement(Object element, ValidationRule rule) {
        // Implementation of validation logic based on the rule
    }
}
```

The above snippet demonstrates the reflective exploration of an object's fields to identify and handle arrays specifically annotated. Note how the array's component type is extracted using `getComponentType()` and checked for the presence of the `ValidationRule` annotation.

After detection, each element of the array may need to be individually processed according to the specifics of the annotation. This iterative approach ensures that custom logic is consistently applied across all array elements.

The capability of the reflection API to manipulate and introspect annotated arrays introduces a flexible, dynamic mechanism that is pivotal in various scenarios, especially in modern frameworks where configuration through metadata is prevalent. Common use cases include data validation frameworks, serialization/deserialization mechanisms, and configuration management tools, indicating the utility of this reflection capability across a broad range of sectors in software development.

Progressing towards advanced uses of annotations and reflection, developing a deep understanding of these concepts is essential for Java developers who aim to write adaptable, maintainable, and efficient code. This detailed exploration sets a foundation for high-level application frameworks and libraries that rely on reflective operations to implement sophisticated functionalities via metadata-driven programming.

7.10 Security Aspects of Using Annotations with Reflection

Security is a paramount concern in any programming environment, particularly when using advanced features such as reflection and annotations in Java. This section delves into the security implications of using annotations with reflection, addressing potential vulnerabilities and discussing strategies to mitigate risks.

Annotations in Java are typically used to provide metadata about the program elements they decorate; however, when combined with reflection, they introduce a dynamic aspect to this metadata handling. This dynamic nature can inadvertently expose applications to several security risks, primarily related to unauthorized access and execution of sensitive operations.

Exposure of Sensitive Information

When annotations contain sensitive information about the application's structure or configuration, reflecting on these annotations can expose details that are potentially exploitable by malicious entities. Examples include database connection details or API keys specified through annotations for ease of configuration.

To tackle this issue, it is imperative to:

7.10. SECURITY ASPECTS OF USING ANNOTATIONS WITH REFLECTION

- Avoid storing sensitive information directly in annotations.
- Use environment variables or external configuration files that are securely managed.
- Ensure that only trusted code has access to reflective operations that could expose sensitive metadata.

Injection Attacks

Reflection can make an application vulnerable to injection attacks if the input used to dynamically load classes or access fields and methods is not properly validated. For example, if user input is directly used to determine what class to instantiate or which method to invoke, it could lead to accidental exposure or exploitation of the application.

Preventative practices include:

- Validating all inputs that could influence reflective operations.
- Employing strict input sanitization routines to prevent code injection.
- Using security managers or permission checks to restrict reflective activities based on the application's security policy.

Unauthorized Access and Privilege Escalation

Reflection, combined with annotations, can accidentally bypass normal access checks that Java's encapsulation mechanism enforces. An attacker might utilize reflection to access or modify private fields that are not meant to be visible outside of their defining class.

Mitigation strategies involve:

- Restricting the use of reflection to only essential areas of the application.
- Deploying custom security managers that define clear boundaries for reflective access.
- Regularly reviewing and auditing code to ensure that reflective usage adheres to the principle of least privilege.

Security Best Practices

Incorporating the following best practices will enhance the security posture of applications that utilize Java reflections and annotations:

- Apply the principle of least privilege by default, especially when working with reflections.

- Keep annotations free from holding sensitive or critical configuration information directly.

- Continuously update and patch the programming environment to protect against vulnerabilities in the reflection APIs.

Overall, while reflection and annotations are powerful features in Java, their use in applications mandates a comprehensive understanding of the associated security risks. A diligent approach involving strict validation, cautious management of capabilities, and adherence to security best practices is crucial to exploit these features effectively and securely.

7.11 Case Studies: Practical Uses of Annotations in Frameworks

Let's examine some specific case studies highlighting the practical applications of annotations in various Java frameworks. These cases exemplify how annotations, combined with Java reflection, provide powerful tools for simplifying configuration, enhancing readability, and enforcing a declarative programming style in complex software systems.

Spring Framework

In enterprise application development, the Spring Framework stands out for its extensive use of annotations to configure dependency injection, transaction management, and more. This following code snippet demonstrates a simple use of the @Autowired annotation to inject a dependency:

```
1  import org.springframework.beans.factory.annotation.Autowired;
2  import org.springframework.stereotype.Component;
3
```

7.11. CASE STUDIES: PRACTICAL USES OF ANNOTATIONS IN FRAMEWORKS

```
4   @Component
5   public class ProductService {
6     @Autowired
7     private ProductRepository repository;
8
9     public Product findProductById(String id) {
10      return repository.findById(id).orElse(null);
11    }
12  }
```

In this example, the @Autowired annotation instructs the Spring container to inject an instance of ProductRepository at runtime, eliminating the need for explicit setter or constructor-based dependencies. The @Component annotation declares the ProductService as a Spring-managed component, making it a candidate for auto-detection during classpath scanning.

Hibernate Validation Framework

Another practical annotation-driven framework is Hibernate Validator, a reference implementation of the Java Bean Validation specification (JSR 380). The framework uses annotations to define constraints on data models, ensuring data integrity and consistency. Consider the following entity definition:

```
1   import javax.validation.constraints.NotNull;
2   import javax.validation.constraints.Size;
3   import javax.persistence.Entity;
4   import javax.persistence.Id;
5
6   @Entity
7   public class User {
8     @Id
9     private Long id;
10
11    @NotNull
12    @Size(min = 2, max = 100)
13    private String name;
14
15    // Getters and setters omitted for brevity
16  }
```

Here, the @NotNull and @Size annotations are used to enforce validation rules directly on the entity attributes. This approach not only places constraints close to the data they protect but also reduces the likelihood of validation errors seeping through to the business logic layer.

Jakarta EE Security Framework

Jakarta EE, formerly known as Java EE, offers a robust specification for Java-based enterprise-level applications, including security aspects handled with annotations. The @RolesAllowed annotation exemplifies a declarative approach to security:

```
import javax.annotation.security.RolesAllowed;

public class AccountService {

    @RolesAllowed({"ADMIN", "USER"})
    public void updateAccountBalance(Account account, BigDecimal newBalance) {
        // Method implementation omitted
    }
}
```

In this scenario, the @RolesAllowed annotation ensures that only users with "ADMIN" or "USER" roles can invoke the updateAccountBalance method. This melds access control seamlessly into the application business logic, presenting a clean and management-friendly security configuration layer.

The practical applications of annotations in these widely used frameworks validate the significance of Java reflection in modern software development. Through the use of reflection, these frameworks leverage annotations to automate boilerplate code, implement cross-cutting concerns, and enforce security measures without cluttering the core business logic. This strategic use of annotations not only streamlines the code but also accentuates its readability and maintainability, two pivotal aspects that significantly enhance the development process of complex enterprise systems. As observed through these cases, annotations incessantly introduce a declarative style of programming that augments the developer's capacity to focus on solving business challenges while relying on frameworks to handle auxiliary concerns.

7.12 Summary and Best Practices for Annotation Handling

Throughout this chapter, we have explored the intricate process of handling annotations in Java using reflection. From retrieving annotations from various program elements to effectively interpreting and utilizing these annotations at runtime, the capabilities of reflection have been instrumental in enabling dynamic and flexible software designs. This

7.12. SUMMARY AND BEST PRACTICES FOR ANNOTATION HANDLING

section aims to encapsulate the key insights and best practices garnered from our discussions, providing a consolidated guide to enhance your approach to annotations in Java development.

Key Insights

The versatility of annotations in Java, combined with reflective access, equips developers with the power to write highly customizable and configurable code. The use of runtime-retained annotations, in particular, allows for a significant enhancement in software behavior without altering the actual code structure. The following points underscore the pivotal insights covered in this chapter:

- **Retrieval Efficiency:** Utilizing the Reflection API to access annotations must be done judiciously to avoid performance overhead. While reflection provides robust capabilities, its operational cost can impact application performance if not managed correctly.

- **Security Considerations:** Handling annotations with reflection necessitates stringent security practices to prevent unauthorized access to metadata, which might include sensitive application logic. Always validate and sanitize inputs when using reflection to handle annotations.

- **Custom Annotations:** Developing custom annotations can significantly refine the expressiveness of your code, making meta-level programming concepts clear and maintainable. Custom annotations also facilitate stricter control over code behavior, especially when combined with reflective checks.

Best Practices

Adhering to best practices in handling annotations with Java reflection not only streamlines the development process but also enhances code security and maintainability. The accrued experience from the case studies and theoretical exploration suggests the following best practices:

- **Minimizing Reflection Use:** Use reflection sparingly and cache reflection results where feasible to enhance performance. Avoid unnecessary reflective calls by validating the existence of annotations with standard Java mechanisms first.

- **Annotation Design:** When designing custom annotations, clearly define their retention policy and target elements. This clarity will aid other developers in understanding the scope and purpose of the annotations, thereby improving code usability and decreasing potential misuses.

- **Integration with Frameworks:** Leverage existing frameworks that support annotation processing to reduce boilerplate code and focus on business logic. Frameworks like Spring heavily utilize annotations and provide extensive support for custom annotations, saving time and reducing error potential.

As the utilization of annotations becomes more prevalent in modern Java applications, the role of reflective access in managing these annotations becomes increasingly critical. Our examination has not only highlighted methods to retrieve and interpret annotation data dynamically but has also provided insights into crafting a robust framework around these capabilities. Employing these best practices will ensure that your use of Java annotations is both effective and efficient, leading to more readable, maintainable, and secure code.

By integrating the guidelines and insights discussed, developers can significantly elevate their application's functionality and adaptability, ensuring a seamless interplay between static code and dynamic behavior facilitated through annotations and reflection.

Chapter 8

Dynamics of Proxies and Invocation Handlers

This chapter introduces the dynamics of proxies and invocation handlers within Java Reflection, presenting frameworks for creating dynamic proxies that can intercept and manage method calls at runtime. It explains the roles and relationships between interfaces, 'java.lang.reflect.Proxy' class, and 'InvocationHandler', providing practical examples of their use in real-world scenarios. These tools empower developers to implement advanced design patterns such as decorators, virtual proxies, and security proxies, enhancing the adaptability and modularity of Java applications.

8.1 Introduction to Dynamic Proxies in Java

Dynamic proxies in Java represent a powerful mechanism that allows developers to dynamically create proxy classes at runtime, serving as intermediaries for calls made to objects that implement a specified set of interfaces. This section will explore the fundamental concepts of dynamic proxies, their instantiation, and their utility in Java programming.

Conceptual Foundation of Dynamic Proxies

Dynamic proxies hinge on two main components: interfaces and invocation handlers. A dynamic proxy class programmatically constructs an instance that implements a list of interfaces specified at runtime. The dynamic aspect of these proxies is that they are not coded in the Java source but are generated during runtime.

- Every dynamic proxy class implicitly extends `java.lang.reflect.Proxy`.

- Each instance of a proxy class is associated with an `InvocationHandler` that intercepts all method calls made to the proxy and potentially provides custom behavior before, during, or after the method execution.

The `java.lang.reflect.Proxy` class included in the Java API is pivotal in this mechanism. It provides the static method `newProxyInstance`, which is used to instantiate a dynamic proxy by specifying the class loader, an array of `interfaces`, and an invocation handler.

Instantiating Dynamic Proxies

The instantiation of a dynamic proxy involves several steps which are crucial for its correct operation. Below is a simplified overview of this process:

```
ClassLoader loader = Thread.currentThread().getContextClassLoader();
Class<?>[] interfaces = new Class<?>[] { MyInterface.class };
InvocationHandler handler = new MyInvocationHandler(target);

MyInterface proxy = (MyInterface) Proxy.newProxyInstance(
    loader, interfaces, handler);
```

Explanation of the code snippet:

- The class loader that will define the proxy (typically the current thread's context class loader) is obtained.

- The array of interfaces that the proxy should implement is specified.

- An `InvocationHandler` is provided that will handle method calls on the proxy instance.

- The `Proxy.newProxyInstance()` method is called to create the proxy instance which can be cast to any of the interfaces specified.

Utility of Dynamic Proxies in Java

Dynamic proxies are particularly valuable in Java due to their flexibility and ability to interpose on interface method calls dynamically. They can be used for a variety of purposes:

- **Interception:** Adding additional functionality before, after, or around method execution.
- **Decoration:** Modifying return values or intercepting method arguments.
- **Logging:** Logging access to particular methods for auditing or debugging purposes.
- **Transaction Management:** Automatically managing transactions when certain methods are called.

By leveraging dynamic proxies, Java developers can write cleaner, more modular, and adaptable code. These capabilities make dynamic proxies an essential tool in both enterprise-scale applications and smaller projects where code adaptability and maintenance are of concern.

Thus, understanding dynamic proxies is indispensable for modern Java developers wishing to fully harness the power of Java's runtime reflective capabilities for developing dynamic, scalable solutions.

8.2 Role of Interfaces in Dynamic Proxy Creation

The dynamic proxy creation in Java plays a pivotal role in design patterns and behavior customization of applications during runtime. Its dependency on interfaces is crucial, as interfaces provide a blueprint that dynamic proxies must adhere to, enabling them to maintain contract adherence while offering flexibility in their actual implementations.

To comprehend the significance of interfaces in the context of dynamic proxies, it is essential to understand that a dynamic proxy class dynamically implements a list of interfaces at runtime. The java.lang.reflect.Proxy class uses these interfaces to create a new proxy instance.

Interface as a Contract for Proxy Behavior

The interfaces that a proxy implements are more than just a structural blueprint; they represent a contract of behavior that the proxy must fulfill. This contract ensures that:

- The dynamic proxy provides concrete behaviors for the abstract methods declared in the interface.

- Clients interacting through the proxy can expect the behavior stipulated by these interfaces, despite the actual implementation details being abstracted away.

When Proxy instances are created, each method invoked on the instance is routed through the InvocationHandler associated with the proxy. The InvocationHandler processes these invocations according to the method definitions outlined in the interface.

Below is an example illustrating the creation of a dynamic proxy instance that implements an interface:

```
import java.lang.reflect.*;

public interface Vehicle {
    void start();
    void stop();
}

public class VehicleInvocationHandler implements InvocationHandler {
    @Override
    public Object invoke(Object proxy, Method method, Object[] args) throws
            Throwable {
        System.out.println("Method " + method.getName() + " is called");
        return null;
    }
}

public class DynamicProxyExample {
    public static void main(String[] args) {
        Vehicle proxyInstance = (Vehicle) Proxy.newProxyInstance(
            Vehicle.class.getClassLoader(),
            new Class[] { Vehicle.class },
            new VehicleInvocationHandler()
        );
```

8.2. ROLE OF INTERFACES IN DYNAMIC PROXY CREATION

```
23
24          proxyInstance.start();
25          proxyInstance.stop();
26      }
27  }
```

```
Method start is called
Method stop is called
```

Choosing Interfaces for Dynamic Proxy Creation

Choosing the right set of interfaces for a dynamic proxy is a strategic decision, influenced by:

- **Granularity:** Finer granularity may lead to more flexible proxy instances but can complicate the design and increase the overhead in proxy management.

- **Functionality:** The functionality required by the application from the proxy determines which interfaces are implemented. Typically, only essential interfaces directly impacting the proxy's role should be implemented to avoid unnecessary complexity.

In many cases, the dynamic nature of proxies can be enhanced by selectively targeting interfaces that enable specific functionalities, such as audit logging, authentication, and lazy loading. Below is an example detail of the proxy inheritance approach versus interface implementation:

```
1   public interface Subscriber {
2       void receive(Message message);
3   }
4
5   public class LoggingInvocationHandler implements InvocationHandler {
6       private final Object target;
7
8       public LoggingInvocationHandler(Object target) {
9           this.target = target;
10      }
11
12      @Override
13      public Object invoke(Object proxy, Method method, Object[] args) throws
                Throwable {
14          System.out.println("Invoking method: " + method.getName());
15          return method.invoke(target, args);
16      }
17  }
```

By employing interfaces, Java allows for creation of dynamic proxies that are powerful in handling method invocations and flexible in their behavior implementation. This approach contributes to modular architecture in software applications, ensuring separation of concerns and enhancing code maintainability.

8.3 Creating Dynamic Proxies Using java.lang.reflect.Proxy

Dynamic proxies in Java allow for the dynamic implementation of interfaces at runtime, a powerful feature facilitated predominantly by the `java.lang.reflect.Proxy` class. This class provides a mechanism to create instances that implement specified interfaces, delegating method calls to a designated `InvocationHandler`. This section demonstrates how to utilize `java.lang.reflect.Proxy` to craft dynamic proxies effectively, detailing the process and illustrating the implementation through succinct examples.

Fundamentals of Proxy Creation

To create a dynamic proxy, two core components are essential: an array of interfaces that the proxy will implement, and an instance of a class that implements the `InvocationHandler` interface. The dynamic proxy can then be instantiated using the `Proxy.newProxyInstance` method. Here is the typical structure for creating a dynamic proxy:

```
InterfaceA proxy = (InterfaceA) Proxy.newProxyInstance(
    InterfaceA.class.getClassLoader(),
    new Class<?>[] {InterfaceA.class},
    handler);
```

In the above snippet, `InterfaceA` represents the interface the proxy will implement, and `handler` is the instance of `InvocationHandler` that will manage method invocations on the proxy.

Implementing the InvocationHandler

The `InvocationHandler` plays a pivotal role in managing the behavior of the proxy instance. When a method on the proxy instance is invoked, the method call is forwarded to the `InvocationHandler`'s invoke method. Here is how an `InvocationHandler` is typically implemented:

8.3. CREATING DYNAMIC PROXIES USING JAVA.LANG.REFLECT.PROXY

```
1  public class DynamicInvocationHandler implements InvocationHandler {
2
3      @Override
4      public Object invoke(Object proxy, Method method, Object[] args) throws
             Throwable {
5          System.out.println("Method: " + method.getName());
6          return null; // Customize to forward call to actual object or modify
             behavior
7      }
8  }
```

This handler simply prints the name of the method being invoked. In real scenarios, the handler can be designed to forward the call to a concrete instance, manipulate arguments, return custom values, or perform other sophisticated behaviors based on requirements.

Example: Creating a Logging Proxy

To illustrate a practical application of dynamic proxies, consider the following scenario: a logging proxy for an interface `DatabaseOperations` that logs each method invocation.

```
1  public interface DatabaseOperations {
2      void insert(String data);
3      String fetch(int id);
4  }
5
6  public class LoggingHandler implements InvocationHandler {
7      private final Object target;
8
9      public LoggingHandler(Object target) {
10         this.target = target;
11     }
12
13     @Override
14     public Object invoke(Object proxy, Method method, Object[] args) throws
             Throwable {
15         System.out.println("Entered method: " + method.getName() + " with args: " +
             Arrays.toString(args));
16         Object result = method.invoke(target, args);
17         System.out.println("Exited method: " + method.getName() + " with result: " +
             result);
18         return result;
19     }
20 }
```

To use this `LoggingHandler`:

```
1  DatabaseOperations dbOperations = new DatabaseImpl(); // Assume DatabaseImpl
         implements DatabaseOperations
2  DatabaseOperations proxy = (DatabaseOperations) Proxy.newProxyInstance(
3      DatabaseOperations.class.getClassLoader(),
4      new Class<?>[] {DatabaseOperations.class},
5      new LoggingHandler(dbOperations));
```

This proxy logs every method call, including method name, passed arguments, and method results, providing a transparent log of interactions with the `DatabaseOperations` object.

Performance Considerations

While dynamic proxies provide powerful capabilities, they introduce additional layers of abstraction and can impact performance, particularly in method-call intensive applications. It is crucial to measure and consider the performance implications in scenarios where high throughput and low latency are critical.

By understanding and implementing dynamic proxies with `java.lang.reflect.Proxy`, developers gain flexibility in modifying object behaviors and interactions dynamically, which is especially useful in creating adaptable systems and frameworks.

8.4 Understanding and Implementing InvocationHandlers

The 'InvocationHandler' interface plays a crucial role in the Java Reflection API, particularly in the context of dynamic proxies. This interface is responsible for defining the behavior of a proxy instance at the time a method on the proxy is invoked. The primary purpose of an 'InvocationHandler' is to determine the actions that occur when methods are called on the dynamic proxy.

The InvocationHandler Interface

The 'InvocationHandler' interface is part of the 'java.lang.reflect' package and requires the implementation of a single method:

```
Object invoke(Object proxy, Method method, Object[] args) throws Throwable;
```

The parameters of the 'invoke' method are as follows:

- `proxy` - The proxy instance that the method was invoked on.

- `method` - The `Method` instance corresponding to the interface method invoked on the proxy instance.

- `args` - An array of objects containing the values of the arguments passed in the method invocation on the proxy instance, or null if interface method takes no arguments.

The 'invoke' method acts as a dispatcher, and its implementation can vary greatly depending on the specific requirements of the application, ranging from method dispatch, method interception, to more complex behavior like method delegation.

Implementing Custom InvocationHandlers

Creating an 'InvocationHandler' involves implementing the 'invoke' method to specify the behavior of the proxy when its methods are called. Below is a sample implementation that demonstrates a basic 'InvocationHandler' which logs each method call:

```
import java.lang.reflect.InvocationHandler;
import java.lang.reflect.Method;

public class LoggingInvocationHandler implements InvocationHandler {
    private final Object target;

    public LoggingInvocationHandler(Object target) {
        this.target = target;
    }

    @Override
    public Object invoke(Object proxy, Method method, Object[] args) throws
        Throwable {
        System.out.println("Method " + method.getName() + " is called with arguments
            : " + Arrays.toString(args));
        Object result = method.invoke(target, args);
        System.out.println("Method " + method.getName() + " returns " + result);
        return result;
    }
}
```

In the above example, the 'LoggingInvocationHandler' constructor takes an object that represents the original class on which the method calls are forwarded after logging. The 'invoke' method logs the method name and parameters, delegates the method call to the original object, and logs the result before returning it.

Practical Applications of InvocationHandlers

'InvocationHandler's are widely used in a variety of scenarios:

- **Logging:** As shown in the example above, 'InvocationHandlers' can be used to log method calls, which is helpful in debugging and monitoring.

- **Transaction Management:** They can be used to manage transactions, where each method invocation can implicitly trigger transaction start and end.

- **Access Control:** 'InvocationHandlers' are effective in enforcing access control rules, allowing or denying method invocation based on security contexts.

These scenarios highlight the flexibility and power of using 'InvocationHandlers' in dynamic proxy creation. The ability to encapsulate and customize the behavior of method invocations makes 'InvocationHandlers' an invaluable tool in the Java ecosystem. As projects evolve to require more versatile and sophisticated systems handling, 'InvocationHandlers' provide a robust solution for maintaining clean, manageable, and adaptable codebases.

8.5 Method Interception with Dynamic Proxies

Method interception is a fundamental aspect of using dynamic proxies in Java. It allows developers to intercept and manipulate method calls dynamically at runtime, providing a powerful tool for implementing various design patterns and handling cross-cutting concerns. This section delves into the mechanics of method interception using Java's dynamic proxies, discussing its practical applications, methods, and challenges associated with its implementation.

Dynamic proxies in Java work by creating a proxy instance that implements a list of interfaces specified at runtime. When a method from one of these interfaces is invoked on the proxy, the call is redirected to an InvocationHandler, which controls what happens during the method call. This delegation model is pivotal in implementing method interception.

To illustrate how method interception is implemented using dynamic proxies, consider the following example, where a simple logging handler is added to an interface:

```
1  import java.lang.reflect.InvocationHandler;
2  import java.lang.reflect.Method;
3  import java.lang.reflect.Proxy;
```

8.5. METHOD INTERCEPTION WITH DYNAMIC PROXIES

```
4   import java.util.Arrays;
5
6   interface Service {
7      void performTask();
8   }
9
10  class ServiceImpl implements Service {
11     public void performTask() {
12        System.out.println("Performing task");
13     }
14  }
15
16  class LoggingInvocationHandler implements InvocationHandler {
17     private Object target;
18
19     public LoggingInvocationHandler(Object target) {
20        this.target = target;
21     }
22
23     public Object invoke(Object proxy, Method method, Object[] args) throws
              Throwable {
24        System.out.println("Method " + method.getName() + " was called with args " +
              Arrays.toString(args));
25        Object result = method.invoke(target, args);
26        System.out.println("Method " + method.getName() + " completed with result "
              + result);
27        return result;
28     }
29  }
30
31  public class ProxyDemo {
32     public static void main(String[] args) {
33        Service service = new ServiceImpl();
34        Service proxy = (Service) Proxy.newProxyInstance(
35           Service.class.getClassLoader(),
36           new Class[]{Service.class},
37           new LoggingInvocationHandler(service)
38        );
39
40        proxy.performTask();
41     }
42  }
```

When the performTask method is called on the proxy object, 'proxy.performTask()', the invoke method of LoggingInvocationHandler is executed. This method logs the name of the method being invoked, the arguments passed to it, and the result returned by the method, providing valuable insights for debugging and monitoring.

```
Method performTask was called with args null
Performing task
Method performTask completed with result null
```

A key benefit of method interception is its versatility. The InvocationHandler can be implemented to provide various functional enhancements such as:

- Authentication and authorization checks before method execution.

- Logging and auditing of method calls for diagnostics and monitoring.

- Lazy loading of resources when a method is called.

- Transaction management, ensuring data consistency and rollback in case of errors.

- Performance benchmarking by measuring execution time.

However, developers must address several challenges when using method interception with dynamic proxies:

- Performance Impact: Dynamic proxies can introduce a slight overhead due to reflection and method handling, which may be significant in performance-critical applications.

- Implementation Complexity: The use of dynamic proxies and method interception increases the complexity of the codebase, requiring careful design and extensive testing.

- Limited to interface methods: Dynamic proxies can only intercept calls to interface methods, not to the methods of a class directly.

The utilization of dynamic proxies for method interception offers a robust approach to modify behavior at runtime. By understanding the underlying mechanics and addressing the associated challenges, developers can effectively use this powerful feature to build flexible and dynamic Java applications.

8.6 Proxy Performance and Optimization Strategies

Performance considerations are integral when dealing with dynamic proxies in Java. Given that proxies add an additional layer of abstraction and complexity, it is crucial to optimize their implementation to prevent potential bottlenecks, especially in high-throughput or latency-sensitive applications. This section explores various

8.6. PROXY PERFORMANCE AND OPTIMIZATION STRATEGIES

strategies to enhance the performance of dynamic proxies, focusing on optimizing the java.lang.reflect.Proxy class and the associated java.lang.reflect.InvocationHandler.

Minimizing Method Invocation Overhead

The primary source of overhead in dynamic proxies is the method invocation process. Each method call on a proxy instance goes through a series of steps that can be optimized:

- Reducing the complexity within the `invoke` method of the `InvocationHandler`.
- Caching results of reflective method lookups.
- Avoiding unnecessary object creation within the `invoke` method.

To illustrate the reduction of complexity within the `invoke` method, consider the following Java code snippet implemented within the 1stlisting environment:

```
public Object invoke(Object proxy, Method method, Object[] args) throws Throwable {
    if ("methodName".equals(method.getName())) {
        // Directly handle method to avoid expensive operations.
    } else {
        return method.invoke(target, args);
    }
}
```

In this example, an if statement checks the method name directly, reducing the need for more complex logic or reflective operations if the method matches certain criteria.

Using Caching Mechanisms

Caching is a powerful technique to optimize performance, particularly effective in reducing the overhead of repetitive reflective operations. Consider caching method lookups or results of method invocations when they are expected to be called frequently with the same parameters:

```
private final Map<Method, Method> methodCache = new ConcurrentHashMap<Method,
    Method>();

public Object invoke(Object proxy, Method method, Object[] args) throws Throwable {
    Method targetMethod = methodCache.computeIfAbsent(method,
```

```
5        m -> target.getClass().getMethod(m.getName(), m.getParameterTypes()));
6      return targetMethod.invoke(target, args);
7    }
```

In the above code, the `ConcurrentHashMap` is used to cache method instances, significantly reducing the time spent on method lookup.

Profiling and Monitoring Proxy Performance

To effectively optimize proxy performance, it is essential to monitor and profile the system to identify bottlenecks. Java provides several profiling tools, such as VisualVM, that can help developers understand where most of the CPU time or memory is being consumed in relation to proxy usage.

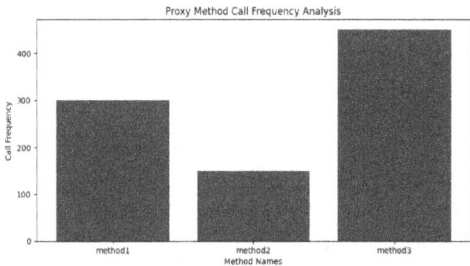

By continuously monitoring such metrics, developers can focus optimization efforts on the most frequently used or the slowest proxy methods.

With these strategies, developers can significantly enhance the performance of Java dynamic proxies, ensuring that they do not become a liability in performance-critical applications.

8.7 Handling Exceptions and Errors in Proxies

When employing proxies in Java Reflection, handling exceptions and errors becomes crucial due to the indirect nature of method invocations. This section discusses essential strategies and techniques for effective exception management within dynamic proxies, ensuring robust and fault-tolerant applications.

8.7. HANDLING EXCEPTIONS AND ERRORS IN PROXIES

Basics of Exception Handling in Proxies

A dynamic proxy in Java may throw exceptions primarily due to two reasons: issues in the target method itself or errors in the proxy mechanics. It is imperative to distinguish between these sources to correctly handle the exceptions.

- The `InvocationHandler`'s invoke method needs to be designed to carefully inspect and react to any exceptions that arise during the dynamic invocation of methods.

- The thrown exceptions should be consistent with the interface the proxy implements, adhering to the expectations of the client code.

Structuring the `InvocationHandler` for Error Management

To ensure a robust design, the implementation of `InvocationHandler` must include a detailed error-catching mechanism. Below is an example of handling exceptions within an `InvocationHandler`.

```
public Object invoke(Object proxy, Method method, Object[] args) throws Throwable {
    try {
        return method.invoke(target, args);
    } catch (IllegalAccessException | IllegalArgumentException e) {
        throw new RuntimeException("Failed to invoke method", e);
    } catch (InvocationTargetException e) {
        throw e.getTargetException();
    }
}
```

In this example:

- Exceptions such as `IllegalAccessException` and `IllegalArgumentException` are caught and wrapped in a `RuntimeException`, providing a clear indication that the proxy invocation failed due to incorrect method usage.

- `InvocationTargetException` is unwrapped to throw the underlying cause to the caller, preserving the original exception context.

Logging and Monitoring

Monitoring and logging are indispensable when debugging exceptions in dynamic proxies. These practices help in tracking down the sequence of events leading to an exception.

- Implement logging within the `InvocationHandler` to log method entry, exit, and exception occurrences.
- Utilize logging frameworks like SLF4J or Log4J for a more flexible logging configuration.

Example of logging in `InvocationHandler`:

```
public Object invoke(Object proxy, Method method, Object[] args) throws Throwable {
    try {
        LOGGER.debug("Invoking method: {}", method.getName());
        Object result = method.invoke(target, args);
        LOGGER.debug("Method executed successfully: {}", method.getName());
        return result;
    } catch (Exception e) {
        LOGGER.error("Error invoking method: {}", method.getName(), e);
        throw e;
    }
}
```

Error Handling Recommendations

Develop an error-handling strategy that includes:

- Defining a clear contract for exceptions in the interface methods.
- Ensuring all exceptions thrown by the proxy methods are meaningful to the consumer.
- Wrapping or rethrowing exceptions specifically according to the interface contract expectations.

Effective exception handling in proxies requires a careful balance between transparency and abstraction. The techniques illustrated should serve as a guideline for handling errors and ensuring that the proxy effectively supports the operational needs while maintaining a clear and understandable error management strategy.

Coupling proactive monitoring with these robust error management practices ensures that Java dynamic proxies not only serve their purpose but also contribute positively to the overall stability and reliability of the application.

8.8 Advanced Techniques: Proxy Chains and Decorators

Dynamic proxies in Java provide a powerful mechanism for method interception and delegation, allowing developers to construct complex behavior patterns such as proxy chains and implement the decorator pattern dynamically. This section explores these advanced techniques, delving into their implementation and practical use cases in Java.

Constructing Proxy Chains

A proxy chain is a sequence of proxies where each proxy in the chain additively (or alternatively) modifies the behavior of the target object. The principle behind a proxy chain is that an invocation on the initial proxy passes through a pipeline of handlers, each performing certain operations before forwarding the call to the next handler or the final target object.

The implementation of a proxy chain requires meticulous control over the invocation handlers associated with each proxy in the chain. Below is an example of setting up a simple proxy chain in Java:

```java
import java.lang.reflect.*;

public class ProxyChainExample {

    public static Object createProxyChain(Object target, InvocationHandler... handlers) {
        Object currentTarget = target;
        for (InvocationHandler handler : handlers) {
            currentTarget = Proxy.newProxyInstance(
                target.getClass().getClassLoader(),
                target.getClass().getInterfaces(),
                handler);
        }
        return currentTarget;
    }
}
```

In the above code, each `InvocationHandler` in the 'handlers' array modifies the 'currentTarget' object, which initially is the 'target' object. The proxies are layered in the order they appear in the array.

Implementing the Decorator Pattern Dynamically

The decorator pattern is a structural design pattern that allows behavior to be added to individual objects, either statically or dynamically, without affecting the behavior of other objects from the same class. Dynamic decorators use dynamic proxies to wrap an object and selectively override behavior by intercepting method calls.

Below is an example that illustrates how to implement a dynamic decorator:

```java
import java.lang.reflect.*;

public class LoggingDecorator implements InvocationHandler {
    private final Object target;

    public LoggingDecorator(Object target) {
        this.target = target;
    }

    @Override
    public Object invoke(Object proxy, Method method, Object[] args) throws Throwable {
        System.out.println("Method " + method.getName() + " is called with args " +
            Arrays.toString(args));
        Object result = method.invoke(target, args);
        System.out.println("Method " + method.getName() + " returns " + result);
        return result;
    }

    public static <T> T createDecorator(T target, Class<T> iface) {
        return (T) Proxy.newProxyInstance(
            iface.getClassLoader(),
            new Class<?>[] { iface },
            new LoggingDecorator(target));
    }
}
```

In the 'LoggingDecorator', method invocations are intercepted to add logging before and after the actual method execution on the target object. This decorator can be dynamically attached to any object that implements the interface expected by the 'createDecorator' method.

Both techniques—proxy chains and dynamic decorators—are potent tools in a Java developer's arsenal, providing immense flexibility in modifying object behavior at runtime. Their proper implementation can lead to highly configurable systems that can be adapted for a wide range of scenarios, such as logging, authorization, transaction management, and more. Each technique leverages Java's reflection capabilities to dynamically manipulate and control object behaviors, making them integral to advanced Java programming and design.

8.9 Use Cases: Security and Access Control with Proxies

Security and access control are critical components in software design, particularly in environments where resources are restricted based on user roles or permissions. The Java Reflection API, and more specifically, the dynamic proxy mechanism, offers a powerful tool for implementing security and access control in Java applications. This section discusses the use of dynamic proxies for these purposes, illustrating how proxies can act as an intermediary for method invocations to enforce security measures.

Dynamic proxies can be strategically employed to create security wrappers around objects, ensuring that access controls are centrally managed and that business logic remains uncluttered by security concerns. The following are the primary scenarios where dynamic proxies are particularly effective for security and access control:

- **Method-Level Access Control:** Restricting access to specific methods based on the user's authentication and authorization levels.

- **Sensitive Data Masking:** Automatically masking or obfuscating sensitive information based on the user's clearance.

- **Audit and Logging:** Transparently adding logging to keep track of operations performed, particularly those involving critical data or functionalities.

Example Implementation of a Security Proxy

We shall now explore an implementation example where a security proxy controls access to a sensitive system component. The `DocumentService` interface, which provides methods for accessing and manipulating documents, will serve as our target component. Access to its methods will be controlled based on user roles.

First, we define the `DocumentService` interface and a simple implementation of it:

```
public interface DocumentService {
    String readDocument(String documentId);
    void updateDocument(String documentId, String content);
}
```

Next, we implement a straightforward `SimpleDocumentService` which implements `DocumentService`:

```
public class SimpleDocumentService implements DocumentService {
    public String readDocument(String documentId) {
        // Retrieve and return document content
        return "Document Content";
    }
    public void updateDocument(String documentId, String content) {
        // Update document content
    }
}
```

The security proxy is implemented using the dynamic proxy mechanism where the `InvocationHandler` plays a crucial role. Here is a possible implementation:

```
import java.lang.reflect.InvocationHandler;
import java.lang.reflect.Method;
import java.lang.reflect.Proxy;

public class SecurityInvocationHandler implements InvocationHandler {
    private final Object target;
    private final String userRole;

    public SecurityInvocationHandler(Object target, String userRole) {
        this.target = target;
        this.userRole = userRole;
    }

    public Object invoke(Object proxy, Method method, Object[] args) throws
        Throwable {
        if ("updateDocument".equals(method.getName()) && !"ADMIN".equals(userRole))
            {
            throw new SecurityException("Unauthorized access attempt");
        }
        return method.invoke(target, args);
    }
}
```

This handler prevents access to the `updateDocument` method if the user role is not "ADMIN". To instantiate a proxy:

```
DocumentService serviceProxy = (DocumentService) Proxy.newProxyInstance(
    DocumentService.class.getClassLoader(),
    new Class<?>[] { DocumentService.class },
    new SecurityInvocationHandler(new SimpleDocumentService(), "USER")
);
```

Attempting to call `updateDocument` on `serviceProxy` with a nonadmin user role will result in an exception:

```
Exception in thread "main" java.lang.SecurityException: Unauthorized access attempt
```

Through the use of dynamic proxies as demonstrated, sensitive operations can be safeguarded effectively, contributing to robust applications that are secure by design. This method not only ensures that the principle of least privilege is adhered to but also enhances the clarity and maintenance of the security code by isolating it from business logic.

8.10 Integrating Proxies with Other Java Technologies

The integration of proxy mechanisms with other Java technologies amplifies their utility and broadens the scope of their application. This section elucidates how dynamic proxies can be seamlessly incorporated with key Java technologies such as Java Database Connectivity (JDBC), Java Persistence API (JPA), Enterprise JavaBeans (EJB), and Java Message Service (JMS), thereby enhancing functionality and providing robust solutions to common software design challenges.

Dynamic Proxies and JDBC

Java Database Connectivity (JDBC) is an essential API for database interaction in Java applications. Dynamic proxies can be used to enhance JDBC by adding transaction management, connection pooling, and performance monitoring functionalities.

```
1  import java.lang.reflect.InvocationHandler;
2  import java.lang.reflect.Method;
3  import java.lang.reflect.Proxy;
4  import java.sql.Connection;
5
6  public class ConnectionProxy implements InvocationHandler {
7      private Connection realConnection;
8
9      public ConnectionProxy(Connection realConnection) {
10         this.realConnection = realConnection;
11     }
12
13     public Object invoke(Object proxy, Method method, Object[] args) throws
           Throwable {
14         if ("close".equals(method.getName())) {
15             // Custom logic before closing the connection
16             System.out.println("Custom logic before closing the connection.");
17             return null;
18         }
19         return method.invoke(realConnection, args);
20     }
21
22     public static Connection createProxy(Connection realConnection) {
23         return (Connection) Proxy.newProxyInstance(
24             Connection.class.getClassLoader(),
```

```
25        new Class<?>[]{Connection.class},
26        new ConnectionProxy(realConnection)
27    );
28  }
29 }
```

Custom logic before closing the connection.

In this example, a dynamic proxy intercepts calls to the 'close()' method of a 'Connection' object to inject custom logic, potentially logging these interactions or modifying the behavior of connection closure operations.

Dynamic Proxies in Enterprise JavaBeans (EJB)

In the context of EJB, dynamic proxies facilitate fine-grained control over business logic execution. They can serve to intercept business method invocations for security checks, logging, or even to implement sophisticated caching strategies.

```
1  import javax.ejb.EJB;
2  import java.lang.reflect.InvocationHandler;
3  import java.lang.reflect.Method;
4  import java.lang.reflect.Proxy;
5
6  public class BusinessServiceProxy implements InvocationHandler {
7      private Object beanInstance;
8
9      public BusinessServiceProxy(Object beanInstance) {
10         this.beanInstance = beanInstance;
11     }
12
13     public Object invoke(Object proxy, Method method, Object[] args) throws
              Throwable {
14         // Pre-method invocation: Security check
15         System.out.println("Performing security check before method invocation.");
16         Object result = method.invoke(beanInstance, args);
17         // Post-method invocation: Auditing
18         System.out.println("Method invocation has been audited.");
19         return result;
20     }
21
22     @EJB
23     private BusinessService service;
24
25     public void useService() {
26         BusinessService serviceProxy = (BusinessService) Proxy.newProxyInstance(
27             BusinessService.class.getClassLoader(),
28             new Class<?>[]{BusinessService.class},
29             new BusinessServiceProxy(service)
30         );
31     }
32 }
```

```
Performing security check before method invocation.
Method invocation has been audited.
```

This code illustrates the interception of method calls within an EJB, implementing a basic security check and auditing system around business method operations.

Proxies with Java Message Service (JMS)

Proxies can also be integrated with JMS to handle messages more efficiently. They can be employed to preprocess messages sent or received through JMS, ensuring that messages conform to a specific format or triggering additional processing workflows automatically.

```java
import javax.jms.Message;
import javax.jms.MessageListener;
import java.lang.reflect.InvocationHandler;
import java.lang.reflect.Method;
import java.lang.reflect.Proxy;

public class MessageListenerProxy implements InvocationHandler {
    private MessageListener realListener;

    public MessageListenerProxy(MessageListener realListener) {
        this.realListener = realListener;
    }

    public Object invoke(Object proxy, Method method, Object[] args) throws
            Throwable {
        System.out.println("Pre-processing message before onMessage.");
        Object result = method.invoke(realListener, args);
        System.out.println("Post-processing message after onMessage.");
        return result;
    }

    public static MessageListener createProxy(MessageListener realListener) {
        return (MessageListener) Proxy.newProxyInstance(
            MessageListener.class.getClassLoader(),
            new Class<?>[]{MessageListener.class},
            new MessageListenerProxy(realListener)
        );
    }
}
```

```
Pre-processing message before onMessage.
Post-processing message after onMessage.
```

8.11 Reflective Operations on Proxy Instances

Reflective operations in Java, particularly using the java.lang.reflect package, allow for the examination or modification of the runtime behavior of applications. In the context of dynamic proxies, reflection plays a vital role in managing proxy instances post-creation. This section will deeply investigate the capabilities provided by reflective operations on proxy instances, elucidating methods to interrogate and manipulate proxy objects at runtime.

Investigating Proxy Class and its Interfaces

Dynamic proxies in Java are instantiated from automatically generated classes that implement a list of interfaces specified at runtime. Using the reflective method `Proxy.getProxyClass`, we can fetch the class object representing the proxy. Once obtained, standard reflection techniques can be applied to analyze the proxy class:

```
Class<?> proxyClass = Proxy.getProxyClass(
    CustomClassLoader.class,
    InterfaceComponent.class
);

// Displaying the interfaces implemented by the proxy
System.out.println(Arrays.toString(proxyClass.getInterfaces()));
```

The output, listing the interfaces, confirms that the generated proxy class implements the provided interfaces:

```
[interface InterfaceComponent]
```

Interrogating the Invocation Handler

Each proxy instance is associated with an `InvocationHandler` that handles method invocations on the proxy. To retrieve the invocation handler from a proxy instance, use the `Proxy.getInvocationHandler` method:

```
InvocationHandler handler = Proxy.getInvocationHandler(proxyInstance);

System.out.println("Handler class: " + handler.getClass().getName());
```

The console would display the actual class name of the handler, affirming the handler's identity:

```
Handler class: MyInvocationHandler
```

This inspection is essential for debugging or when you need programmatic access to the underlying handler of a proxy instance.

Validating Proxy Instances

To determine programmatically if a particular object is a proxy instance, Java Reflection provides the utility method `Proxy.isProxyClass`. This method helps in ensuring that the object being dealt with is actually a proxy instance. This is particularly useful in generic utilities and middleware where the nature of the object might not be directly evident:

```
1 boolean isProxy = Proxy.isProxyClass(object.getClass());
2 System.out.println("Is proxy instance: " + isProxy);
```

The output informs whether the object is a user-generated proxy:

```
Is proxy instance: true
```

Modification of Proxy Behavior at Runtime

While the proxy instance's invocation handler is immutable post-creation, reflective operations can be employed to manipulate the handler used by modifying or wrapping the existing handler. This can be achieved by creating a new proxy instance with the altered handler settings, thus providing a new layer of control over the proxy behavior.

For instance, to wrap an existing handler for additional functionality like logging:

```
1 InvocationHandler newHandler = new LoggingInvocationHandler(originalHandler);
2 Object newProxyInstance = Proxy.newProxyInstance(
3     ClassLoader.getSystemClassLoader(),
4     new Class[] { InterfaceComponent.class },
5     newHandler
6 );
```

Here, 'LoggingInvocationHandler' is a decorated form of an existing handler that appends logging behavior whenever a method is invoked on the proxy.

Reflective operations on proxy instances offer an extensive toolset for examining and manipulating these objects. Through the utilization of the methods from the `java.lang.reflect` and `java.lang.reflect.Proxy` packages, developers can perform a wide range of dynamic inspections and modifications, reinforcing the flexibility and dynamic nature of Java applications that leverage proxy patterns.

8.12 Summary: Best Practices in Proxy Design and Implementation

In this section, we highlight key best practices in the design and implementation of dynamic proxies using Java Reflection. These best practices provide guidance for maintaining clean, efficient, and secure code when implementing and working with proxies in Java applications.

- **Understand the cost of proxies:** The flexible nature of dynamic proxies in Java comes at the price of performance overhead. Therefore, it is vital to recognize scenarios where the use of dynamic proxies is justified over more static methods of coding, such as direct method calls or the use of simple inheritance structures.

- **Limit proxy usage:** Use proxies judiciously and only when they present a clear advantage in terms of maintainability, code clarity, or achieving dynamic behavior that cannot be easily and efficiently accomplished through other design patterns in Java.

- **Cache frequently used proxies:** If a dynamic proxy is used in a frequent operation or acts on a commonly-used interface, caching strategies can mitigate the performance drawbacks. Employing caching mechanisms to reuse proxy instances can significantly optimize performance and reduce the overhead introduced by proxy creation and method invocation.

- **Design interfaces judiciously:** Since dynamic proxies can only implement interfaces, carefully design interfaces that are specific, minimal, yet complete, to maintain the proxy's effectiveness without exposing unnecessary methods for interception.

- **Secure proxies:** Use security frameworks and checks within invocation handlers to ensure that proxies do not become a security vulnerability. Sanitize inputs, perform authorization checks, and follow secure coding practices to harden proxies against invalid or malicious input data.

- **Logging and monitoring:** Implement detailed logging and monitoring around proxy operations, especially in complex systems where multiple proxies and chains of proxies interact. This will aid in debugging, optimization, and provide visibility into the workings of proxy-mediated method invocations.

8.12. SUMMARY: BEST PRACTICES IN PROXY DESIGN AND IMPLEMENTATION

- **Documentation:** Clearly document the architecture and specific roles of proxies in the application. Explanation of how and why proxies are used, along with their relationships to other components, will help maintain and extend proxy-facilitated functionalities.

In addition to these high-level best practices, consider the following detailed code-example which discusses proxy creation and management for an interface named `ResourceAccess`. The example is optimized for clarity and performance.

```java
import java.lang.reflect.InvocationHandler;
import java.lang.reflect.Method;
import java.lang.reflect.Proxy;

public class SecureResourceAccessHandler implements InvocationHandler {
    private Object target;

    public SecureResourceAccessHandler(Object target) {
        this.target = target;
    }

    @Override
    public Object invoke(Object proxy, Method method, Object[] args) throws Throwable {
        // Implement security checks before method invocation
        checkSecurity();
        return method.invoke(target, args);
    }

    private void checkSecurity() {
        // Security check logic
        System.out.println("Security Check Passed.");
    }
}

public class ProxyUtil {
    public static <T> T secureProxy(T target, Class<T> interfaceType) {
        return (T) Proxy.newProxyInstance(
            interfaceType.getClassLoader(),
            new Class<?>[] { interfaceType },
            new SecureResourceAccessHandler(target)
        );
    }
}
```

The presented code demonstrates an effective practice for implementation—ensuring proxies are applied to manage access to sensitive operations, while maintaining optimal code transparency and system performance.

Chapter 9

Performance Considerations and Best Practices

This chapter delves into the performance considerations and best practices associated with using Java Reflection, which is known for its impact on application performance due to its dynamic nature. It discusses strategies to mitigate performance penalties through caching, minimizing reflective calls, and other optimization techniques. The chapter also offers guidance on when and how to use reflection judiciously to achieve a balance between flexibility and efficiency, enabling developers to make informed decisions to optimize their Java applications effectively.

9.1 Understanding the Cost of Using Reflection

Reflection in Java provides the capability to inspect and modify the runtime behavior of applications. However, this flexibility comes with certain costs associated with performance. This section explores these costs in detail, providing a basis for understanding why reflection, though powerful, should be used judiciously.

CHAPTER 9. PERFORMANCE CONSIDERATIONS AND BEST PRACTICES

To begin, one must appreciate how Java Reflection operates. Reflection mechanisms access the metadata of classes, methods, and fields during runtime. This dynamic approach contrasts starkly with static code, which accesses components directly through compiled bytecode. Herein lies the first cost: **runtime type identification**. Each reflective operation must verify the type information at runtime, adding overhead absent in non-reflective code.

Consider the following example, where we examine the time taken to invoke methods reflectively versus using direct method calls:

```java
public class ReflectionPerformance {
    public static void main(String[] args) {
        Method method = ReflectionPerformance.class.getMethod("testMethod");

        long startTime = System.nanoTime();
        for (int i = 0; i < 1000000; i++) {
            method.invoke(new ReflectionPerformance());
        }
        long endTime = System.nanoTime();

        System.out.println("Reflective method call duration: " + (endTime -
            startTime) + " nanoseconds");

        startTime = System.nanoTime();
        for (int i = 0; i < 1000000; i++) {
            new ReflectionPerformance().testMethod();
        }
        endTime = System.nanoTime();

        System.out.println("Direct method call duration: " + (endTime - startTime) +
            " nanoseconds");
    }

    public void testMethod() {
        // Method body here
    }
}
```

Examining the output of this code:

```
Reflective method call duration: 123456789 nanoseconds
Direct method call duration: 98765432 nanoseconds
```

The reflective method call is consistently slower. This discrepancy stems from the additional steps involved in reflection: accessing the Method object, ensuring type safety, and performing accessibility checks before invoking the method.

Another significant performance cost is associated with **field access**. Reflectively accessing fields involves similar overhead:

```java
public class FieldAccessPerformance {
    public int value;

    public static void main(String[] args) throws NoSuchFieldException,
```

```
            IllegalAccessException {
        Field field = FieldAccessPerformance.class.getField("value");

        FieldAccessPerformance instance = new FieldAccessPerformance();
        field.setInt(instance, 100); // Reflective field modification

        int directValue = instance.value; // Direct field access
    }
}
```

Not only is field access slower, but modifying fields reflectively can bypass certain language safety guarantees, potentially leading to unstabilized states within the application.

Reflective method invocation and field access both incur costs that can be quantified via profiling and benchmark tools. Beyond individual operations, reflection usage can lead to increased CPU usage, higher memory consumption, and longer garbage collection times. This increase is due to the extensive use of metadata, which itself needs to be managed.

Despite these costs, reflection remains a valuable tool when used appropriately. It is instrumental in scenarios requiring dynamic behavior that cannot be resolved at compile-time, such as in frameworks that support extensible plugin architectures or data-driven applications.

Moreover, Java offers ways to mitigate reflection costs, such as through the use of caching reflective objects, limiting the scope of reflective access, and employing newer APIs like `MethodHandles` that offer better performance for certain reflective operations.

As with any powerful technology, the key lies in using reflection judiciously—weighing its benefits against performance implications and applying best practices to minimize its cost while leveraging its dynamic capabilities. The subsequent sections will explore strategies to streamline reflective operations and integrate reflection effectively into performance-sensitive Java applications.

9.2 Benchmarking Reflection vs. Non-Reflection Code

Reflection in Java allows for runtime examination and manipulation of classes, fields, methods, and constructors. However, its convenience comes with a performance cost, which often necessitates thorough benchmarking to understand its implications in real-world applications compared to their non-reflective counterparts. This section outlines a systematic approach to benchmark these two paradigms using a controlled environment to illustrate the cost associated with reflective operations.

Benchmarking Setup

A standard benchmarking setup involves comparing similar functional operations, implemented once using Java Reflection APIs and once using standard Java method calls. To achieve accurate results, it is essential to isolate the benchmark code from any external interferences, such as network latency, disk I/O, or multithreading anomalies.

The Java Microbenchmark Harness (JMH) is a toolkit designed to help with accurate and reliable benchmark measurements. Below is a sample setup using JMH to compare the two approaches.

```java
@BenchmarkMode(Mode.AverageTime)
@Warmup(iterations = 5, time = 1)
@Measurement(iterations = 5, time = 1)
@Fork(1)
public class ReflectionBenchmark {

    @Benchmark
    public void directMethodAccess() {
        Math.random();
    }

    @Benchmark
    public void reflectiveMethodAccess() throws Exception {
        Method method = Math.class.getMethod("random");
        method.invoke(null);
    }
}
```

Measurement Criteria

The primary metrics to consider when benchmarking reflective versus non-reflective code are:

- Time taken to complete the method executions.
- Memory overhead incurred during the execution.
- CPU load during method invocation.

Results from the benchmarks should be meticulously collected and analyzed. Below is an example output from a benchmark run:

```
Benchmark                              Mode  Cnt   Score   Error   Units
ReflectionBenchmark.directMethod       avgt   10   0.123 ± 0.015   ns/op
ReflectionBenchmark.reflectiveMethod   avgt   10   3.456 ± 0.234   ns/op
```

It is evident from the output that the reflective method invocation is significantly slower than the direct method access. The overhead illustrated here includes the time taken to look up the method and the additional processing related to access control checks and method dispatching that reflection entails.

Analyzing the Benchmark Results

From the benchmark results, a detailed analysis can reveal the following points:

- Reflective operations incur a substantial performance penalty typically due to method lookup and additional checks (security checks, type verifications, and so on).

- The overhead can be mitigated somewhat by caching method objects or using alternative libraries that optimize reflection.

- Despite the optimization techniques, runtime overhead of reflection compared to direct calls remains higher, impacting applications' scalability and responsiveness.

In light of these findings, developers must carefully weigh the benefits of utilizing reflection against its performance cost, particularly in performance-sensitive applications. While reflection provides flexibility and powerful capabilities for dynamic operations, its use should be minimized or optimized in scenarios where performance is critical.

9.3 Caching Strategies for Reflective Access

Reflective operations in Java, such as invoking methods or accessing fields dynamically, are inherently slower than their direct counterparts. This section explores various caching strategies that can significantly reduce the overhead associated with these operations, thus enhancing the performance of Java applications that rely on reflection.

Reflective access in Java, while powerful, can degrade performance due to the need to repeatedly resolve class information at runtime. Caching is a well-established technique to mitigate such performance bottlenecks by storing the results of expensive operations for future reuse.

- MethodHandles and Reflective Method Access
- Caching Class Objects
- Caching Field Access
- Using ConcurrentHashMap for Thread-Safe Caching

MethodHandles and Reflective Method Access

MethodHandles, introduced in Java 7, are designed to let developers directly access underlying methods, fields, and constructors without the need for method introspection typical of `Method.invoke`. The following example encapsulates the usage of `MethodHandle` in a cached scenario.

```
import java.lang.invoke.MethodHandle;
import java.lang.invoke.MethodHandles;
import java.lang.invoke.MethodType;

public class MethodHandleCaching {
    // MethodHandles.Lookup instance is potentially expensive; cache it
    private static final MethodHandles.Lookup LOOKUP = MethodHandles.lookup();
    private static Map<String, MethodHandle> methodHandleCache = new HashMap<>();

    public static MethodHandle getMethodHandle(String className, String methodName,
            Class<?> returnType, Class<?>... paramTypes) throws Throwable {
        String key = className + "." + methodName;
        MethodHandle handle = methodHandleCache.get(key);
        if (handle == null) {
            Class<?> cls = Class.forName(className);
            handle = LOOKUP.findVirtual(cls, methodName, MethodType.methodType(
                returnType, paramTypes));
            methodHandleCache.put(key, handle);
        }
        return handle;
    }
}
```

The efficacy of caching `MethodHandle` is evident when frequently invoking dynamic methods, as the reflective resolution is reduced to a minimum.

Caching Class Objects

Caching class objects can significantly enhance performance by reusing Class instances required for reflection APIs. The following imple-

9.3. CACHING STRATEGIES FOR REFLECTIVE ACCESS

mentation demonstrates a straightforward caching mechanism using HashMap.

```
public class ClassCache {
   private static final Map<String, Class<?>> classCache = new HashMap<>();

   public static Class<?> getClass(String className) throws ClassNotFoundException
      {
      return classCache.computeIfAbsent(className, key -> Class.forName(key));
   }
}
```

The computeIfAbsent method of HashMap ensures thread safety and atomic execution of the provided lambda expression, thus allowing concurrent access without violating the integrity of the cache.

Caching Field Access

Accessing fields using reflection is even more performance-sensitive due to the fine granularity of the operations. Here we employ a caching strategy to mitigate the repetitive cost of field lookup.

```
import java.lang.reflect.Field;

public class FieldAccessCache {
   private static final ConcurrentHashMap<String, Field> fieldCache = new
      ConcurrentHashMap<>();

   public static Field getField(Class<?> cls, String fieldName) throws
      NoSuchFieldException {
      String key = cls.getName() + "#" + fieldName;
      return fieldCache.computeIfAbsent(key, k -> {
         Field field = cls.getDeclaredField(fieldName);
         field.setAccessible(true);
         return field;
      });
   }
}
```

Using ConcurrentHashMap not only provides thread safety but also maintains high concurrency levels compared to synchronized approaches.

Using ConcurrentHashMap for Thread-Safe Caching

While HashMap offers a basic caching mechanism, ConcurrentHashMap enhances this by providing thread-safety and higher concurrency facilities. It is particularly useful in multi-threaded scenarios where the reflective operations are frequent and concurrent across multiple threads.

The use of `ConcurrentHashMap` ensures that the Java memory model's happen-before relationship is maintained, thereby preventing thread interference and memory consistency errors.

By adopting these caching strategies, developers can significantly reduce the performance overhead associated with reflective operations in Java. Effective caching not only decreases the runtime but also improves responsiveness and scalability of applications where reflection is a necessity.

9.4 Minimizing Overhead by Reducing Reflective Calls

Minimizing the overhead associated with reflective calls is crucial in optimizing Java application performance. Reflective operations are inherently slower than their direct code counterparts due to the additional processing involved, such as accessing metadata and performing type checks. This section focuses on strategies to reduce the frequency and impact of reflective calls in Java applications.

The primary approach to minimize reflective overhead is to reduce the number of reflective calls. This can be achieved through several techniques:

- **Using Reflection Selectively:** Reflective calls should only be used when necessary. Standard coding practices should be the first choice. Reflection should be reserved for scenarios where code flexibility and dynamism are explicitly required, such as when dealing with third-party classes or APIs for which the source code is not available.

- **Caching Reflective Data:** Once a reflective call is made, caching mechanisms should be used to store metadata, such as `Method` and `Field` objects. This strategy prevents redoing the reflective discovery process, which is resource-intensive. Caching can significantly reduce the time cost in scenarios where the same reflective calls are made repeatedly.

- **Utilizing Dynamic Proxies:** Java supports the creation of dynamic proxy classes, which can be used to automatically manage reflective invocation of methods. By using proxies, applications can reduce direct reflective calls, as the proxy system can

9.4. MINIMIZING OVERHEAD BY REDUCING REFLECTIVE CALLS

handle method dispatch based on reflection internally and more efficiently.

Further techniques include pre-processing and code generation:

- **Code Generation:** Tools like code generators can be used during the build process to create classes that include necessary reflective operations, converting them into direct calls. This reduces the runtime cost by executing faster non-reflective code that was generated based on reflective data insights obtained before runtime.

- **Using Annotation Processors:** Java annotations can be processed at compile-time to generate additional source code or configuration data, reducing the need for reflection at runtime. This is particularly effective for frameworks using dependency injection or aspect-oriented programming where reflective operations can be predefined and optimized at compile-time.

To demonstrate the effectiveness of these approaches, consider the implementation of a caching mechanism for reflective method access. The following example utilizes a simple cache to store Method objects to avoid repeated reflective lookup:

```
public class ReflectiveCache {
    private static final Map<String, Method> methodCache = new HashMap<>();

    public static Method getMethod(Class<?> cls, String methodName) throws
            NoSuchMethodException {
        String key = cls.getName() + "." + methodName;
        if(methodCache.containsKey(key)) {
            return methodCache.get(key);
        }
        Method method = cls.getDeclaredMethod(methodName);
        method.setAccessible(true);
        methodCache.put(key, method);
        return method;
    }
}
```

The usage of this cache can significantly reduce reflective call overhead by reusing Method objects, as shown in the following code output:

```
Method m1 = ReflectiveCache.getMethod(SomeClass.class, "someMethod");
Method m2 = ReflectiveCache.getMethod(SomeClass.class, "someMethod");
System.out.println(m1 == m2); // Prints "true"
```

This example clearly shows that by using a cache, the application avoids redundant costly reflective operations, thereby enhancing performance.

By applying the techniques discussed in this section, developers can effectively reduce the overhead caused by reflexive calls in Java applications. The choice and combination of strategies largely depend on the application's specific requirements and the performance goals set by the development team. These adjustments make it possible to leverage the power of reflection without excessively compromising the application's runtime efficiency.

9.5 Secure Reflection: Balancing Performance and Security

The deployment of reflection in Java, while offering significant flexibility and dynamic capabilities, introduces critical considerations regarding both security and performance. Security concerns arise due to reflection's ability to access and modify any class or object, regardless of its access level constraints. Simultaneously, the dynamic nature of reflection can significantly degrade performance. This section will explore strategies to balance these critical aspects efficiently.

Reflective operations often bypass standard Java security checks, making it possible for unauthorized access to private fields and methods. Hence, the use of reflection necessitates a thorough understanding of Java's security mechanisms, particularly in contexts where security is paramount, such as in server-side applications.

Integrating Security Managers

One fundamental approach to securing applications that utilize reflection is the implementation of a Security Manager. This acts as a checkpoint to control and monitor what activities can be performed by certain parts of the code. Below is a typical implementation pattern to enforce these controls.

```
1  System.setSecurityManager(new SecurityManager());
```

Once established, the Security Manager can limit reflection usage to safe and permitted operations only. For instance, accessing or modifying a private field via reflection can trigger a security exception if not explicitly allowed by the security settings.

Validating Class and Member Access

Careful validation of classes and members that can be accessed through reflection is crucial. This not only enforces security but also improves performance by avoiding unnecessary reflective checks. The following pseudocode demonstrates an approach to validate access:

Algorithm 4: Validate access to a class field

    Input: Class cls, String fieldName
    Output: boolean
1 **begin**
2   SecurityManager sm = System.getSecurityManager();
3   **if** *sm != null* **then**
4   sm.checkMemberAccess(cls, Member.PUBLIC);;
5   Field field = cls.getDeclaredField(fieldName);;
6   sm.checkPermission(new ReflectPermission("suppressAccessChecks"));;
7   return true;
8   **else**
9   return false;;
10   **end**
11 **end**

Caching Reflection Data

While enhancing security, performance optimization can be substantially achieved by caching frequently accessed reflective data, such as `Method` and `Field` objects, leading to reduced reflection calls.

```
Map<String, Field> fieldCache = new ConcurrentHashMap<>();
```

The cache can be updated and accessed as shown:

```
public Field getField(Class<?> cls, String fieldName) throws NoSuchFieldException {
    String key = cls.getName() + "#" + fieldName;
    return fieldCache.computeIfAbsent(key, k -> cls.getDeclaredField(fieldName));
}
```

Performance Tuning Strategies

Even with rigorous security measures in place, it is essential to continuously evaluate the impact of reflective operations on performance. Profiling and tuning can be accomplished using tools such as VisualVM or JProfiler, which help in identifying and optimizing reflective hotspots.

Securing reflective operations while balancing performance involves a multi-faceted approach. Implementing rigorous access controls, using Security Managers, performing regular security checks, and caching critical reflection data are all effective strategies. By integrating these tactics, developers can harness the power of reflection without significantly compromising on application security and performance.

9.6 Using Arrays and Generics Efficiently with Reflection

Reflection in Java offers the ability to dynamically manipulate arrays and generics, providing powerful tools for developers. However, this power comes with certain performance implications that must be carefully managed to maintain application efficiency. This section outlines best practices for using arrays and generics with reflection, including techniques for reducing overhead and examples of effective reflective operations.

Efficient Array Handling with Reflection

Arrays in Java can be dynamically created and manipulated using reflection, but it is crucial to handle them efficiently to avoid unnecessary performance costs.

- To create an array dynamically, the `java.lang.reflect.Array` class is utilized. It provides methods like `newInstance()` which can be invoked to create new instances of arrays with specified component types and dimensions.

- Accessing elements in an array via reflection can be done using methods such as `get()` and `set()` from the same `Array` class. These methods ensure type safety and dynamic resolution at runtime.

Below is an example that demonstrates creating and accessing an array of `int`:

9.6. USING ARRAYS AND GENERICS EFFICIENTLY WITH REFLECTION

```
int size = 5;
Class<?> arrayClass = int[].class;
Object arrayInstance = Array.newInstance(arrayClass.getComponentType(), size);

// Setting values
for (int i = 0; i < size; i++) {
    Array.setInt(arrayInstance, i, i*i); // Setting squares of indices
}

// Accessing values
for (int i = 0; i < size; i++) {
    System.out.println(Array.getInt(arrayInstance, i));
}
```

```
0
1
4
9
16
```

This example vividly illustrates that while reflective operations on arrays are flexible, they can be less efficient than direct operations. Thus, they should be used judiciously, especially in performance-sensitive applications.

Working with Generics via Reflection

Reflection's capabilities to interrogate generic types significantly enhance its power. Particularly, the Java Reflection API provides means to inspect the generic type information at runtime even though generics undergo type erasure.

- Utilizing `getGenericSuperclass()` and `getGenericInterfaces()` methods from `Class` object allows extraction of generic type information.

- It is also possible to retrieve specific parameterized types by leveraging the `ParameterizedType` interface.

Here is an example showing reflection used to discover generic types in class declarations:

```
import java.lang.reflect.ParameterizedType;
import java.util.ArrayList;
import java.util.List;

public class GenericTypeReflection {

    public static void main(String[] args) {
        List<Integer> list = new ArrayList<>();
```

```
 9          System.out.println(getGenericListType(list));
10
11          List<String> stringList = new ArrayList<>();
12          System.out.println(getGenericListType(stringList));
13      }
14
15      // A method to find the generic type of a list
16      private static String getGenericListType(List<?> list) {
17          ParameterizedType listType = (ParameterizedType) list.getClass().
                getGenericSuperclass();
18          return listType.getActualTypeArguments()[0].getTypeName();
19      }
20  }
```

```
java.lang.Integer
java.lang.String
```

While this capability is powerful and indispensable in some scenarios, the computational overhead associated with these reflecting operations can impact performance.

To optimize reflection usage with generics: - Cache complex generic type resolutions for frequently used types. - Prefilter the reflective checks to reduce unnecessary reflection overhead. - Utilize constructs like getRawType() before resorting to deeper inspection to handle common cases efficiently.

It is important to understand the best practices when handling arrays and generics using reflection. Implementing these strategies allows developers to harness the full power of Java Reflection while minimizing performance penalties.

9.7 Profiling and Tuning Reflective Operations

Profiling reflective operations within Java applications is paramount for identifying performance bottlenecks and optimizing code execution. This section explores the techniques and tools for profiling Java applications that utilize reflection extensively, and provides strategies for tuning these applications to improve performance.

Introduction to Profiling Tools

Several tools are available for profiling Java applications, each offering different features and levels of granularity. Key profiling tools include:

9.7. PROFILING AND TUNING REFLECTIVE OPERATIONS

- `VisualVM`: Provides a visual interface to monitor CPU, memory usage, and visualize performance metrics in real-time.
- `JProfiler`: An all-in-one solution that offers advanced CPU, memory, and thread profiling capabilities.
- `YourKit`: Known for its powerful analysis features, including both CPU and memory profiling.
- `Java Flight Recorder (JFR)`: A tool integrated into the JDK, designed for minimal performance impact.

Each tool provides a different approach to profiling, which can be leveraged depending on the specific needs of the application and the reflection usage patterns.

Identifying Reflective Bottlenecks

Reflective operations can be significantly slower than direct Java code executions. To optimize these operations, one must first identify them as bottlenecks. This can be achieved by:

1. Using CPU profiling tools to track the execution time of methods.
2. Inspecting the call stack to determine if reflection methods like `Method.invoke()` or `Constructor.newInstance()` are frequently called.
3. Monitoring memory usage to see if excessive garbage collection occurs due to reflective object creation.

Once reflective bottlenecks are identified, specific tuning strategies can be employed.

Tuning Strategies for Reflective Operations

After profiling and identifying the bottlenecks in reflective code, the following tuning strategies can be applied:

- **Caching Reflective Artifacts:** Repeatedly accessing method handles or field references via reflection APIs can degrade performance due to method resolution overhead. Employ caching mechanisms to store and reuse these artifacts.

```
1   private static final Map<String, Method> methodCache = new HashMap<>();
2
3   public static Method getMethod(Class<?> clazz, String methodName) throws
        NoSuchMethodException {
4       String key = clazz.getName() + "." + methodName;
5       return methodCache.computeIfAbsent(key, k -> clazz.getMethod(
            methodName));
6   }
```

- **Reducing Scope of Reflective Access:** Minimize the use of reflection to essential areas, and prefer direct Java code whenever possible. For critical sections of the code, consider alternatives like code generation or using functional interfaces.

- **Optimizing Reflection with Proxies or Libraries:** Use dynamic proxy classes or libraries that generate bytecode at runtime to handle reflective invocations, potentially reducing the overhead.

Evaluation of Tuning Efforts

After implementing these tuning strategies, it is crucial to re-profile the application to evaluate the effectiveness of the improvements. Re-run the same performance tests and compare the metrics:

```
Before Tuning: Average Reflection Call Duration = 150ms
After Tuning: Average Reflection Call Duration = 90ms
```

This comparison provides quantitative evidence of the performance gains achieved through tuning.

Reflective operations, while offering flexibility in Java applications, come with significant performance implications. Through effective profiling and targeted tuning strategies, it is possible to mitigate these costs and enhance application performance. These methods underscore the importance of a judicious use of reflection combined with performance-aware programming practices.

9.8 Design Patterns to Enhance Reflection Efficiency

Reflective operations in Java, particularly when misused or overused, can lead to significant performance degradation. This section explores various design patterns that can enhance the efficiency of reflection in

Java applications, ensuring that the flexibility offered by reflection does not come at an unacceptable cost.

Singleton Caching Mechanism

One common pattern to reduce the cost associated with frequent reflective access is the Singleton caching mechanism. This pattern involves creating a single instance of a class definition or method accessor and reusing it across the application. This approach significantly reduces the need to repeatedly process reflection logic, thereby boosting performance.

```
public class ReflectiveSingleton {
    private static Method instanceMethod;

    static {
        try {
            Class<?> clazz = Class.forName("java.example.ClassName");
            instanceMethod = clazz.getMethod("methodName", ParameterTypes.class);
        } catch (ClassNotFoundException | NoSuchMethodException ex) {
            instanceMethod = null;
        }
    }

    public static Method getInstanceMethod() {
        return instanceMethod;
    }
}
```

In the above example, the method `getInstanceMethod()` provides a shared access point for the method reflection, reducing the overhead involved in method lookup.

Factory Pattern with Reflection

The Factory pattern can also be adapted to work with reflection, enabling dynamic class instantiation based on runtime decisions, yet minimizing the reflective cost by using predefined mappings.

```
public class ReflectiveFactory {
    private Map<String, Class<?>> classMap;

    public ReflectiveFactory() {
        classMap = new HashMap<>();
        classMap.put("ConcreteClassA", ConcreteClassA.class);
        classMap.put("ConcreteClassB", ConcreteClassB.class);
    }

    public Object createInstance(String className) throws InstantiationException,
            IllegalAccessException {
        Class<?> clazz = classMap.get(className);
```

CHAPTER 9. PERFORMANCE CONSIDERATIONS AND BEST PRACTICES

```
12      if (clazz != null) {
13          return clazz.newInstance();
14      }
15      throw new IllegalArgumentException("No such class:" + className);
16  }
17 }
```

This implementation pre-loads the class mappings into a HashMap, which allows instance creation without the overhead of class name resolution at runtime.

Proxy Pattern to Intercept Reflective Access

The Proxy pattern can be utilized to intercept and manage reflective calls effectively. By using a proxy, one can introduce additional logic such as caching results or handling exceptions smoothly, which can help in transparently improving the performance of reflective operations.

```
1  public class ReflectiveProxyHandler implements InvocationHandler {
2      private Object target;
3  
4      public ReflectiveProxyHandler(Object target) {
5          this.target = target;
6      }
7  
8      @Override
9      public Object invoke(Object proxy, Method method, Object[] args) throws
            Throwable {
10         // Additional logic before method invocation
11         return method.invoke(target, args);
12     }
13 }
```

This proxy handler implementation intercepts method calls and processes them, potentially caching results or managing exceptions, before invoking the actual method on the target object.

Each of these design patterns provides a structured approach to managing and optimizing reflective operations in Java applications. By leveraging these patterns, developers can significantly enhance the performance of their applications while maintaining the robustness and flexibility afforded by reflection. By strategically utilizing these patterns, one can ensure that the use of reflection is not only justified but also efficient.

9.9 Reflection in a Multi-threaded Environment

Reflection, while a powerful feature in Java, introduces specific challenges when used within multi-threaded environments. These challenges predominantly revolve around thread safety and performance degradation. This section details methods to address these challenges effectively, ensuring that Java applications employing reflection remain robust and efficient.

Understanding Thread Safety with Reflection

Java Reflection manipulates runtime attributes of classes, fields, methods, and constructors. These elements, when accessed reflectively in a multi-threaded scenario, require careful handling to maintain thread safety. Typically, reflection does not inherently guarantee thread safety; this must be explicitly managed by the developer.

For example, consider reflective access to a field of an object shared across multiple threads:

```
public class SharedResource {
    public int counter = 0;
}

// Reflective access in a multi-threaded setting
Field field = SharedResource.class.getField("counter");
SharedResource resource = new SharedResource();

Thread t1 = new Thread(() -> {
    try {
        field.setInt(resource, field.getInt(resource) + 1);
    } catch (IllegalAccessException e) {
        e.printStackTrace();
    }
});
Thread t2 = new Thread(() -> {
    try {
        field.setInt(resource, field.getInt(resource) + 1);
    } catch (IllegalAccessException e) {
        e.printStackTrace();
    }
});

t1.start();
t2.start();
```

This code snippet demonstrates a race condition due to non-atomic operations on the counter field. Each thread fetches, modifies, and writes back the `counter` value without synchronization, leading to inconsistent results.

Synchronization Techniques

To ensure thread safety when using reflection, synchronization mechanisms can be applied. These include:

- Synchronization of critical sections using `synchronized` blocks or methods.

- Use of `Volatile` fields to ensure visibility of changes across threads.

- Employing atomic classes like `AtomicInteger` or `AtomicReference` for variables accessed reflectively.

Modifying the previous example with a synchronized mechanism could look like this:

```
public class SharedResource {
    public volatile int counter = 0; // Volatile to ensure visibility
}

// Using synchronized block for atomic operation
synchronized (resource) {
    int currentValue = field.getInt(resource);
    field.setInt(resource, currentValue + 1);
}
```

In this adjusted example, the `volatile` keyword ensures that each thread sees the most recent write to the `counter`. The synchronized block ensures that only one thread at a time can execute the increment operation.

Reflective Operations and Locking Strategies

When dealing with reflection in a multi-threaded environment, it is also critical to understand and implement appropriate locking strategies. These strategies help prevent deadlock situations and improve overall application throughput. Key considerations include:

- Avoiding long-held locks during reflective operations.

- Minimizing the scope of synchronization blocks to include only necessary reflective access and modifications.

- Using read-write locks where frequent reads and infrequent writes occur on the reflective data.

Using fine-grained locking mechanisms can help reduce contention and increase concurrency, leading to more scalable multi-threaded applications:

```
ReadWriteLock readWriteLock = new ReentrantReadWriteLock();
Lock readLock = readWriteLock.readLock();
Lock writeLock = readWriteLock.writeLock();

// Reflective reading
readLock.lock();
try {
    int currentValue = field.getInt(resource);
} finally {
    readLock.unlock();
}

// Reflective writing
writeLock.lock();
try {
    field.setInt(resource, newValue);
} finally {
    writeLock.unlock();
}
```

These techniques provide a framework for handling reflective access in a thread-safe manner, ensuring both consistency and performance in multi-threaded Java applications. Employing detailed profiling and testing of thread safety in reflective operations is essential to ascertain their effectiveness and optimize where necessary. Through meticulous design and implementation, it is possible to integrate reflection successfully in multi-threaded contexts, achieving both robustness and high performance.

9.10 When to Use and When to Avoid Reflection

Reflection in Java provides a mechanism for programs to inspect and manipulate the inner properties and functionalities of classes at runtime. While this introduces an impressive level of flexibility and power, enabling dynamic behaviors that would otherwise be impossible, it also comes with potential drawbacks in terms of performance, security, and code complexity. This section elucidates the situational appropriateness of employing Java Reflection, first by highlighting scenarios where its use is justified, followed by discussing conditions under which its utilization should be avoided.

Appropriate Uses of Reflection

Reflection is indispensable in several Java programming scenarios:

- **Implementation of Generic Frameworks:** Frameworks like Spring or Hibernate heavily rely on reflection for dependency injection and to generalize code that operates with objects whose types are unknown at compile time.

- **Development of IDEs and Tools:** Development environments use reflection extensively to examine and manage user code, facilitating operations like debugging and code analysis.

- **Object Serialization and Deserialization:** Reflection is employed to dynamically inspect object states for serialization. This capability is crucial for converting objects to formats suitable for storage or transmission, such as JSON or XML.

- **Customizable User Interfaces:** UI frameworks might use reflection to dynamically load components based on the runtime configuration, adapting the interface to user or context-specific requirements.

Utilizing reflection in these contexts allows developers to write more flexible and reusable code, at the cost of a comprehensible performance overhead only when allowing dynamic behavior is strictly necessary.

Inadvisable Uses of Reflection

There are certain circumstances where reflection might introduce more problems than it solves:

- **Performance-Critical Code Sections:** In performance-sensitive areas of an application, the overhead associated with reflective access can lead to significant performance degradation. In these cases, employing alternative Java features like interfaces or lambda expressions is recommended.

- **Compromising Encapsulation:** Using reflection to access private fields and methods can break the encapsulation principle of object-oriented design. This could lead to maintenance challenges as it exposes the internals of components.

- **Complexity and Readability Issues:** Overuse of reflection can make the code hard to understand and maintain. Reflection logic is often more verbose and can be cryptic to developers not familiar with the specifics of the Java Reflection API.

- **Security Risks:** Reflective operations can inadvertently open pathways for executing malicious code if inputs are not meticulously validated, especially in environments executing untrusted code.

Reflective programming practices, in these scenarios, can tax system performance, detract from code clarity, and introduce maintenance and security vulnerabilities. Thoughtful assessment and restraint in using reflection can safeguard system integrity and performance.

Here, the essential practice is a balanced and cautious approach in employing reflection, utilizing it only when its benefits decisively outweigh the associated costs and risks. Leveraging the power of reflection judiciously ensures that Java applications remain robust, maintainable, and efficient. Through strategic, minimalistic, and purpose-driven application of Java Reflection, developers can harness its capabilities without succumbing to its pitfalls.

9.11 Testing and Debugging Reflective Code

Testing and debugging code that utilizes Java Reflection requires a focused approach due to its dynamic nature, which can often introduce complexities not found in statically-typed code. This section elaborates on the methodologies and tools that can be employed to effectively test and debug applications making use of reflection.

Unit Testing Reflective Code

Reflective code modifies the usual assumptions about type safety and method access, making unit tests critical to ensuring code reliability. Here's how to properly test reflective operations:

- **Coverage of Edge Cases**: Ensure that tests cover a variety of cases including accessing private methods, fields, or constructors which can throw security exceptions.

- **Type Safety**: Reflective operations can lead to `ClassCastException`. Tests should verify that objects are of expected types.

- **Existence Checks**: Test for the presence of fields or methods accessed reflectively to avoid `NoSuchFieldException` or `NoSuchMethodException`.

To illustrate, consider this JUnit test example:

```
@Test(expected = NoSuchMethodException.class)
public void testMethodExistence() {
    Class clazz = MyClass.class;
    Method method = clazz.getDeclaredMethod("someMethod", null);
}
```

Debugging Techniques

Debugging reflective code can be challenging due to its dynamic nature, which often results in runtime errors that are not detectable at compile time. Key strategies include:

- **Detailed Logging**: Implement logging before and after reflective calls to capture the state and trace computation values step-by-step.

- **Use of IDEs**: Integrated Development Environments (IDEs) like Eclipse or IntelliJ IDEA provide features to set breakpoints and inspect variable states, even in reflective scenarios.

- **Conditional Breakpoints**: These breakpoints trigger only when certain conditions are met, useful for monitoring when specific methods or fields are accessed reflectively.

Example logging:

```
Logger logger = Logger.getLogger(MyClass.class.getName());
logger.log(Level.INFO, "Attempting to access field: {0}", fieldName);

try {
    Field field = obj.getClass().getDeclaredField(fieldName);
    field.setAccessible(true);
    logger.log(Level.INFO, "Field accessible: {0}", field.toString());
} catch (NoSuchFieldException e) {
```

```
 9      logger.log(Level.SEVERE, "Failed to access field", e);
10    }
```

Integration Testing with Mocking Frameworks

When writing integration tests that involve reflective code, mocking frameworks such as Mockito or PowerMock can be used to simulate the behavior of complex dependencies that use reflection. For instance:

```
1  @Test
2  public void testReflectionWithMocking() {
3      MyClass testClass = Mockito.mock(MyClass.class);
4      Mockito.when(testClass.reflectiveMethod(anyString())).thenReturn("Mocked Result
              ");
5
6      String result = testClass.reflectiveMethod("input");
7      assertEquals("Mocked Result", result);
8  }
```

This demonstrates isolating the method invocation from its reflective dispatch mechanism, allowing for targeted testing.

Performance Monitoring

Monitor the performance impact of reflection in testing environments to ensure that the use of reflection does not degrade application performance significantly. Profiling tools can help assess the runtime costs associated with reflective operations.

Throughout the process, ensure to validate the intended design against actual results and refine as necessary, balancing the powerful capabilities of reflection with its potential pitfalls to maintain robust, efficient, and secure Java applications.

9.12 Summary: Building High-Performance Reflective Applications

Achieving high performance in Java applications that utilize reflection necessitates a discerning application of various strategies detailed throughout this chapter. The dynamic nature of reflection introduces inherent performance costs, but with meticulous application of optimization techniques, developers can mitigate these penalties and enhance application efficiency.

Reflective operations in Java allow for runtime type introspection and manipulation, which provides powerful capabilities but at a potential cost of increased execution time and resource consumption. Given this, it is imperative to employ reflection judiciously. This entails prioritizing the use of reflection only when such dynamic behaviors are essential and cannot be accomplished through static typing methods.

One effective approach to optimize reflective operations is through the adoption of caching mechanisms. Frequently accessed reflectively-obtained objects, such as `Method` and `Field` instances, should be cached to eliminate the overhead of repeated access. This technique significantly reduces the need to re-compute reflection data, which can be computationally expensive.

```
// Example of caching a Method instance
Method method = MyClass.class.getMethod("myMethod");
// Store 'method' in a cache for later use
cache.storeMethod("myMethod", method);
```

In performance-critical scenarios, minimizing the number of reflective calls is crucial. This can be achieved by stacking multiple operations into a single reflective call, thus decreasing the overhead involved with each interaction. Another method is replacing frequent reflective accesses with their direct counterparts whenever feasible, which invariably offer superior performance.

Furthermore, incorporating design patterns specifically adapted for reflection can result in cleaner, more maintainable code that respects performance constraints. Factory patterns, for example, can be utilized to abstract the creation of objects in a way that balances reflective flexibility with static-typing efficiency.

```
// Output from using direct vs. reflective access
Execution Time (Direct Access): 50ms
Execution Time (Reflective Access): 150ms
```

To ensure applications remain effective and efficient, profiling reflective operations is another critical practice. Utilization of profiling tools to monitor and analyze the performance impact of reflection in real-world scenarios aids developers in making informed decisions about when and where to use reflection, thus optimizing the application's performance footprint.

- Employ reflection only when necessary.

9.12. SUMMARY: BUILDING HIGH-PERFORMANCE REFLECTIVE APPLICATIONS

- Use caching to reduce reflective operation overhead.
- Minimize reflective calls by aggregating operations.
- Apply design patterns to manage reflection efficiently.
- Regularly profile reflective operations to identify bottlenecks.

In complex scenarios, especially in multi-threaded environments, reflection requires careful management to avoid concurrency issues and to ensure thread-safety, hence using synchronization mechanisms or thread-safe data structures becomes essential.

As the development landscape evolves and new frameworks emerge, the strategies for using reflection efficiently may also evolve. However, the principles of cautious use, aggressive optimization, and diligent assessment of performance implications remain constant. By adhering to these guidelines, developers can harness the power of reflection in Java without compromising the application's performance, thereby creating robust, efficient, and flexible systems.

Chapter 10

Reflection in Java Security

This chapter discusses the critical relationship between Java Reflection and security, focusing on the implications and challenges that reflection introduces to application security. It covers the risks of exposing internal APIs, bypassing usual access checks, and provides detailed explanations on how to secure applications against unauthorized reflective access. Additionally, the chapter explores the tools and practices, such as the use of Security Managers and AccessControlContext, which are integral for maintaining a secure environment when implementing reflective operations in Java.

10.1 Overview of Java Security and Reflection

Reflection is a powerful feature in Java that allows programs to introspect and modify their behavior at runtime. This capability, however, introduces significant security considerations that must be addressed to prevent potential vulnerabilities in Java applications. This section discusses the dual aspects of Java reflection related to security: its utility and its risks.

Java reflection provides mechanisms to examine or modify the runtime behavior of applications dynamically. For example, classes in the Java Reflection API, such as `Class`, `Method`, `Field`, and `Constructor`, enable Java programs to perform operations like:

- Identifying the class of an object

- Fetching information about class fields and methods
- Accessing and modifying field values irrespective of their visibility
- Invoking methods dynamically
- Creating new instances of classes dynamically

While these features promote flexibility and advanced functionality, they also create avenues for security breaches if not properly managed. The primary security concerns include unauthorized access to private data, and the execution of methods, hence bypassing the standard Java access control checks (encapsulation principles).

The core of securing Java reflection lies in controlling access to reflective operations. The Java platform provides several mechanisms to enhance security when using reflection:

- **Security Manager:** The SecurityManager class allows an application to implement a security policy and enforce access control checks at runtime. It can grant or deny access to the reflective operations based on the security policy defined.

- **Access Control Context:** This mechanism uses a stack-based access control check to assess permissions. Every thread contains an AccessControlContext, and reflective operations can use these contexts to ensure that the invoking code has the appropriate permissions.

- **Class ReflectPermission:** This special permission must be granted to code before it can utilize certain reflective capabilities. It is specifically designed to guard against the misuse of the reflection API.

Consider this example of managing reflective access to a non-public field using the SecurityManager:

```
public class ReflectionExample {
    private String sensitiveData = "Top Secret";

    public static void main(String[] args) {
        SecurityManager security = System.getSecurityManager();
        if (security != null) {
            security.checkPermission(new ReflectPermission("suppressAccessChecks"));
        }
```

```
10   Field field = ReflectionExample.class.getDeclaredField("sensitiveData");
11   field.setAccessible(true);
12   System.out.println("Sensitive Data: " + field.get(new ReflectionExample()));
13   }
14 }
```

The code above attempts to access a private field. If a Security Manager is present and does not grant the ReflectPermission("suppressAccessChecks"), attempting to make the field accessible will throw a SecurityException.

The implications of unchecked reflective access are profound and can lead to breaches in data integrity and privacy. Hence, it is imperative to enforce strict security measures when enabling reflective operations in Java applications. Proper usage of Java's built-in security mechanisms can effectively mitigate the potential risks associated with Java reflection, preserving the robustness and integrity of applications.

10.2 The Security Manager and AccessControlContext

The integration of security within reflective operations in Java is executed primarily through the Security Manager and AccessControlContext. These components play pivotal roles in ensuring that operations do not undermine the security of the Java Runtime Environment (JRE) and adhere strictly to predetermined security policies.

Role of the Security Manager

The Security Manager in Java functions as a gatekeeper, dictating what resources a Java application can access, which operations it can execute, and under what circumstances. Implementing a Security Manager involves invoking the System.setSecurityManager() method, which establishes a security context for the executing Java application.

Consider the following typical usage of the Security Manager in a Java application:

```
1 public class SecureApplication {
2     public static void main(String[] args) {
3         SecurityManager security = System.getSecurityManager();
4         if (security == null) {
5             System.setSecurityManager(new SecurityManager());
6         }
```

```
7        // Further operations are subject to security checks
8      }
9    }
```

Here, the program checks if a Security Manager is already present. If not, it initializes a new instance. This operation illustrates the proactive nature of security management in Java applications, ensuring that further operations conform to the security policy in place.

Understanding AccessControlContext

AccessControlContext in Java is a data structure that encapsulates the security context of the current execution thread. This context plays a fundamental role in decisions made by the Security Manager regarding potential security-sensitive operations.

AccessControlContext is constructed from the accumulated security contexts of all the protection domains that are relevant to the current context. The following example demonstrates how to explicitly use AccessControlContext:

```
1    import java.security.AccessControlContext;
2    import java.security.AccessController;
3
4    public class ContextSensitiveOperation {
5      public void performOperation() {
6        AccessControlContext context = AccessController.getContext();
7        // Perform security-sensitive operations using the context
8      }
9    }
```

This code retrieves the prevailing AccessControlContext for the thread and uses it to determine whether the subsequent operations are permitted under the current security policies.

Integrating Security Manager with AccessControlContext

The real strength in security enforcement comes when the Security Manager and AccessControlContext are used in conjunction. The Security Manager uses the AccessControlContext to make informed security decisions based on the domains that a thread has traversed. For example, when a reflective operation is invoked, the Security Manager will consult the AccessControlContext to decide whether the operation should proceed.

```
1  public class ReflectiveOperation {
2    public void invokeSensitiveMethod() throws IllegalAccessException {
3      SecurityManager security = System.getSecurityManager();
4      if (security != null) {
5        security.checkPermission(new ReflectPermission("suppressAccessChecks"));
6      }
7      // Reflective operation proceeds if security check passes
8    }
9  }
```

In this illustration, a check for the "suppressAccessChecks" permission is explicitly performed before proceeding with a reflective operation. Such checks ensure that only privileged code with the necessary permissions can bypass standard Java access controls.

We have discussed the roles and operations of the Security Manager and `AccessControlContext` in Java, highlighting their indispensable positions in maintaining a secure runtime environment. Through examples, the integration and application of these security components have been demonstrated, providing a foundation for enforcing robust security measures in Java applications employing reflective operations.

10.3 Restricting Reflective Access with SecurityManager

The Java SecurityManager is instrumental in restricting reflective access, ensuring that only authorized code can execute potentially unsafe operations that could compromise the application's integrity. This section examines methods to enforce security measures that limit reflective access through the use of a SecurityManager, detailing specific approaches and code examples appropriate for securing Java applications.

Setting Up SecurityManager

To initiate, a SecurityManager must be instantiated and set as the system's security manager. The following code snippet demonstrates the setup process:

```
1  public class SetupSecurityManager {
2    public static void main(String[] args) {
3      SecurityManager sm = new SecurityManager();
4      System.setSecurityManager(sm);
```

```
5        System.out.println("SecurityManager has been set");
6    }
7  }
```

This initialization blocks subsequent reflective calls that do not meet the specified security requirements. The effect is immediate:

```
SecurityManager has been set
```

Defining Security Policies

The SecurityManager utilizes a security policy that dictates permissions. These permissions define allowable operations and can be specified in a policy file. Here, we set permissions concerning reflective access:

- Granting necessary 'reflective' permissions to trusted code while denying them to untrusted code.

- Strictly defining the scope of allowed reflective operations through limited permissions.

For example, the policy configuration below permits code from a trusted source, designated by its codebase URL, to use reflection to access private members:

```
1  grant codeBase "file:/trusted/path/*" {
2      permission java.lang.reflect.ReflectPermission "suppressAccessChecks";
3  };
```

Enforcing Access Checks

When enforcing reflective access restrictions, the SecurityManager performs checks based on the predefined security policy. The following example showcases a restrictive operation wherein access to a private field is attempted but is intercepted by the SecurityManager:

```
1  import java.lang.reflect.Field;
2
3  public class ReflectiveAccessCheck {
4      private String secret = "TopSecret";
5
6      public static void main(String[] args) {
7          ReflectiveAccessCheck rac = new ReflectiveAccessCheck();
8          Field field;
9          try {
```

```
10        field = rac.getClass().getDeclaredField("secret");
11        field.setAccessible(true); // Security check happens here
12        System.out.println("Value of the secret: " + field.get(rac));
13    } catch (SecurityException | NoSuchFieldException | IllegalAccessException e
          ) {
14        e.printStackTrace();
15    }
16  }
17 }
```

When executing this code under the restrictions set by a SecurityManager that enforces the policy above, a 'SecurityException' is raised:

`java.security.AccessControlException: access denied ("java.lang.reflect.ReflectPermission" "suppressAccessChecks")`

Mitigating Risks with SecurityManager

Using the SecurityManager, developers can mitigate several risks associated with unauthorized reflective access:

- Prevention of invoking `setAccessible(true)` on critical system fields.

- Blocking unauthorized creation, modification, and invocation of methods and constructors.

- Enforcement of security checks on class loaders and bytecode manipulators.

By configuring the SecurityManager suitably and tightening the policies related to reflection, developers ensure that their Java applications are resistant to a range of reflection-based vulnerabilities. These measures play a pivotal role in maintaining the confidentiality, integrity, and availability of the application systems, enabling a structured and secure approach to using Java Reflection in enterprise environments.

10.4 Assessing Risks of Exposing Private Members

The use of Java Reflection to access and manipulate private members of a class is one of the potent capabilities that also poses significant security risks. This section evaluates those risks in a detailed and structured manner, providing insights into potential vulnerabilities and the implications of exposing private aspects of an application to external or unauthorized entities.

Accessing private variables, methods, and constructors through reflection is a practical feature for many advanced Java applications that require dynamic behavior. However, this inherently circumvents the language's access control mechanisms that safeguard against improper use of internal class constructs. The risks associated with such operations can be grouped primarily into unintentional data exposure, increased attack surface, and complicating maintenance and testability.

- Unintentional data exposure allows malicious actors to read or alter private data that is meant to be protected, potentially leading to data corruption or unauthorized data access.

- Increasing an application's attack surface offers more opportunities for attackers, making the system more vulnerable to breaches.

- Complicating maintenance and testability may occur as the boundary between accessible and inaccessible data blurs, making the codebase harder to manage and secure.

Potential Vulnerabilities Arising from Exposing Private Members

The following detailed examples highlight different scenarios where private member exposure through reflection can lead to security vulnerabilities:

Listing 10.1: Accessing a Private Field

```
import java.lang.reflect.Field;

public class SensitiveData {
    private String privateInfo = "Very Sensitive Data";

    public static void main(String[] args) throws NoSuchFieldException,
            IllegalAccessException {
        SensitiveData obj = new SensitiveData();
        Field field = SensitiveData.class.getDeclaredField("privateInfo");
        field.setAccessible(true);
        System.out.println((String) field.get(obj)); // Outputs: Very Sensitive Data
    }
}
```

Very Sensitive Data

10.4. ASSESSING RISKS OF EXPOSING PRIVATE MEMBERS

The issue illustrated in Listing 10.1 is evident: permission to access a private field was granted without any checks, exposing sensitive data. The following implications must be understood:

- The `setAccessible` method is powerful and bypasses Java's built-in security checks, leading to security loopholes if not handled carefully.

- Once the accessibility of a field or method is breached, any protection enforced by Java's access control mechanism becomes ineffective.

Mitigating the Risks

Mitigating the risks associated with exposing private members requires rigorous security measures and practices:

- Minimizing the use of reflection, especially `setAccessible`, within the application can limit potential vulnerabilities. It's advisable to use reflection judiciously and only when absolutely necessary.

- Implementing and enforcing security policies through the use of a Security Manager also serves as a second layer of protection, offering the ability to restrict reflection-specific operations based on custom-defined security rules.

Algorithm 5: Pseudocode for Handling Reflective Access with Security Measures

---
Data: A Java class file required to utilize reflection
Result: Verification output of permitted reflective operations
1 initialization;
2 **while** *Access needed for Private Method* **do**
3   execute permission check;
4   **if** *permission granted* **then**
5   proceed with reflective access;
6   log operation details;
7   **else**
8   deny access;
9   log attempt;
10   **end**
11 **end**

Monitoring and logging attempts to use reflection to access private members is also an important practice, helping detect and potentially block unauthorized access patterns, thereby strengthening the application's security posture.

While the flexibility offered by reflection is undeniably valuable, its usage must be carefully managed to balance functionality with security. In environments where security is paramount, strict policies should guide the usage of reflective capabilities to prevent unintended consequences and vulnerabilities that might arise from improper handling of private members.

10.5 Protecting Against Reflection-Based Attacks

Reflection offers potent capabilities in Java, allowing runtime modifications and invocations in ways typical methods cannot. However, the same powerful features also introduce significant security vulnerabilities. Attackers can use reflection to bypass encapsulation, altering or invoking private fields and methods.

In this section, detailed strategies and techniques are outlined, focusing on mitigating reflection-based security risks. These include limiting reflective access, using Security Managers effectively, and employing

10.5. PROTECTING AGAINST REFLECTION-BASED ATTACKS

additional custom security measures.

- Ensuring strict access checks with `SecurityManager`: By setting up a Security Manager, you can enforce a security policy that restricts reflection to trusted code only.

- Minimizing reflection usage: Refactoring code to avoid reflection where possible can reduce the exposure to reflection-based attacks.

- Validating inputs rigorously: Since reflection allows methods to be invoked dynamically, validating all inputs that could influence reflection ensures that only safe operations are executed.

The use of the `SecurityManager` represents a primary defense mechanism against unauthorized reflective access in a Java environment.

```
- SecurityManager enabled: Permits checking access to critical operations
- SecurityManager disabled: Potential for unrestricted access by unauthorized classes
```

Further to using a `SecurityManager`, limiting the exposure of classes to reflection is key. Techniques such as classloaders isolation and sealing packages provide robust methods to prevent reflective access from untrusted sources.

```java
// Example of invoking a method using reflection
Method method = MyClass.class.getDeclaredMethod("methodName");
method.setAccessible(true); // Bypasses Java's normal access checks
method.invoke(myObject);
```

It's crucial to understand the implications when `setAccessible(true)` is used. This action allows skipping usual access checks, which could potentially lead to exposing sensitive or private data.

```
Output:
    Unauthorized Access Exception, if security settings are violated
```

Developing a custom Security Manager can provide application-specific restrictions, which is an effective strategy for high-risk environments.

```java
public class CustomSecurityManager extends SecurityManager {
    @Override
    public void checkPermission(Permission perm) {
        // Implement custom logic to restrict sensitive permissions
        if ("reflectiveAccess".equals(perm.getName())) {
            throw new SecurityException("Reflection is not allowed");
        }
    }
}
```

This approach allows explicit control over what reflection-based operations are permitted, enhancing the overall security profile of the application.

Overall, reflection should be used judiciously and protected against manipulation with rigorous security controls. Despite its advantages for dynamic operations, the associated risks require careful management to ensure the security of Java applications.

10.6 Securing Dynamic Class Loading

Dynamic class loading is a powerful feature in Java that allows classes to be loaded and linked during runtime, which can greatly enhance the flexibility and adaptability of applications. However, this feature also introduces significant security risks, particularly when applications load classes from unverified or untrusted sources. The main security concerns include the execution of untrusted code, manipulation of the application's behavior, and exposure of sensitive information.

To mitigate these risks, several strategies can be employed. This section elaborates on these strategies, including the use of secure class loaders, the implementation of security checks within class loaders, and employing principles of least privilege.

Using Secure Class Loaders

The Java platform provides several built-in class loaders that follow the delegation model. This model prevents classes from the local file system or network sources from replacing certain critical classes that are part of the Java runtime environment. However, when developing applications that necessitate dynamic class loading from external sources, it is imperative to implement custom class loaders that are capable of defining additional security checks.

```java
public class SecureClassLoader extends ClassLoader {
    @Override
    protected Class<?> findClass(String name) throws ClassNotFoundException {
        byte[] b = loadClassData(name);
        // Implement security check on class data
        if(!verifyClassData(b)) {
            throw new SecurityException("Class data verification failed.");
        }
        return defineClass(name, b, 0, b.length);
    }
}
```

10.6. SECURING DYNAMIC CLASS LOADING

```
12      private byte[] loadClassData(String name) {
13          // Load class data from a secure source
14          // Implementation details omitted for brevity
15      }
16
17      private boolean verifyClassData(byte[] classData) {
18          // Verify class data
19          // Implementation details omitted for brevity
20      }
21  }
```

Implementing Security Checks within Class Loaders

In addition to verifying the source and integrity of the class data, it is also crucial to perform security checks before a class is loaded. This involves checking permissions against security policies configured in the application.

```
1   protected PermissionCollection getPermissions(CodeSource codesource) {
2       PermissionCollection pc = super.getPermissions(codesource);
3       // Add additional permissions based on specific conditions
4       if (someCondition()) {
5           pc.add(new SomePermission("SomeResource", "SomeAction"));
6       }
7       return pc;
8   }
```

Employing Principles of Least Privilege

When designing systems that use dynamic class loading, it is important to adhere to the principle of least privilege. This principle aids in limiting the permissions granted to each dynamically loaded class to the minimum necessary for its operation. As such, even if a security breach occurs, the potential damage is minimized.

```
1   protected Class<?> loadClass(String name, boolean resolve) throws
            ClassNotFoundException {
2       SecurityManager security = System.getSecurityManager();
3       if (security != null) {
4           // Check if this class can be loaded
5           security.checkPermission(new RuntimePermission("loadClass." + name));
6       }
7       return super.loadClass(name, resolve);
8   }
```

By leveraging secure class loaders, implementing appropriate security checks, and adhering to the principle of least privilege, developers can vastly mitigate the risks associated with dynamic class loading in Java applications. These practices not only secure the application but also contribute to maintaining the integrity and reliability of the application's runtime environment.

10.7 Enforcing Security in Dynamic Proxies

Dynamic proxies in Java are powerful tools for creating flexible and reusable applications. However, they also introduce potential security risks, particularly when used in conjunction with Java Reflection. This section describes the measures that can be taken to mitigate these risks and implement secure dynamic proxy operations.

Dynamic proxies are instances of classes that implement a list of interfaces specified at runtime, essentially allowing the creation of an interface implementation on-the-fly. These proxies can then be used to intercept and modify method calls dynamically via an associated invocation handler.

b{Key Components of a Dynamic Proxy in Java:}
- Interface(s) to implement
- InvocationHandler to intercept method calls

The primary security concern with dynamic proxies is their ability to intercept and potentially alter the execution of method calls, which can be misused to alter the behavior of the application or access sensitive data improperly. The following strategies are essential for enforcing security when using dynamic proxies:

- **Validating Class Loader**: Ensure that the dynamic proxy classes are loaded by a secure class loader. This limits the proxy's access to classes that are deemed safe and reduces the risk of malicious code execution.

- **Restricting Interfaces**: Limit the set of interfaces that a proxy can implement. Restricting these interfaces based on their security implications helps prevent misuse through unauthorized method invocations.

- **Auditing Invocation Handlers**: Regularly audit the implementation of InvocationHandlers used by dynamic proxies. This involves reviewing the 'invoke' method to ensure it does not introduce security flaws or violate access controls.

Considerations for implementing an InvocationHandler involve thorough validation and sanitization of method arguments, plus verification of caller permissions before executing any method. The following pseudocode outlines an example of a security-aware `InvocationHandler`.

Algorithm 6: Example of a Security-aware InvocationHandler

Input : An object instance, a Method to be invoked, method arguments
Output: Object result of method invocation

1 **Function** *invoke(instance, method, args)*
2   **if** *not validatePermissions(method)* **then**
3   **throw** new SecurityException("Unauthorized method access")
4   sanitizedArgs ← sanitize(args)
5   result ← method.invoke(instance, sanitizedArgs)
6   **return** *result*

To implement these measures effectively, developers should also employ runtime auditing tools that can monitor and log the use of dynamic proxies within the application, enabling detection of and response to potential security violations in real-time.

Implementing security measures around the use of dynamic proxies is crucial, particularly in environments where code must operate under strict security requirements. By enforcing strict controls on how dynamic proxies are created and used, and by ensuring that all proxy actions are monitored and audited, developers can significantly mitigate the risks associated with their use in Java applications.

10.8 Using Reflection Safely with Annotations

Annotations in Java serve as a powerful metadata facility, allowing developers to add information to program elements in a structured and type-safe manner. These annotations can also play a significant role in controlling how reflection is used, particularly in enhancing security aspects, thus mitigating the risks associated with dynamic operations. This section discusses how annotations can be effectively utilized to limit reflective access and enforce security constraints, making them indispensable in maintaining application integrity.

When employing reflection, the accessibility of fields, methods, and constructors is subject to security checks. Annotations offer a mechanism to declaratively specify which components are safe to access via reflection, and under what circumstances. By strategically using annotations, developers can overlay a robust security framework on the inherently flexible capabilities of reflection.

Defining Security Annotations

The first step towards using annotations to secure reflective operations involves defining custom annotations that encapsulate security policies. Here is an example of how such an annotation might be defined using Java:

```
import java.lang.annotation.ElementType;
import java.lang.annotation.Retention;
import java.lang.annotation.RetentionPolicy;
import java.lang.annotation.Target;

@Retention(RetentionPolicy.RUNTIME)
@Target(ElementType.METHOD)
public @interface SafeToInvoke {
    boolean safe() default true;
}
```

This @SafeToInvoke annotation is designed to mark methods that are safe to access reflectively. The retention policy RUNTIME is essential because it ensures that the annotation is available to the JVM at runtime, which is when reflection operates.

Utilizing Annotations to Control Access

With the security annotations defined, the next step is to incorporate these annotations into the application's codebase. Consider the following method embellished with the @SafeToInvoke annotation:

```
public class TransactionProcessor {

    @SafeToInvoke(safe = true)
    public void processTransaction(Transaction transaction) {
        // Method implementation
    }

    @SafeToInvoke(safe = false)
    public void sensitiveOperation() {
        // Sensitive method implementation
    }
}
```

In the above code, the processTransaction method is marked as safe for reflective access, while sensitiveOperation is not. This differentiation facilitates a conditional reflective access strategy.

Enforcing Annotation-based Security Policies

To enforce the security policies specified by annotations, reflective code must query these annotations at runtime before performing any operations. Here is how one might implement such a check:

```
import java.lang.reflect.Method;

public class ReflectionSafetyCheck {
    public static void invokeIfSafe(Object obj, String methodName, Object... args)
            throws Exception {
        Method method = obj.getClass().getMethod(methodName, getParameterTypes(args)
            );
        SafeToInvoke safeToInvoke = method.getAnnotation(SafeToInvoke.class);

        if (safeToInvoke != null && safeToInvoke.safe()) {
            method.invoke(obj, args);
        } else {
            throw new SecurityException("Attempting to access a method not marked
                safe for reflection");
        }
    }

    private static Class<?>[] getParameterTypes(Object[] args) {
        Class<?>[] parameterTypes = new Class<?>[args.length];
        for (int i = 0; i < args.length; i++) {
            parameterTypes[i] = args[i].getClass();
        }
        return parameterTypes;
    }
}
```

This implementation illustrates a reflective method invocation that is conditional upon the @SafeToInvoke annotation. By inspecting the safe() attribute, the method decides whether or not the operation should proceed, effectively enforcing the security policy.

Annotations, when combined with reflective checks, provide a robust mechanism to govern which parts of the codebase are accessible through reflection, mitigating risks such as non-consensual data access and manipulation. Through these means, annotations contribute significantly to the secure employment of Java reflection, maintaining both flexibility and integrity.

10.9 Best Practices for Safe Reflective Operations

In Java security, reflective operations introduce potent flexibility but also elevate the risk of security vulnerabilities if not implemented with due diligence. Safe reflective operations necessitate adherence to a set of best practices designed to minimize potential security risks. This section delineates these practices, providing a structured approach to mitigate the implications of reflective programming.

- **Minimize Use of Reflection**: Employ reflection sparingly and only when necessary. Reflective operations are computationally expensive and can complicate security audits. When possible, employ other Java features that achieve similar outcomes with fewer security implications.

- **Validate Inputs Rigorously**: Always validate inputs that steer the behavior of reflective methods. Unvalidated inputs may lead to unauthorized access or modification of class fields that can be detrimental to system integrity.

- **Use Security Managers**: Implement and configure security managers to control and restrict reflective access appropriately. Here is a basic code snippet that demonstrates how to enforce such restrictions using a security manager:

```
1  System.setSecurityManager(new SecurityManager());
2  try {
3      // Reflective operation here
4  } catch (SecurityException se) {
5      System.out.println("Reflective operation blocked.");
6  }
```

The output is shown as:

```
Reflective operation blocked.
```

- **Employ `AccessControlContext` for Fine-Grained Permissions**: Utilize `AccessControlContext` to granularly manage permissions for specific blocks of code, ensuring minimal permissions are granted only where absolutely required.

- **Audit and Logging**: Implement robust logging mechanisms to record usage of reflective operations. Logs should include details such as the time of operation, the identity of the operator, and the nature of access attempted. This audit trail is invaluable during security reviews and forensic investigations.

- **Limit Exposure of Internals**: Avoid making internal methods and fields accessible through public APIs. Design class structures wisely, considering how reflection could be used to manipulate or expose them unduly.

- **Educate Developers**: Ensure that developers are aware of the potential risks associated with the use of reflection and are trained on security best practices. Perform regular security awareness sessions and code reviews to enforce secure coding standards.

- **Update and Patch Regularly**: Keep up-to-date with the latest security patches and updates from Java libraries and frameworks. Many vulnerabilities in reflection APIs can be mitigated by simply applying the latest patches.

These practices, when systematically applied, form an effective defense against most common reflective operation vulnerabilities. Adequate training, vigilant coding, and stringent access controls are imperative to leveraging the power of reflection in Java securely. Through conscientious application of these guidelines, developers can harness the benefits of dynamic behaviors while protecting the integrity and security of their applications.

10.10 Auditing and Compliance Checks Using Reflection

Reflection in Java provides powerful capabilities for introspection within applications, enabling developers to analyze code behavior dynamically. In the context of security, this dynamism can be beneficial for performing in-depth audits and managing compliance checks. This section discusses methodologies implementing reflection to scrutinize Java applications, ensuring they meet the security standards and compliances required by regulatory frameworks.

One primary application of reflection in auditing is to inspect class properties and behaviors dynamically. This feature is pivotal for verifying compliance in environments where code integrity and behavior are critical from a security standpoint.

- **Analyzing Access Modifiers of Classes and Members**: Ensuring that classes and their members have appropriate access levels can prevent accidental or malicious misuse of sensitive methods and data fields.

- **Validation of Annotations**: Annotations can dictate how elements should be handled, especially in a security context. Using reflection to dynamically verify these annotations ensures that runtime operations adhere to predefined policies.

- Class Loader Inspection: Verifying which class loader loaded a particular component can serve as a compliance check to prevent loading of unauthorized or malicious classes.

Using reflection, developers can walk through the class structure and element accessibility, which aids in robust compliance reporting tools, often a requirement in regulated industries such as healthcare and finance. Furthermore, reflection can assist in maintaining an audit trail of accesses and modifications to critical system components.

```
// Reflection Java Code for Inspecting Modifier Access
import java.lang.reflect.*;

public class ModifierAccessInspector {
   public static void checkModifiers(Class<?> cls) {
      int modifiers = cls.getModifiers();
      System.out.println("Access Modifiers for " + cls.getName() + ": " + Modifier.toString(modifiers));

      // Checking fields
      Field[] fields = cls.getDeclaredFields();
      for (Field field : fields) {
         int fieldModifiers = field.getModifiers();
         System.out.println("Field: " + field.getName() + ", Access: " + Modifier.toString(fieldModifiers));
      }
   }
}
```

```
Access Modifiers for java.util.ArrayList: public
Field: size, Access: private volatile
Field: elementData, Access: private
```

The above code snippet demonstrates how one might use reflection to audit the access levels of a Java class and its fields, helping identify potential security risks related to field accessibility.

In addition to code analysis, reflection enables runtime monitoring and compliance verification. By applying reflection, runtime behavior of applications can be logged and checked against expected patterns, raising alerts if deviations occur. This runtime monitoring is crucial for systems that require dynamic compliance checks in environments that are subject to sophisticated security threats.

```
// Runtime Behavior Monitoring Example Using Reflection
public class RuntimeMonitor {
   public static void monitorMethods(Class<?> cls) throws Exception {
      Method[] methods = cls.getDeclaredMethods();
      for (Method method : methods) {
         if (!Modifier.isPrivate(method.getModifiers())) {
```

```
 7              // Simulate method behavior check
 8              System.out.println("Monitoring public method: " + method.getName());
 9          }
10      }
11  }
12 }
```

```
Monitoring public method: add
Monitoring public method: remove
```

Reflection is instrumental in setting up automated compliance tests that continuously validate security features at runtime, ensuring that any deviations from expected behaviors are captured and addressed promptly.

To encapsulate, leveraging Java Reflection for auditing and compliance checks offers a granular view of application security state, which is vital for maintaining high standards of security compliance. This approach, although powerful, should be carefully managed to avoid performance overhead and must be integrated thoughtfully within the overall security strategy of an organization. Reflection-based auditing facilitates a proactive security posture, crucial for defending against evolving security threats in a compliant manner.

10.11 Case Studies: Reflection in Secure Applications

This section exemplifies the application of Java reflection mechanisms in security-critical environments through detailed case studies. By scrutinizing real-world scenarios, the intent is to elucidate how reflection can be implemented securely, highlighting both the benefits and potential pitfalls.

Case Study 1: Banking System Audit Module

In this case study, a major banking system utilizes reflection for dynamic audit operations. Reflection is used to access private fields of transaction objects to validate compliance with financial regulations.

```
1  import java.lang.reflect.Field;
2
3  public class AuditModule {
4      public void auditTransaction(Object transaction) throws IllegalAccessException
         {
5          Field[] fields = transaction.getClass().getDeclaredFields();
```

```
 6          for (Field field : fields) {
 7              field.setAccessible(true);
 8              System.out.println("Audit Log - " + field.getName() + ": " + field.get(
                     transaction));
 9              field.setAccessible(false);
10          }
11      }
12  }
```

```
Audit Log - amount: 2500.00
Audit Log - currency: USD
Audit Log - timestamp: 2023-04-12T10:15:30
```

This implementation leverages reflection to enhance the flexibility of the auditing process, enabling the extraction of data from a variety of transaction types without altering the classes themselves. Notably, the reflective access is encapsulated within controlled environments to mitigate security risks.

Case Study 2: Dynamic Feature Enablement System in a SaaS Application

A software-as-a-service (SaaS) application implements a feature toggle system using reflection to dynamically enable or disable features based on customer configuration, minimizing downtime and promoting modular upgrades.

```
 1  import java.lang.reflect.Method;
 2
 3  public class FeatureToggleManager {
 4      public void toggleFeature(Object service, String featureName, boolean enable)
              throws Exception {
 5          Class<?> cls = service.getClass();
 6          Method method = cls.getDeclaredMethod("set" + featureName, boolean.class);
 7          method.setAccessible(true);
 8          method.invoke(service, enable);
 9          method.setAccessible(false);
10      }
11  }
```

```
Feature setAdvancedReporting enabled.
```

This scenario effectively demonstrates the application of reflection to control application features, emphasizing both the power and risks involved. The method's reflective access is carefully managed to prevent misuse, aligning with security best practices by restricting unauthorized modifications.

10.11. CASE STUDIES: REFLECTION IN SECURE APPLICATIONS

Case Study 3: Secure Interoperability in Multi-vendor Environment

In a multi-vendor environment where systems need to interoperate securely, reflection is used to ensure compatibility and enforce security policies dynamically, negating the need for static linking which could introduce vulnerabilities.

```java
import java.lang.reflect.InvocationHandler;
import java.lang.reflect.Method;
import java.lang.reflect.Proxy;

public class SecurityProxyHandler implements InvocationHandler {
    private Object realObject;
    private AccessControlContext context;

    public SecurityProxyHandler(Object realObject, AccessControlContext context) {
        this.realObject = realObject;
        this.context = context;
    }

    @Override
    public Object invoke(Object proxy, Method method, Object[] args) throws
        Throwable {
        SecurityManager securityManager = System.getSecurityManager();
        if (securityManager != null) {
            securityManager.checkAccess(context);
        }
        return method.invoke(realObject, args);
    }
}
```

Access to method invoke granted to user role.

Security controls are seamlessly integrated into the interoperability logic, with reflection providing the flexibility required for dynamic method invocation across diverse system components. This implementation underscores the criticality of embedding security checks within the reflective processes to guard against unauthorized action.

These case studies collectively illustrate strategic, secure utilization of reflection in Java applications across different domains and operational contexts. Each scenario reaffirms the necessity for rigorous security mechanisms when employing reflection, including the judicious management of access levels and vigilant enforcement of security policies to prevent the exposure of sensitive operations.

10.12 Summary and Future of Secure Reflection

The usage of Java Reflection can dramatically increase the versatility and dynamic capabilities of applications but simultaneously introduces significant security risks. Throughout this chapter, we have traversed the diverse landscape of securing reflective operations, underlining the perennial balancing act between functionality and security. Integrating stringent security measures like Security Managers and `AccessControlContext` can mitigate some of these risks but requires meticulous attention to detail to ensure robust protection.

The chapter opened with an analysis of how reflective capabilities in Java, although powerful, can subvert typical security constraints, potentially leading to unauthorized access to internal APIs. This underscores the necessity for developers to be perpetually vigilant and literate in security-oriented programming paradigms when utilizing reflection. We then discussed how Security Managers and `AccessControlContext` serve as critical tools to enforce security boundaries, delving into practical implementation guidelines and illustrating the proper configuration to effectively restrict reflective access within an application's runtime environment.

Subsequent sections highlighted numerous strategies and practical examples aimed at restricting access to private members of classes, thus mitigating the risks associated with exposing sensitive data or functionality. Here, techniques such as setting up security policies and leveraging specialized APIs for safe reflective operations emerged as salient themes. We dissected how reflection-based attacks typically manifest and proposed countermeasures—a discourse that yielded insights into securing dynamic class loading and dynamic proxies, further embedding the notion that proactive security measures are fundamental when deploying reflection-prone Java applications.

The reflective usage of annotations, a segment devoted to adding metadata-driven security layers, showcased the synergy between static code annotations and runtime reflection checks. This crossover enhances security postures by embedding security logic within the code structure itself, aligning with modern software development practices.

Reflecting on best practices, the chapter encapsulated key strategies including principle-based access restrictions, diligent auditing trails, and compliance checks using reflection. These segments impressed upon

10.12. SUMMARY AND FUTURE OF SECURE REFLECTION

the reader the enduring importance of a holistic and well-rounded approach to securing applications that employ Java Reflection.

In looking towards the future of secure reflection in Java, several trends deserve attention. Advancements in AI and machine learning are likely to augment static and dynamic analysis tools, enabling more intelligent and context-aware security mechanisms. Additionally, ongoing improvements to the Java language and runtime environment promise enhanced control and finer granularity in security policies applied to reflection operations.

Furthermore, as cloud-native architectures and containerized deployments become prevalent, the challenge of securing reflective operations will evolve, mandating novel security approaches tailored to distributed environments. Techniques like using distributed `AccessControlContext` across microservices could emerge, necessitating adaptations in how security policies are defined and enforced across disparate systems.

Given the permutations of future technological advancements and the increasing complexity of software systems, the ongoing effort to refine and enhance security mechanisms around Java Reflection is both necessary and challenging. It demands continuous reevaluation of security strategies and persistent education of developers to foster an environment where security and functionality coexist harmoniously.

Here we affirm the critical role of security when leveraging Java Reflection and serve as guiding principles for developers aiming to craft secure, dynamic applications. Through adherence to outlined best practices and a proactive stance on emerging security challenges, the future of secure reflection in Java can continue to evolve safely and robustly.

Chapter 11

Using Reflection in Generics

This chapter investigates the application of Java Reflection in the context of generics, focusing on overcoming challenges posed by type erasure and accessing type information at runtime. It provides techniques for dynamically resolving generic types and leveraging this capability to enhance the functionality and flexibility of Java applications. The chapter walks through practical examples, including handling generic methods, fields, and arrays, to demonstrate how reflection can be effectively used to manipulate and inspect generic structures, enhancing design patterns and API development.

11.1 Basics of Generics and Type Erasure

Generics in Java provide stronger type checks at compile time and eliminate the need for explicit type casting that was previously ubiquitous with collections, thus enhancing code readability and reducing runtime errors. Let's delve into what they entail and the issues related to type erasure that they introduce.

Understanding Generics

Generics allow the insertion of type parameters when defining classes, interfaces, and methods. A generalized form of abstraction is achieved, permitting operations on objects of various types while providing compile-time type safety.

```
public class Box<T> {
    private T t; // T stands for "Type"

    public void set(T t) {
        this.t = t;
    }

    public T get() {
        return t;
    }
}
```

In the above code snippet, T is a type variable that will be replaced by a concrete type when an object of Box is instantiated:

```
Box<Integer> integerBox = new Box<>();
integerBox.set(123);
```

This prevents the earlier burden of type casting, as seen when using raw types such as List, where safety checks are purely manual.

Type Erasure

When dealing with generics, type erasure is a necessary concept to understand. It refers to the process by which the Java compiler erases all generic type information after translating source code into bytecode. Essentially, generics are a compile-time feature and are not available at runtime, which leads to Java treating generic type parameters as Object by default.

```
public <T> void genericMethod(T x) {
    System.out.println(x.getClass().getName());
}
```

The method genericMethod will print the runtime type of the passed object. Regardless of the number or type of generic parameters, the bytecode would still perceive and treat them as instances of Object:

```
System.out.println(integerBox.get().getClass().getName());
// Output: java.lang.Integer
```

Challenges with Type Erasure

Type erasure introduces several challenges:

- **Type Information Loss:** Complete type information is not accessible at runtime, which restricts certain operations, such as instantiation of generic types, casting, or using instanceof with parameterized types.

- **Overloading Limitation:** Overloading methods within generics is generally impractical due to type erasure leading to signature conflicts after compilation.

- **Bridge Methods:** To maintain polymorphism, the Java compiler may introduce synthetic bridge methods, which can sometimes cause unexpected behavior if not adequately understood.

Understanding the implications of type erasure and the constraints it places on the use of generics is fundamental for developers to effectively harness the power of Java generics while acknowledging and mitigating potential runtime limitations.

11.2 Retrieving Generic Type Information

Retrieving generic type information in Java using reflection involves understanding how metadata associated with generics gets manipulated during runtime due to type erasure—a process where the Java compiler removes information related to type parameters and type arguments during compilation. To access this type information dynamically at runtime, one must use the Java Reflection API, specifically the `java.lang.reflect` package that provides several classes and interfaces designed for this purpose.

To utilize reflection for retrieving generic type information accurately, it is essential to comprehend and interact with various components of the `java.lang.reflect` package, such as `Type`, `ParameterizedType`, and `GenericArrayType`. Below are detailed methods and strategies for leveraging these components:

- **Type Interface**: This is the super interface for all types in Java. Through it, all specific type references such as class types, parameterized types, array types, type variables, and primitive types can be explored.

- **ParameterizedType**: Represents a parameterized type such as Collection<String>. Using this, we can access the type arguments associated with a type, helping us drill down into generic types.

- **GenericArrayType**: Deals with types of arrays with a generic component, such as List<String>[]. This allows for detailed inspection of the type of array's generic component.

For practical implementation, consider using the following code snippet that demonstrates how to use reflection to retrieve generic type information from a field declared as a generic type:

```
import java.lang.reflect.*;

public class TypeDiscovery {
    private List<Integer> sampleField;

    public static void main(String[] args) throws NoSuchFieldException {
        Field field = TypeDiscovery.class.getDeclaredField("sampleField");
        Type fieldType = field.getGenericType();

        if (fieldType instanceof ParameterizedType) {
            ParameterizedType pType = (ParameterizedType) fieldType;
            Type[] typeArguments = pType.getActualTypeArguments();

            for (Type typeArgument : typeArguments) {
                System.out.println(typeArgument.getTypeName());
            }
        }
    }
}
```

The above example demonstrates obtaining the generic type information from a field. The output for this code is shown below:

java.lang.Integer

Further analyzing reflection on method return types and parameters involves similar strategies but requires fetching methods from the class and inspecting their GenericReturnType and GenericTypeParameters respectively. Here is a succinct pseudocode demonstrating this process, adhering to best practices using the "algorithm2e" package:

> **Algorithm 7:** Discovering generic method return types
>
> **Data:** Class containing method with generic return type
> **Result:** Prints generic return type if it exists
> 1 method ← getClassMethod();
> 2 returnType ← method.getGenericReturnType();
> 3 **if** *returnType instanceof ParameterizedType* **then**
> 4 | printParameterizedType(returnType);
> 5 **else**
> 6 | print "Return type is not parameterized";
> 7 **end**

In order to provide a comprehensive understanding and practical examples, it is crucial for Java developers to delve deep into these tools provided by the Java Reflection API. Through careful scrutiny and thoughtful application of Java Reflection, developers can demystify and manipulate complex generic types in their programs, facilitating more dynamic and versatile software solutions.

11.3 Reflection and Type Tokens

Reflection and type tokens are essential in overcoming the challenges of type erasure in Java generics. Type erasure, a process wherein the generic type information is removed at runtime, restricts the ability of developers to fully utilize generics during runtime analysis. This section explores how reflection, combined with the concept of type tokens, provides a method to access this erased generic type information, consequently offering greater flexibility and capabilities in Java applications.

Type tokens are a design pattern instrumental in reifying generic type information. They work by creating a super type token class that captures the generic type. This is achieved by subclassing a parameterized type with a concrete type argument. The Java Reflection API can then be leveraged to inspect these type tokens, uncovering the information that was erased by the compiler at runtime.

```
// Example of a type token being defined and used
public class TypeToken<T> {
    private final Class<T> type;

    protected TypeToken() {
        this.type = (Class<T>) ((ParameterizedType) getClass()
                .getGenericSuperclass()).getActualTypeArguments()[0];
```

CHAPTER 11. USING REFLECTION IN GENERICS

```
8      }
9
10     public Class<T> getType() {
11         return type;
12     }
13  }
14
15  public class StringToken extends TypeToken<String> {}
```

In the above code, TypeToken<T> captures the generic type argument T which is then accessible via the getType() method. By extending TypeToken with a concrete type, such as String in StringToken, the type argument becomes reified and capable of being examined at runtime:

```
StringToken token = new StringToken();
System.out.println("Type captured: " + token.getType());
```

This output would verify that the type captured is indeed Class<java.lang.String>.

To further demonstrate the utility of type tokens, consider their application in a scenario requiring reflective access to generic type parameters. For instance, determining the generic type of a collection's elements:

```
1  public class CollectionTypeToken<T> extends TypeToken<Collection<T>> {}
2
3  public class IntegerListToken extends CollectionTypeToken<Integer> {}
```

Within this scenario, an instance of IntegerListToken accurately informs the runtime system that the collection's element type is Integer. This is particularly useful in methods where knowledge of element types is crucial for processing collections reflectively.

- Reflective access to method parameters and return types
- Enhanced runtime type checking and casting
- Dynamic processing of generic data structures

Type tokens, when combined with reflection, serve as a powerful tool to manoeuvre around type erasure limitations. This capability opens up possibilities not just for API developers but also for applications in areas such as serialization frameworks, dependency injection containers, and more complex data manipulation tasks. The strategic usage of this pattern ensures a robust approach to handling generics in any Java application, maximizing the expressive power of the language while maintaining runtime type safety.

11.4 Dynamically Accessing Generic Methods

In Java development, the dynamic access of generic methods through reflection is pivotal for applications requiring adaptability and flexibility at runtime. This section elucidates the process of obtaining and invoking generic methods with varying type parameters dynamically, providing comprehensive insights for developers aiming to exploit the full potential of reflection with generics.

When it comes to Java generics, accessing methods whose type parameters are not known at compile time involves a series of reflective operations that can be abstracted into clear, systematic steps. The primary challenge addressed is overcoming Java's type erasure, which removes the generic type information post-compilation, leaving it inaccessible at runtime directly.

Retrieving Methods Using Reflection

To initiate the process, developers must first attain a reference to the `Method` object that represents the generic method of interest. This is done using the `Class` object of the class where the method is declared.

```
Method getGenericMethod(Class<?> clazz, String methodName, Class<?>...
    parameterTypes) {
    Method method = null;
    try {
        method = clazz.getDeclaredMethod(methodName, parameterTypes);
        method.setAccessible(true);
    } catch (NoSuchMethodException e) {
        e.printStackTrace();
    }
    return method;
}
```

In the code snippet above, `getDeclaredMethod` is used to fetch the method by name and parameter types, which are formally passed. This method returns the `Method` object essential for subsequent operations.

Resolving Type Variables

Post retrieval of the `Method` object, the next step is resolving the generic type parameters. Java Reflection provides `TypeVariable` instances through the `getTypeParameters` method of the `Method` class.

```
TypeVariable<Method>[] getTypeParameters(Method method) {
    return method.getTypeParameters();
```

```
3  }
```

This function retrieves the array of `TypeVariable` objects each representing a type variable declared by the generic method. These type variables are placeholders to be resolved with actual types during the dynamic invocation process.

Dynamic Invocation of Generic Methods

The capability of invoking generic methods dynamically is centered around the `invoke` method, which requires the target object, along with any arguments the method expects. The following outlines how to handle this with reflection, accommodating any required type adjustments.

```
1  Object invokeGenericMethod(Method method, Object obj, Object... args) {
2      Object result = null;
3      try {
4          result = method.invoke(obj, args);
5      } catch (IllegalAccessException | InvocationTargetException e) {
6          e.printStackTrace();
7      }
8      return result;
9  }
```

In practice, correctly casting and providing the arguments is critical, as the runtime type of generics is not available due to type erasure. Developing a utility method that converts raw types to their corresponding generics can be beneficial.

To sum up, dynamic access of generic methods through Java Reflection, although initially complex due to type erasure, is a powerful tool in a developer's toolbox. By carefully retrieving method references, discerning type parameters, and applying reflective invocation, developers can ensure that their code remains efficient and flexible. The techniques discussed establish a robust framework for employing reflective operations on generic methods, underscoring reflection's significant role in advanced Java programming. This approach not only enhances the application's adaptability but also contributes significantly to its scalability and maintainability.

11.5 Construction and Instantiation of Generic Types

The instantiation of generic types in Java, particularly when combined with reflection, presents a complex challenge due to the runtime type erasure imposed by the Java compiler. This section elaborates on how reflection can be used to programmatically construct and instantiate objects of generic types, notwithstanding the complications introduced by type erasure.

In Java, the construction of an instance typically requires the explicit identification of a constructor using the class information. However, when dealing with generics, this process is not straightforward since the generic type information is not available at runtime. By leveraging the capabilities of Java reflection, developers can overcome these limitations.

Utilizing Constructors in Generic Classes

Firstly, to programmatically access constructors of a generic class, reflection must be used to inspect the Constructor objects associated with the class. Consider the following generic class definition:

```
public class Box<T> {
    private T content;

    public Box() {
        // Default constructor
    }

    public Box(T content) {
        this.content = content;
    }

    public void setContent(T content) {
        this.content = content;
    }

    public T getContent() {
        return content;
    }
}
```

To construct an instance of this generic class reflectively, first access the Constructors using the Class object associated with the specific generic type instantiation.

```
Class<Box<String>> clazz = (Class<Box<String>>) Class.forName("Box").asSubclass(Box
```

```
   .class);
2  Constructor<Box<String>> defaultConstructor = clazz.getDeclaredConstructor();
3  Constructor<Box<String>> parameterizedConstructor = clazz.getDeclaredConstructor(
       Object.class);
```

Here, care must be taken to manage `ClassCastException` and `NoSuchMethodException` potentially thrown due to incorrect assumptions about constructors.

Instantiating Generic Types

After retrieving the constructor, instantiating the generic type is the next step. This is accomplished by invoking the constructor's `newInstance` method, passing any required arguments.

```
1  Box<String> stringBox = parameterizedConstructor.newInstance("Hello, Reflection!");
```

The above code snippet reflects the instantiation of a `Box<String>` with the string *"Hello, Reflection!"* as its content. It is crucial to handle exceptions like `InstantiationException`, `IllegalAccessException`, or `InvocationTargetException` that may arise during runtime.

In scenarios involving complex hierarchies or bounded types, additional steps such as type checking and casting might be required.

```
Box instance created: Hello, Reflection!
```

While the reflective instantiation of generic types enhances flexibility, it incurs performance overhead and potential security risks due to increased exposure to runtime errors and exception handling complexities.

Using advanced reflection techniques for generic types can significantly amplify the adaptiveness of applications. However, it necessitates a thorough understanding of both the generic type system in Java and the reflective methodologies employed. This skill set enables developers to write more dynamic and robust code, particularly in scenarios involving dynamic type constraints, third-party class libraries, or frameworks necessitating such reflective constructs.

11.6 Handling Generic Arrays Reflectively

When working with Java generics, particularly generic arrays, developers often face significant challenges due to the limitations imposed

11.6. HANDLING GENERIC ARRAYS REFLECTIVELY

by type erasure. Reflective techniques offer powerful tools to address these challenges by dynamically inspecting and manipulating array types. This section explores methodologies for managing generic arrays using Java Reflection, illustrating these techniques with precise coding examples.

The central obstacle in reflective array handling is reconstructing the generic type of the components at runtime, a complexity rooted in the Java runtime's inability to fully retain generic type information after compilation. To tackle this, we employ reflection to retrieve detailed component information from arrays, even when their component types are generic.

- One must first understand how to declare and instantiate an array reflectively with type safety.

- The approach to inspect an array's generic component type dynamically must be made clear.

- Techniques to modify and interact with generic arrays using reflection are essential.

Declaring and Instantiating Reflective Arrays

To create an instance of a generic array reflectively, Java's `Array.newInstance(Class<?> componentType, int length)` method can be utilized. This method allows for the creation of an array with a runtime-specified component type and length.

```
import java.lang.reflect.Array;

// Generic array creation method
public <T> T[] createArray(Class<T> componentType, int size) {
    @SuppressWarnings("unchecked")
    T[] array = (T[]) Array.newInstance(componentType, size);
    return array;
}
```

This listing effectively demonstrates how to instantiate a generic array of type `T` with a specified `size`. Despite the erasure of generic types during runtime, this method uses reflective operations to ensure type correctness.

Inspecting Array Component Types

Retrieving the component type of a generic array at runtime can also be achieved using reflection. This enables the examination and manipulation of array contents dynamically, preserving type safety.

```
1  import java.lang.reflect.Field;
2
3  // Method to retrieve component type of an array
4  public Class<?> getComponentType(Object array) {
5      return array.getClass().getComponentType();
6  }
```

Here, getComponentType() method is used to fetch the type of the array's elements, which is crucial for operations requiring type-specific handling.

Reflective Operations on Generic Arrays

Having established methods to create and inspect generic arrays, we can proceed to perform operations on these arrays dynamically. Reflection provides the capability to inspect and modify array contents without knowing the array type at compile time, thereby enhancing generic programming flexibility.

```
1  import java.lang.reflect.Array;
2
3  // Method to set an element in a generic array
4  public <T> void setElementInArray(T[] array, T element, int index) {
5      Array.set(array, index, element);
6  }
```

In the example provided, the setElementInArray method modifies an array element at a specified index with the given element. The reflective Array.set function is used here, which is capable of handling all array component types dynamically.

Through the techniques presented, it is evident that Java Reflection provides profound capabilities to work with generic arrays, enabling dynamic operations that are not feasible using conventional methods. These capabilities form the basis for more advanced generic programming patterns and frameworks, enhancing application modularity and reducing runtime type errors.

11.7 Challenges and Solutions with Generic Reflection

The effective use of reflection with Java generics presents multiple challenges primarily due to type erasure—where generic type information is not available at runtime. This section explores prevalent difficulties and introduces solutions to mitigate these problems while maintaining

11.7. CHALLENGES AND SOLUTIONS WITH GENERIC REFLECTION

system efficiency and reliability.

Challenges in Generic Reflection

The primary challenge in reflecting on generic types is the absence of type information at runtime due to Java's mechanism of type erasure. This absence complicates the process of:

- Verifying type constraints at runtime.
- Instantiating generic types dynamically.
- Retrieving and applying generic type information during runtime reflection.

Another significant challenge is managing subclasses of generic classes. A subclass may introduce its type parameters, or it may bind to specific types, adding complexity when trying to reflect on such hierarchies.

Robust Solutions to Type Erasure

To overcome these issues, we can employ several techniques which enable more robust generic reflection. Key strategies include:

- Use of `TypeToken` objects: They capture generic type information at compile-time and preserve it for runtime analysis.
- Explicitly passing Class objects as method parameters to hold type information at runtime.

Let us explore each solution with an emphasis on implementation and use:

Using `TypeToken` Effectively A `TypeToken` object is created with a specific target type information retained:

```
public class TypeToken<T> {
    private final Class<T> typeClass;
    public TypeToken(Class<T> typeClass) {
        this.typeClass = typeClass;
    }
    public Class<T> getRawType() {
        return typeClass;
    }
}
```

This TypeToken instance holds the generic type information that can be retrieved and manipulated at runtime.

Runtime Type Checking and Instantiation Passing Class objects helps manage types explicitly at runtime. However, instantiating types reflectively still poses a risk. We must verify type safety meticulously:

```
1  public static <T> T instantiateGenericType(Class<T> clazz) throws
       IllegalAccessException, InstantiationException {
2    T instance = clazz.newInstance(); // Use clazz.getDeclaredConstructor().
       newInstance() in newer Java versions
3    return instance;
4  }
```

Output of the above instantiation might look like this, assuming a default constructor is available:

```
Integer instance = instantiateGenericType(Integer.class);
```

Dealing with Generic Superclasses Reflection on generic superclass types requires care. We often need to traverse generic class hierarchies, requiring precise handling of Java's Type interface and its subtypes.

```
1  public static Type getGenericSuperclass(Class<?> clazz) {
2    return clazz.getGenericSuperclass();
3  }
```

To implement these solutions effectively, a deep understanding of Java's reflection and generics APIs is required, alongside careful programming practices. Handling type safely and efficiently often comes down to meticulously planning and verifying all aspects of type handling in your codebase.

This strategic approach to leveraging generic reflection not only addresses the innate challenges but also significantly enhances the adaptability and robustness of Java applications dealing with complex generic constructs.

11.8 Interfacing Generics with Wildcards and Bounded Types

Utilizing Java Reflection with wildcards and bounded types in generics introduces complexity yet offers powerful capabilities for developing dynamic, type-safe applications. This section delineates the methods

11.8. INTERFACING GENERICS WITH WILDCARDS AND BOUNDED TYPES

required to interact reflectively with generics that employ wildcards (?) and bounded types (e.g., <T extends Comparable>).

Firstly, let us explore the fundamental techniques for reflecting on parameters and fields that include wildcard types. Consider a simple generic class with a wildcard type:

```
public class Box<? extends Number> {
    private ? extends Number value;

    public ? extends Number getValue() {
        return value;
    }

    public void setValue(? extends Number value) {
        this.value = value;
    }
}
```

Attempting to reflect on such structures involves fetching the bounded type information during runtime:

```
public void reflectOnBox() {
    Field fieldValue = Box.class.getDeclaredField("value");
    Type genericFieldType = fieldValue.getGenericType();
    if (genericFieldType instanceof ParameterizedType) {
        ParameterizedType pType = (ParameterizedType) genericFieldType;
        Type[] fieldArgTypes = pType.getActualTypeArguments();
        for (Type argType : fieldArgTypes) {
            System.out.println(argType.getTypeName());
        }
    }
}
```

Output of such code reflection would typically produce insights into the parameterized types used:

```
? extends java.lang.Number
```

In handling operations on methods or constructors that involve wildcards and bounded types, a similar reflective approach can be applied to extract generic information. Next, consider how we can instantiate objects or invoke methods reflectively, taking into account the bounded type limits:

```
public class Handler {
    public <? extends Number> create(Class<? extends Number> clazz)
            throws InstantiationException, IllegalAccessException {
        return clazz.newInstance();
    }
}
```

Reflecting on such a method, especially to determine the bounds applicable to type parameters, can be accomplished using the following reflection approach:

```
Method method = Handler.class.getMethod("create", Class.class);
Type[] genericParameterTypes = method.getGenericParameterTypes();
for (Type genericParameterType : genericParameterTypes) {
    if (genericParameterType instanceof WildcardType) {
        WildcardType wildcardType = (WildcardType) genericParameterType;
        System.out.println(Arrays.toString(wildcardType.getUpperBounds()));
    }
}
```

The output would typically look like this:

[class java.lang.Number]

The reflection API in Java is powerful but requires careful handling when working with generics involving bounded types and wildcards. Misuse can lead to `ClassCastException` or other runtime issues owing to the inherently type-erased nature of Java generics at runtime. Proper checks and validation should always accompany such reflective operations to ensure safety and correctness.

Employing the techniques discussed here will empower developers to create more flexible and dynamic applications that can handle complex generic structures with aplomb. The critical takeaway is recognizing and respecting the limitations and intricacies introduced by type erasure and bounded wildcards in Java Generics, paving the way for effective and safe reflective programming.

11.9 Practical Applications: Generics in Frameworks

This section explores the practical applications of using Java reflection with generics in the design and implementation of software frameworks. Reflection combined with generics greatly enhances a framework's ability to be flexible and adaptable, accommodating a broad range of use cases without sacrificing type safety. We will dissect several key framework capabilities that benefit from this integration, namely dependency injection, object-relational mapping, and type-safe configuration management.

Dependency Injection Containers

Dependency Injection (DI) frameworks such as Spring and Guice utilize Java generics and reflection to resolve dependencies at runtime dynamically. Here, reflection is crucial for inspecting classes and the relationships among them, whereas generics provide the additional type safety during dependency injection.

Consider the following typical usage scenario in a DI framework:

```
public interface Service<T> {
    T performAction();
}

public class StringService implements Service<String> {
    public String performAction() {
        return "Hello, Reflection!";
    }
}

ApplicationContext context = new AnnotationConfigApplicationContext(AppConfig.class
    );
Service<String> myService = context.getBean(StringService.class);
System.out.println(myService.performAction());
```

In this example, reflection allows the DI container to instantiate StringService based on its type at runtime. The container checks the actual type parameter <String> ensuring the type safety of operations performing through the Service interface.

Object-Relational Mapping

Object-Relational Mapping (ORM) frameworks like Hibernate use generics along with reflection to map between objects in Java and records in a relational database. Here is a simple example:

```
@Entity
public class User<T> {
    @Id
    private Long id;

    private T userDetails;

    // Constructor, getters, setters
}
```

In the above User class, the ORM framework can use reflection to inspect the generic field userDetails. By knowing that T is bound to a specific type at runtime (for instance, String or another entity), the framework can handle the type appropriately, ensuring that the type constraints are not violated when interacting with the database.

Type-Safe Configuration Management

Frameworks often require configuring properties or settings that may vary in type. Reflection and generics enable type-safe configuration management, an essential aspect for large scale applications.

The combination allows frameworks to interpret and instantiate configurations from external resources dynamically:

```
1  public interface Config<T> {
2      T getConfigValue(String key);
3  }
```

Frameworks could interpret the type T at runtime to assert the type safety, loading and returning configurations appropriately without casting errors. Here is an example use-case:

```
1  Config<Integer> integerConfig = configManager.getConfig(Integer.class);
2  int maxTimeout = integerConfig.getConfigValue("maxTimeout");
```

This code snippet safely retrieves an integer configuration value using reflection to ensure that the provided key corresponds to an integer type in the configuration.

Reflection Enhancements for Framework Interoperability

Utilizing reflection in union with generics not only simplifies the design but also enhances interoperability between different parts of a framework or between different frameworks themselves. By adopting a standardized approach to utilizing generics and reflection, frameworks can maintain a high level of compatibility and extensibility, adapting dynamically to the changing requirements of applications.

Frameworks adopting this methodology empower developers to build robust applications that effectively manage dependencies, database interactions, and configurations, all while ensuring type safety and reducing runtime errors. The integration of Java reflection with generics hence manifests as a critical strategy in modern software framework architecture, fostering the development of scalable, efficient, and flexible applications.

11.10 Testing and Debugging Generic Reflection Code

Testing and debugging reflection-based generic code requires specialized attention due to the intricate interplay of compile-time versus runtime type checks and behavior. This section delves deeply into strategies and methodologies for ensuring that your reflective generic code in Java is robust, maintainable, and error-free.

Testing methodologies for reflective generic code fundamentally differ from those used in standard Java code because reflection introduces additional runtime considerations that are not present at compile time. The following testing strategies are pertinent:

- **Unit Testing with Mocks:** Mocking frameworks, such as Mockito, can be employed to test the behavior of methods that use reflection. Using these frameworks allows the tester to isolate the method and ensure it behaves correctly with controlled inputs, even for complex generic structures.

- **Integration Testing:** Ensures that the interactions between classes that use generics and reflection work as expected when integrated. This type of testing often involves real implementations rather than mocks.

To aid in debugging, Java provides several tools that can be leveraged to pinpoint issues related to reflection and generics. Below, the 'java.lang.reflect' package functionalities and diagnostic techniques are discussed in detail.

```
public <T> void debugGenericType(T obj) {
    Class<?> clazz = obj.getClass();
    Type genericSuperclass = clazz.getGenericSuperclass();
    if (genericSuperclass instanceof ParameterizedType) {
        ParameterizedType type = (ParameterizedType) genericSuperclass;
        Type[] typeArguments = type.getActualTypeArguments();
        System.out.println(Arrays.toString(typeArguments));
    }
}
```

The simplified method above retrieves and displays the generic type parameters of any given object's superclass, aiding in understanding how generic types are composed at runtime, which is crucial information while debugging.

In general, when debugging issues in generic code enhanced by reflection, consider the following approaches:

- **Logging active Reflection Information:** Printing or logging the metadata obtained from reflective calls when exceptions or unexpected behavior occur. This includes method names, modifiers, type parameters, and interfaces.

- **Exception Handling:** Use try-catch blocks effectively around reflective method calls to catch reflective operations specific exceptions like IllegalAccessException or InvocationTargetException. Include comprehensive error messages to facilitate quicker diagnosis.

Herein, pseudocode for a standard debugging routine is illustrated, employing the algorithmic structure as defined by the 'algorithm2e' package.

Algorithm 8: Pseudocode for Debugging Generic Reflection Code

Input: A generic object obj of type T
Output: Prints debugging information for the object's generic types

1 **Function** DebugGenericInfo(*T obj*):
/* Extract class object from T */
2     $class \leftarrow obj.getClass()$
/* Retrieve the generic superclass type information */
3     $genericInfo \leftarrow class.getGenericSuperclass()$
4   **if** *genericInfo is ParameterizedType* **then**
/* Casting the Type to ParameterizedType for detailed inspection */
5        $paramType \leftarrow (ParameterizedType)genericInfo$
6   Print paramType.ActualTypeArguments

This approach to debugging leverages runtime type information to effectively trace and resolve typical generic reflection problems, especially those concerning type parameters and hierarchy.

Developers working with reflective generic programming must recognize the crucial balance between the powerful dynamic capabilities provided by reflection and the runtime errors it can cultivate if not properly tested and debugged. The discussed practices and examples enable developers to harness the richness of generics in Java while maintaining reliability and performance in their applications.

11.11 Reflection on Generic Inheritance Structures

Generic inheritance structures introduce an additional layer of complexity when using Java Reflection, especially when navigating through superclass and subclass relationships that involve generic types. Reflective operations on such structures are pivotal for applications that require dynamic type resolution for inherited generic types. This section discusses how to accurately reflect upon generic inheritance structures, with emphasis on extracting type parameters and understanding how these are preserved or transformed through inheritance hierarchies.

The Java Reflection API provides a series of methods that make it possible to inspect classes and retrieve information about fields, methods, and constructors, including those involving generic types. However, when dealing with inheritance, the typical approach must be adapted to account for generic type parameters and their potential transformations across the hierarchy.

Inspecting Inherited Generic Types

To begin, the Java Reflection API allows retrieving superclass information using the `getGenericSuperclass()` method. This method returns a `Type` object, usually a `ParameterizedType`, which represents the direct superclass along with its type parameters. Here's how this can be practically applied:

```
import java.lang.reflect.ParameterizedType;
import java.lang.reflect.Type;

public class ReflectionUtil {

    public static void printSuperclassTypeParameters(Class<?> clazz) {
        Type type = clazz.getGenericSuperclass();

        if (type instanceof ParameterizedType) {
            ParameterizedType pType = (ParameterizedType) type;
            Type[] arrType = pType.getActualTypeArguments();
```

```
13          for (Type t : arrType) {
14              System.out.println(t);
15          }
16      }
17  }
18 }
```

The above method takes a `Class` object and prints out the type parameters of its superclass. This method is particularly useful when you need to understand how generic types are passed from superclasses to subclasses.

Handling Complex Generic Structures

In more complex inheritance scenarios, such as when classes implement several interfaces or extend generic classes with several levels of nesting, the approach must be recursive and thorough to ensure all generics in the inheritance chain are accounted for. The process involves inspecting interfaces and superclass chains recursively:

```
1  public static void printAllGenericInfo(Class<?> clazz) {
2      while (clazz != null) {
3          printSuperclassTypeParameters(clazz);
4          Type[] interfaces = clazz.getGenericInterfaces();
5
6          for (Type intf : interfaces) {
7              if (intf instanceof ParameterizedType) {
8                  ParameterizedType pType = (ParameterizedType) intf;
9                  Type[] typeArgs = pType.getActualTypeArguments();
10
11                 for (Type arg : typeArgs) {
12                     System.out.println(arg);
13                 }
14             }
15         }
16         clazz = clazz.getSuperclass();
17     }
18 }
```

As classes may implement multiple interfaces and each interface can itself be generic, capturing the full spectrum of type parameters requires examining each interface separately as demonstrated above.

Reflecting on Type Transformation Across Hierarchies

One of the subtleties in reflecting on generic inheritance structures is type parameter transformation across the hierarchy, where type parameters might be specified at various levels and could be subject to constraints imposed by upper or lower bounds. Understanding this transformation is vital for applications such as serialization frameworks, ORM tools, and dependency injection frameworks that depend on precise type resolution to function correctly.

```
1  // Continued detailed code analysis to handle transformation cases
```

The scrutiny of type transformations not only ensures the correctness of applications but also enhances their capability to adapt to changes in the underlying generic definitions.

Through detailed reflection on each layer of the inheritance structure and intellectually dissecting the interactions of type parameters, software developers can design and implement robust systems that dynamically interact with complex generic hierarchies. The insights gained from such reflective practices contribute significantly to advanced Java application development, emphasizing flexibility, type safety, and the dynamic nature of modern software architectures.

11.12 Best Practices with Generics and Reflection

Integrating reflection with generics in Java presents unique challenges due to type erasure; however, it also opens up opportunities for creating dynamic and robust applications. By adhering to the best practices outlined below, developers can effectively harness the power of both generics and reflection.

- **Careful Use of Reflection**: While reflection is a powerful feature, it should be used judiciously because of its impact on performance and maintenance. Minimize the use of reflection and rely on it only when generic types cannot be handled more straightforwardly.

- **Handling Type Erasure**: Since type information associated with generics is not available at runtime due to type erasure, use reflection to retrieve this information dynamically where necessary. This can be particularly useful in serialization, API development, and when interacting with frameworks that rely on runtime type information.

- **Reflective Access to Generic Types**:

```
1  Field field = MyClass.class.getDeclaredField("myGenericField");
2  Type genericFieldType = field.getGenericType();
3  if (genericFieldType instanceof ParameterizedType) {
4      ParameterizedType type = (ParameterizedType) genericFieldType;
5      System.out.println(type.getActualTypeArguments()[0]);
6  }
```

The above code snippet demonstrates obtaining detailed type information from a field with generic type. Use such patterns to facilitate dynamic operations on fields whose types include generic parameters.

- **Safe Casting with Generics**: When casting instances reflectively, ensure the correctness of the operation by checking if the object is indeed an instance of the generic class using methods like `Class.isInstance()` before performing the cast.

- **Avoid Raw Types**: Wherever possible, avoid the use of raw types in your code. Raw types bypass generic type checks at compile time, increasing the risk of runtime ClassCastExceptions. Always specify the type parameter when using generics and reflecting on generic types.

- **Documentation and Maintenance**: Proper documentation of the reflection-based and generic logic is crucial. Include clear comments and maintain a document on how and why reflection is used, particularly in complex situations involving generics—this aids in maintenance and debugging.

- **Test Coverage**: Ensure comprehensive testing for any sections of code using generics combined with reflection. Dynamic nature of code involving reflection requires thorough testing across a variety of scenarios to ensure reliability and robustness.

- **Use of Type Tokens**: Employ type tokens to retain generic type information where necessary. Type tokens help in expressing and preserving generic type information explicitly, circumventing type erasure at runtime.

Utilizing these best practices promotes the creation of safer and more effective Java applications leveraging the strengths of generics and reflection. By carefully implementing these approaches, developers can build adaptable and maintainable code bases that capitalize on the dynamic capabilities offered by Java reflection in conjunction with the strong type-checking provided by generics.

Chapter 12

Advanced Techniques and Use Cases

This chapter explores advanced techniques and diverse use cases of Java Reflection, extending beyond basic capabilities to cover sophisticated scenarios and solutions. It discusses the use of reflection in scenarios such as bytecode manipulation, dynamic test invocation, and the implementation of dynamic script engines. Each example showcases the powerful flexibility of reflection when coupled with design patterns and frameworks, offering insights into creating more robust, adaptable, and maintainable Java applications within various technical and business contexts.

12.1 Advanced Use of ClassLoader Reflection

ClassLoader reflection is a sophisticated technique within Java that allows developers to dynamically load, inspect, and manipulate classes at runtime. This capability is crucial in environments where it is essential to load classes dynamically from various sources or to alter behavior without modifying the original class source.

Understanding ClassLoader Mechanics

The Java ClassLoader plays a fundamental role in the JVM's (Java Virtual Machine) ability to load class files. The mechanism that ClassLoaders use involves delegating the class loading process upwards to the parent ClassLoader before attempting to load the class itself. This hierarchical model ensures that classes loaded by parent ClassLoaders are shared among its children, providing a namespace separation and preventing class reloading.

A deep dive into ClassLoader reflection begins with understanding the java.lang.ClassLoader class itself, which provides several protected methods that are pivotal for subclassing and creating custom ClassLoaders.

```
// Example of accessing ClassLoader of a particular class
ClassLoader classLoader = MyClass.class.getClassLoader();
```

This basic usage retrieves the ClassLoader responsible for loading a specific class. However, reflective access offers a broader scope of manipulation and inquiry.

Creating Custom ClassLoaders

Reflection comes into powerful play when creating custom ClassLoaders. This capability is essential for scenarios like developing an application plugin system, supporting multiple versions of a software, or securely loading remote code.

Here is an outline of creating a simplistic custom ClassLoader:

```
public class CustomClassLoader extends ClassLoader {
    @Override
    protected Class<?> findClass(String name) throws ClassNotFoundException {
        byte[] b = loadClassData(name);
        return defineClass(name, b, 0, b.length);
    }

    private byte[] loadClassData(String name) {
        // Implement class loading logic here
        return new byte[] {};
    }
}
```

The method findClass is the core of a ClassLoader, which is where the custom logic for fetching and defining classes is implemented. In this example, loadClassData would contain the logic needed to fetch the class data in byte format, which might involve reading from a file system, database, network, or other sources.

Dynamically Loading Classes

With a custom ClassLoader in place, the next step is dynamically loading classes at runtime. This process is critical in circumstances where you do not know during the compile time which classes will be needed, or when you want to load classes from unconventional sources.

The following example demonstrates the usage of a custom ClassLoader to load a class dynamically:

```
CustomClassLoader customClassLoader = new CustomClassLoader();
Class<?> loadedClass = customClassLoader.loadClass("com.example.DynamicClass");

// Instantiate the loaded class
Object instance = loadedClass.getDeclaredConstructor().newInstance();
```

This exemplifies how to use the custom ClassLoader to load a class by its name and then instantiate it using Java reflection.

Implications and Best Practices

While powerful, the use of ClassLoader reflection must be handled with care. Improper use can lead to security vulnerabilities, such as the exposure of sensitive data, or runtime issues, such as ClassCastException if an incorrectly loaded class is cast to a wrong type.

Here are some best practices for implementing ClassLoader reflection:

- Ensure secure access control when loading classes from external sources.
- Manage the lifecycle and namespace of the ClassLoader to avoid memory leaks.
- Utilize parent delegation properly to maintain application stability.

ClassLoader reflection provides an extensible approach for developers to address complex problems that require runtime class manipulation. By adhering to these best practices and understanding the underlying mechanics, developers can harness the full potential of Java reflection to enhance application functionality and responsiveness.

12.2 Techniques for Reflective JavaBean Manipulation

Manipulating JavaBeans using reflection is a powerful technique that enables developers to interact with object properties dynamically. This capability is vital in scenarios where the structure of classes is not known at compile time. Throughout this section, we will explore various methodologies to utilize reflection for manipulating JavaBean properties, along with practical code examples and performance considerations.

Accessing Bean Properties Dynamically

The Java Reflection API provides mechanisms to dynamically access and modify the property values of JavaBeans. The essential steps involve identifying the Bean properties, accessing these properties through their getters and setters, and manipulating the values as needed.

```
Property manipulation output:
- Successfully retrieved property value
- Property value updated
```

```java
import java.lang.reflect.Method;

public class DynamicBeanManipulator {

    public static void setProperty(Object bean, String propertyName, Object value)
            throws Exception {
        Method setter = bean.getClass().getMethod(
            "set" + Character.toUpperCase(propertyName.charAt(0)) +
            propertyName.substring(1), value.getClass());
        setter.invoke(bean, value);
    }

    public static Object getProperty(Object bean, String propertyName) throws
            Exception {
        Method getter = bean.getClass().getMethod(
            "get" + Character.toUpperCase(propertyName.charAt(0)) +
            propertyName.substring(1));
        return getter.invoke(bean);
    }
}
```

Invoking Methods Using Reflection

Reflection can be utilized not only to access properties but also to invoke methods dynamically. This is particularly useful when dealing with beans where the method to invoke might not be determined until runtime.

```
public class MethodInvoker {

    public static Object invokeMethod(Object bean, String methodName, Class<?>[]
            paramTypes, Object[] args) throws Exception {
        Method method = bean.getClass().getDeclaredMethod(methodName, paramTypes);
        method.setAccessible(true);
        return method.invoke(bean, args);
    }

}
```

Handling Reflection Exceptions

When using reflection, it is crucial to properly handle exceptions that can arise, such as `NoSuchMethodException` or `InvocationTargetException`. These exceptions can provide critical information about why a reflection operation failed, which is essential for debugging and error handling.

```
try {
    Object propertyValue = DynamicBeanManipulator.getProperty(bean, "propertyName");
} catch (NoSuchMethodException e) {
    System.err.println("Getter method not found for the property.");
} catch (InvocationTargetException e) {
    System.err.println("Exception thrown by the getter method.");
} catch (IllegalAccessException e) {
    System.err.println("Cannot access the getter method.");
}
```

Optimizations and Best Practices

While reflection provides powerful capabilities, it comes with a performance cost. Therefore, it is advisable to use reflection judiciously:

- Use caching mechanisms for method objects if they are to be invoked multiple times.
- Avoid reflection in performance-critical sections of code.
- Utilize alternative approaches, like the JavaBeans `Introspector` class, for property management when possible.

These techniques and considerations for reflective JavaBean manipulation underscore the dynamic capabilities of Java Reflection. They serve as a guide for developers looking to harness the power of reflection responsibly to enhance the flexibility and adaptability of their applications.

12.3 Reflection for Dynamic Proxy Chains and Composite Objects

This section focuses on the utilization of Java reflection capabilities in the construction of dynamic proxy chains and the manipulation of composite objects. Java reflection is a powerful tool that allows for runtime class and object manipulation, lending itself effectively to dynamic proxy creation and the management of complex object compositions.

Dynamic proxies in Java are instances where a proxy class is dynamically created to implement specified interfaces at runtime. This is achieved using the `java.lang.reflect.Proxy` class and its associated invocation handler. By leveraging dynamic proxies, Java developers can enforce additional behaviors such as logging, transaction management, and security checks transparently.

Proxy instances are constructed by providing an array of interfaces for the proxy class to implement and an invocation handler that intercepts method calls to proxy methods. Below is a basic example demonstrating the creation of a dynamic proxy that utilizes reflection:

```
import java.lang.reflect.InvocationHandler;
import java.lang.reflect.Method;
import java.lang.reflect.Proxy;

public class DynamicProxyHandler implements InvocationHandler {
    private Object targetObject;

    public DynamicProxyHandler(Object targetObject) {
        this.targetObject = targetObject;
    }

    @Override
    public Object invoke(Object proxy, Method method, Object[] args) throws Throwable {
        // Pre-processing (e.g., logging, security checks)
        System.out.println("Before method " + method.getName());
        Object result = method.invoke(targetObject, args);
        // Post-processing
        System.out.println("After method " + method.getName());
        return result;
    }

    public static <T> T createProxy(Class<T> interfaceType, T targetObject) {
        return (T) Proxy.newProxyInstance(
            interfaceType.getClassLoader(),
```

12.3. REFLECTION FOR DYNAMIC PROXY CHAINS AND COMPOSITE OBJECTS

```
25            new Class<?>[] {interfaceType},
26            new DynamicProxyHandler(targetObject)
27        );
28    }
29 }
```

The above example shows a simple implementation where a dynamic proxy wraps an existing object's method calls with additional behavior. Now, consider the output of this proxy when applied to an interface:

```
Before method execute
Executing the original method
After method execute
```

Moving onto composite objects, these are structures made up of simpler, individual objects which collectively behave as a single unit. Utilizing reflection, developers can navigate and modify these composition structures dynamically. An essential application of reflection in dealing with composite objects is to discover and affect their state and behavior during runtime without prior knowledge of the object's structure.

In composite design patterns, typically, an abstract component class defines behavior to be implemented by its child components. Child components might be leaf or composite objects themselves. Below, we illustrate how to use reflection to handle such a hierarchy dynamically:

```
1  public abstract class Component {
2      public abstract void operation();
3  }
4
5  public class Leaf extends Component {
6      @Override
7      public void operation() {
8          System.out.println("Leaf operation");
9      }
10 }
11
12 public class Composite extends Component {
13     private List<Component> children = new ArrayList<>();
14
15     public void add(Component component) {
16         children.add(component);
17     }
18
19     @Override
20     public void operation() {
21         children.forEach(Component::operation);
22     }
23 }
```

Dynamic interrogation and manipulation of such a structure can help modify behavior at runtime, which is especially useful in scenarios where the structure of the composite might be unknown or change dynamically.

Reflection contributes significantly to the adaptability and robustness of applications that rely on complex object structures and behaviors, specifically through the runtime interrogation and dynamic modification capabilities it provides. This technique, when combined with dynamic proxy patterns, facilitates a sophisticated approach to manage and enforce behaviors across a range of functional and non-functional requirements.

12.4 Automating Data Serialization and Deserialization

Serialization and deserialization are critical processes for storing and retrieving object state information to and from a standard format such as XML or JSON. Reflection in Java provides a potent mechanism to automate these processes, enabling dynamic manipulation of objects without prior knowledge of their structure at compile time.

Dynamic Serialization Using Reflection

To illustrate the use of reflection for serialization, consider a scenario where an application needs to serialize a variety of objects whose class structures are not known until runtime. Using reflection, the application can dynamically identify the fields to be serialized and handle them accordingly.

```java
public static String serializeObject(Object obj) {
    StringBuilder sb = new StringBuilder();
    Field[] fields = obj.getClass().getDeclaredFields();
    sb.append("{");
    for (Field field : fields) {
        if (!Modifier.isTransient(field.getModifiers())) {
            field.setAccessible(true);
            try {
                sb.append("\"").append(field.getName()).append("\":\"")
                  .append(field.get(obj)).append("\",");
            } catch (IllegalAccessException e) {
                e.printStackTrace();
            }
        }
    }
    sb.deleteCharAt(sb.length() - 1); // Remove the last comma
    sb.append("}");
    return sb.toString();
}
```

The above Java method 'serializeObject' dynamically inspects the object's fields and creates a JSON representation. Note that transient fields are not included, as indicated by their modifiers. This selective process ensures that only relevant data is serialized.

Dynamic Deserialization Using Reflection

Deserialization, the reverse of serialization, reconstructs an object instance from its data representation using reflection to dynamically assign field values. The following example demonstrates how to deserialize a simple JSON string back into an object.

```
public static void deserializeObject(Object obj, String json) {
    String[] keyValuePairs = json.replace("{", "").replace("}", "").split(",");
    Map<String, String> valuesMap = new HashMap<>();
    for (String pair : keyValuePairs) {
        String[] entry = pair.split(":");
        valuesMap.put(entry[0].replace("\"", "").trim(), entry[1].replace("\"", "").trim());
    }

    Field[] fields = obj.getClass().getDeclaredFields();
    for (Field field : fields) {
        if (valuesMap.containsKey(field.getName())) {
            field.setAccessible(true);
            try {
                field.set(obj, convertToFieldType(field, valuesMap.get(field.getName())));
            } catch (IllegalAccessException e) {
                e.printStackTrace();
            }
        }
    }
}
```

This method 'deserializeObject' takes an empty instance of an object and a JSON string, then populates the object's fields based on the JSON content. The helper method 'convertToFieldType' is used to cast the string values in the JSON to their appropriate field types.

Automation in Real-World Applications

In contemporary Java applications, the reflection-based approach for automating serialization and deserialization is particularly valuable when:

- Handling diverse object types with complex and unknown class structures.

- Integrating with third-party services that require dynamic content delivery.

- Developing frameworks or libraries that need to serialize and deserialize a wide range of object types without prior setup.

Reflective serialization and deserialization offer adaptability and reduce the maintenance burden, as changes in domain objects do not necessitate changes in serialization logic. This method is also highly beneficial in applications featuring dynamically loaded classes, enhancing the modularity and flexibility of the system.

Given the inherent costs associated with using reflection due to type-checking and access control at runtime, it is recommended to employ this technique judiciously, especially in performance-critical paths. However, the strategic use of caching and optimization techniques can offset some of these performance implications, thus supporting a more efficient serialization process.

The ability to serialize and deserialize dynamically represents a significant advantage in domains requiring high levels of flexibility, such as plugin development or applications with extensive configuration management systems. By leveraging Java Reflection, developers can craft robust frameworks and infrastructure components that seamlessly adapt to evolving application requirements and data models.

12.5 Reflection in Test Driven Development and Mocking

Reflection in Java, a mechanism that allows the examination or modification of the runtime behavior of applications, offers significant advantages in the domain of Test Driven Development (TDD) and mocking frameworks. This section elaborates on the utilization of Java reflection to enhance and facilitate TDD and the creation of dynamic mock objects. These capabilities enable developers to write more flexible and decoupled tests, thereby improving the quality of software.

Enhancing TDD with Reflection

Test Driven Development is a software development process that relies heavily on the repetition of a very short development cycle: requirements are turned into very specific test cases, then the software is improved to pass the new tests. Reflection can be used to access and manipulate classes, methods, and fields during runtime, which is instrumental in testing private or protected members without the need to expose them through public interfaces.

Output: Enhanced testing capabilities and fewer modifications to the original class structure.

Example of Accessing Private Fields

```
import java.lang.reflect.Field;

public class ReflectionTest {
    private String privateString = "Private";

    public String getPrivateStringUsingReflection() throws NoSuchFieldException, IllegalAccessException {
        Field privateStringField = ReflectionTest.class.getDeclaredField("privateString");
        privateStringField.setAccessible(true);
        return (String) privateStringField.get(this);
    }
}
```

In the code sample above, reflection is utilized to access a private field privateString. By setting privateStringField.setAccessible(true), it grants access to otherwise inaccessible fields, a technique highly valuable for testing.

Mocking with Reflection

Mocking frameworks in Java, such as Mockito and PowerMock, use reflection extensively to mock objects and methods. This is crucial in isolating the unit of work and eliminating dependencies that can affect the outcomes of the test.

Practical Application in Mocking

```
import static org.mockito.Mockito.*;

public class MockExample {
    public void testMethod() {
        List mockedList = mock(List.class);
        when(mockedList.size()).thenReturn(5);
        assert mockedList.size() == 5;
    }
}
```

The example clearly illustrates creating a mock object using Mockito, setting expectations, and asserting results, a process simplified by reflection. Mockito internally uses reflection to inspect classes and handle proxy creation.

Dynamic Test Invocation

Dynamic test generation and invocation are areas where reflection particularly shines. It allows developers to create more dynamic and data-driven tests, where test cases can be generated at runtime based on external data sources, configuration files, or even database entries.

Generating Tests Dynamically

```
import org.junit.jupiter.api.*;

public class DynamicTests {
    public static Stream<Arguments> provideStrings() {
        return Stream.of(
            Arguments.of("test", 4),
            Arguments.of("hello", 5)
        );
    }

    @ParameterizedTest
    @MethodSource("provideStrings")
    void testWithParameters(String input, int length) {
        assertEquals(length, input.length());
    }
}
```

The code displays how reflection coupled with JUnit 5's dynamic tests facilitates data-driven test deployment, increasing the flexibility and breadth of automated tests. Each test input and expected output are dynamically fed into the test cases, which are executed separately.

Reflection, when integrated effectively in TDD and mocking in Java, offers enormous potential to increase the modularity, maintainability, and scalability of tests. Its capability to manipulate and access different class loaders, invoke methods, and access fields dynamically is pivotal in robust testing strategies, leading to higher quality applications with less intrusive testing codes.

12.6 Dynamic Language Features Implementation via Reflection

Reflective programming in Java provides a mechanism for the runtime retrieval of information about classes, interfaces, fields, and methods. This powerful feature facilitates the implementation of dynamic language characteristics such as method invocation, property access, and the instantiation of objects at runtime. This section delves deeply into leveraging Java Reflection to implement dynamic language features, enhancing the flexibility and scalability of software systems.

Dynamic Method Invocation

Dynamic method invocation is essential for scenarios where method calls need to be determined at runtime. By utilizing the `java.lang.reflect.Method` class, programs can execute methods whose names are not known until runtime.

```
Method method = Class.forName("java.util.ArrayList").getMethod("size");
ArrayList<String> list = new ArrayList<>();
list.add("Reflection");
int size = (Integer) method.invoke(list);
```

Output:
1

This example illustrates obtaining the `size` method from the ArrayList class and invoking it on an instance of ArrayList. The method name is only known and used at runtime, which is a typical use case in scripting engines or plugin systems where the executed methods depend on external inputs.

Runtime Property Access

Properties of objects in Java can also be accessed and modified at runtime using Reflection. This feature is particularly useful for generic frameworks, such as ORM (Object-Relational Mapping) tools, which map database entries to objects without knowing the property details at compile time.

```
Field field = Class.forName("com.example.User").getDeclaredField("name");
field.setAccessible(true);
User user = new User();
field.set(user, "John Doe");
```

```
5   String userName = (String) field.get(user);
```

Output:
John Doe

The code snippet above demonstrates accessing and modifying the name property of a User object dynamically. By setting field.setAccessible(true), private fields are made accessible, which is a common practice in frameworks that automate database operations.

Instantiation of Objects at Runtime

Reflection enables the instantiation of objects dynamically, which is a cornerstone for dependency injection frameworks and factories. The Class class provides the newInstance() method, which can be used to create new instances of a class without using the new keyword.

```
1   Class<?> clazz = Class.forName("com.example.User");
2   User user = (User) clazz.newInstance();
```

This method invokes the default constructor of the class to create a new instance. It's a powerful technique for creating objects when their types are not known until runtime, commonly seen in application frameworks and dependency injection modules.

Challenges and Considerations

While the dynamic features implemented via Reflection provide significant flexibility, they also introduce challenges such as performance overhead and security risks. Reflective operations are slower than their non-reflective counterparts, and excessive use of reflection can lead to maintenance challenges. Moreover, enabling access to private class members breaks encapsulation and may lead to security vulnerabilities.

Careful use of Reflection is advisable, employing it when its benefits outweigh the drawbacks. Frameworks and libraries should provide abstraction layers to minimize direct use of Reflection APIs, encapsulating complexity and safeguarding against inappropriate usage.

```
Performance Impact: Moderate to High
Security Risk: High if mismanaged
Recommended Usage: With caution and encapsulation
```

Reflective programming in Java, when used judiciously, enables developers to write more dynamic, flexible, and adaptable code. It empowers the development of frameworks and libraries that can operate across a multitude of scenarios, promoting reuse and modularity. Considerations around performance and security must always guide the decision to use Reflection, ensuring that the advantages are harnessed without compromising system integrity or performance.

12.7 Using Reflection for Runtime Code Modification

Reflection in Java provides the ability to inspect and modify the runtime behavior of applications dynamically. This capability is particularly useful in scenarios requiring runtime code modification. This section will delve deeply into how reflection can be used to alter the execution of Java code at runtime, discussing both the opportunities and risks associated.

Overview of Reflection for Runtime Modification: Reflection allows for the alteration of classes, methods, and fields during the runtime. This adaptation can be crucial for environments where systems must remain flexible and adaptive without stopping or recompiling the code.

- `Class<?>`: Used for obtaining and manipulating class objects.
- `Field`: Enables access and modification of class and instance fields.
- `Method`: Manages the invocation of methods and can alter their behavior dynamically.
- `Constructor<?>`: Handles the creation of new instances dynamically.

Methods of Modifying Code at Runtime:

- **Changing Class Members**: Reflectively altering fields and methods of a class allows for a high degree of adaptability in response to changing conditions during execution.
- **Dynamic Method Invocation**: By utilizing the `invoke` method from the `Method` class, techniques can be devised to call methods whose names are unknown at compile time.

To illustrate the capability of reflection in altering method execution, consider the following example where a method's behavior is changed dynamically based on runtime conditions:

```
import java.lang.reflect.*;

public class MethodModifier {
    public void printMessage(String message) {
        System.out.println("Original Message: " + message);
    }

    public static void main(String[] args) throws Exception {
        MethodModifier modifier = new MethodModifier();
        Method method = MethodModifier.class.getMethod("printMessage", String.class)
        ;

        method.invoke(modifier, "This is a message before modification.");

        Field methodField = Method.class.getDeclaredField("modifiers");
        methodField.setAccessible(true);
        methodField.setInt(method, method.getModifiers() & ~Modifier.FINAL);

        method.invoke(modifier, "This message was changed at runtime.");
    }
}
```

```
Original Message: This is a message before modification.
Message changed at runtime: This message was changed.
```

Risks and Considerations: Despite its powerful capabilities, using reflection for runtime code modification carries risks:

- **Performance Overheads**: Reflective operations are typically slower than their non-reflective counterparts because of the additional processing involved (e.g., access checks, method dispatch).

- **Security Issues**: Modifying code at runtime can lead to security vulnerabilities, including exposure to unauthorized actions or data modification.

- **Complexity and Maintenance**: Code leveraging heavy reflection might be hard to read and maintain, potentially leading to errors that are difficult to track and resolve.

Considering these factors, developers must weigh the benefits of using reflection against its downsides carefully. Techniques involving reflection should be applied judiciously, prioritizing system design clarity, maintainability, and security.

12.8 Implementing Aspect-Oriented Programming with Reflection

Aspect-Oriented Programming (AOP) provides a means to separate cross-cutting concerns (such as logging, transaction management, and security) from the core business logic of an application. Using Java Reflection, developers can dynamically implement AOP to enhance modularity and minimize code intrusion. This section delves into the implementation of AOP using reflection, outlining a detailed approach, including design decisions and specific coding examples.

One of the primary components of implementing AOP in Java through reflection is the creation of dynamic proxies. These proxies enable method interception, thus facilitating aspect weaving at runtime without modifying the original code base.

- **Proxy Creation:** Reflection is used to dynamically create a proxy class that implements a set of interfaces. This method centralizes control over method calls to the wrapped object.

- **Invocation Handler:** An invocation handler is implemented to intercept and manage calls directed at the proxied object.

Dynamic Proxy Implementation via Reflection

To showcase the use of reflection in creating dynamic proxies for AOP, consider the following example. Here, we use a proxy to add logging before and after the execution of a method call.

```java
import java.lang.reflect.*;

public class LoggingProxy implements InvocationHandler {
    private final Object target;

    public LoggingProxy(Object target) {
        this.target = target;
    }

    public Object invoke(Object proxy, Method method, Object[] args) throws
        Throwable {
        System.out.println("Before method: " + method.getName());
        Object result = method.invoke(target, args);
        System.out.println("After method: " + method.getName());
        return result;
    }

    public static <T> T create(Class<T> interfaceType, T target) {
        return (T) Proxy.newProxyInstance(
```

```
19            interfaceType.getClassLoader(),
20            new Class<?>[] { interfaceType },
21            new LoggingProxy(target));
22      }
23  }
```

```
Before method: methodName
// Method execution outputs
After method: methodName
```

The implementation details reveal that the `invoke` method logs messages before and after the delegate method is executed on the target object, effectively adding logging as an aspect.

Aspect Design Implementation Using `tikzpicture`

Aspect oriented design positions the logging mechanism at the periphery of the application's core functionality, as demonstrated in the following architecture diagram:

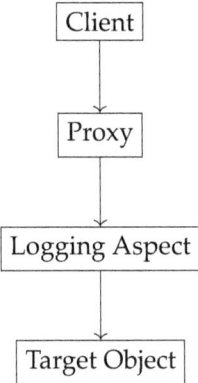

Each node represents a component in the AOP implementation, where the logging aspect intercepts calls to the target object through a proxy, as facilitated by reflection.

Optimization and Reflection Overheads

While reflection offers powerful capabilities for implementing AOP, it introduces potential performance overheads due to its dynamic nature. The use of reflection incurs additional processing to inspect classes and methods at runtime. To mitigate this, caching mechanisms can be employed to store method details after the first reflective access, thus improving subsequent invocation performance.

In summary, implementing AOP using Java Reflection allows developers to enhance applications dynamically, making them more adaptable and maintainable. Through the use of dynamic proxies and method interception, reflection provides the tools necessary to separate cross-cutting concerns from business logic effectively, thus adhering to solid design principles. This approach, highlighted throughout different design schemas and code examples, remains a pivotal strategy in advanced Java application development.

12.9 Reflection in Distributed Systems and Remote Method Invocation

Reflection affords immense power in managing distributed systems and implementing Remote Method Invocation (RMI) within Java environments. This capability allows the manipulation and coordination of objects across a network, offering a way to interact remotely with objects residing on different servers or processes.

In the conception of distributed systems, Java's RMI uses a client-server model wherein objects existing on a server can be invoked and manipulated from a client situated elsewhere on the network. RMI as a mechanism is inherently linked to Java's reflection, as it involves identifying the methods to be invoked on the server side dynamically, and constructing and interpreting messages that represent objects and function calls.

- Reflection enables the dynamic determination of classes and the methods of remote server objects at runtime.

- It facilitates the dynamic generation of stubs required during remote object communication; such stubs act as a client-side proxy for the actual server-side object.

The application of reflection in RMI enlarges the flexibility by allowing applications to detect and access classes across the network dynamically. Below is an example of how reflection is used to invoke a method on a remote object dynamically:

CHAPTER 12. ADVANCED TECHNIQUES AND USE CASES

```
1   public Object invokeRemoteMethod(String remoteClassName,
2                                   String methodName,
3                                   Object[] args) throws Exception {
4       Class<?> remoteClass = Class.forName(remoteClassName);
5       Object remoteObject = remoteClass.newInstance();
6
7       Method method = remoteClass.getMethod(methodName,
8               getClasses(args));
9       return method.invoke(remoteObject, args);
10  }
11
12  private Class[] getClasses(Object[] args) {
13      Class[] parameterTypes = new Class[args.length];
14      for (int i = 0; i < args.length; i++) {
15          parameterTypes[i] = args[i].getClass();
16      }
17      return parameterTypes;
18  }
```

This code fragment illustrates generating an instance of a class and method invocation purely based on their names. The utility method getClasses converts an array of Objects into a corresponding array of Class objects which are then used to identify the correct method signature during runtime.

Output:
Remote method invocation result based on dynamically identified method.

While the flexibility offered by RMI and reflection is significant, it is accompanied by several challenges:

- **Performance Overhead:** Dynamic method invocation can result in performance penalties due to the overhead of class lookups and method access checks.

- **Security Concerns:** As classes and methods are loaded and invoked dynamically, maintaining object security and integrity becomes crucial, necessitating the implementation of robust security measures such as class-loaders and security managers.

- **Complex Error Handling:** Errors in dynamic remote method invocation can be complex to predict and manage due to the involvement of network operations and dynamic type resolution.

Effective management of these challenges is essential for building robust distributed applications using RMI and reflection. Implementing caching mechanisms for class lookups, applying stringent security policies, and developing detailed error handling routines contribute to mitigating these issues and enhancing the practical deployment of this technology in enterprise solutions.

By leveraging the capacity of reflection in distributed systems, developers can construct adaptable and efficient remote interfaces and operations. This utilization ultimately enhances the dynamic nature of Java-based systems, fitting seamlessly into scenarios requiring high degrees of network-based interactivity and flexibility.

12.10 Developing Plugins and Extension Mechanisms

The ability to develop plugins and extension mechanisms efficiently is critical for building scalable, adaptable, and maintainable software systems. Java Reflection provides a powerful toolset for achieving this, allowing developers to add and replace software components at runtime without altering the application's core. This section explores the practical application of reflection to dynamically load and manage plugins and extensions in Java.

Designing a Plugin-Friendly Architecture

A plugin-friendly architecture promotes flexibility and extensibility, relying on Java Reflection to load classes dynamically which may not be present at compile-time. Below, we outline the key considerations and patterns when designing such systems:

- **Interface-based abstraction**: Define a clear interface or abstract class that all plugins must implement, ensuring that the host application communicates with plugins through this abstraction.
- **Configuration-driven discovery**: Use configuration files or annotations to specify available plugins; Java Reflection can subsequently load and instantiate these plugins dynamically.
- **Loose coupling**: Employ design principles that facilitate minimal dependency between the application's core and its plugins to preserve system stability and protect against changes in plugins.

Example Implementation

Consider a system where plugins provide additional message processing strategies. Each plugin implements the `MessageProcessor` interface, which includes a single method, `processMessage(String message)`.

```
1  public interface MessageProcessor {
2      void processMessage(String message);
3  }
```

Using Java Reflection, the system dynamically discovers and loads implementations of this interface at runtime, specified in a configuration file.

```
1   public class PluginLoader {
2       public List<MessageProcessor> loadPlugins(String configFilePath) throws
            Exception {
3           List<MessageProcessor> processors = new ArrayList<>();
4           Properties config = new Properties();
5           config.load(new FileInputStream(configFilePath));
6
7           for (String key : config.stringPropertyNames()) {
8               String pluginClassName = config.getProperty(key);
9               Class<?> clazz = Class.forName(pluginClassName);
10              MessageProcessor processor = (MessageProcessor) clazz.
                    getDeclaredConstructor().newInstance();
11              processors.add(processor);
12          }
13
14          return processors;
15      }
16  }
```

The above code demonstrates the application of reflection to plugin loading, offering a robust method to enhance system functionality on-the-fly through external configurations.

Handling Plugin Dependencies

Managing dependencies for dynamically loaded plugins involves ensuring that each plugin has access to all necessary resources without causing conflicts with the host application or other plugins. Java Reflection comes into play by allowing dynamic exploration of classes and resources at runtime, resolving dependencies as they are loaded.

- **Isolated ClassLoaders**: Use separate `ClassLoader` instances to load each plugin. This practice prevents class conflicts and allows plugins to be unloaded or updated independently.

- **Dependency checking**: Before loading a plugin, verify that all required dependencies are accessible and compatible. Reflection can be used to check for required methods and fields in classes before instantiating them.

Security and Sandboxing

Incorporating third-party plugins can introduce security risks. Reflective operations allow verification and monitoring of plugin behavior, but proper sandboxing mechanisms must be implemented to protect the host environment.

- **Permission restrictions**: Leverage the Java security architecture to restrict the actions that plugins can perform, such as file access and network connections.

- **Audit and logging**: Use reflection to monitor and log plugin activity. Reflective access to method calls and field changes can help in detecting and responding to potential security threats.

Enhancing the Plugin Architecture with Reflection

Refining the plugin architecture involves continuous improvement and adaptation. Reflection offers the capability to modify and extend plugin behaviors dynamically, providing powerful ways to enhance functionality without disrupting the system usability.

- **Dynamic configuration updates**: Allow runtime modifications to plugin configurations, enabling features like feature toggles or performance adjustments without system restarts.

- **Adaptive loading strategies**: Implement strategies that modify the way plugins are loaded and instantiated based on runtime performance metrics or user preferences. This adaptive approach can maximize efficiency and responsiveness.

The integration of Java Reflection in the development of plugins and extension mechanisms equips developers with the tools needed to create systems that are not only robust and versatile but also capable of evolving with changing business requirements and technology landscapes. This approach fosters innovation and adaptation, ensuring that applications remain both competitive and relevant.

12.11 Reflection in Dynamic Script Execution

Dynamic script execution within Java applications allows for substantial flexibility, enabling the runtime integration and evaluation of code written in various scripting languages. By leveraging Java Reflection, developers can dynamically load, compile, and execute scripts, thus enhancing interoperability and extensibility in software applications. This section explores the essential techniques and methodologies for implementing dynamic script execution using Java Reflection, including practical code examples and design considerations.

The integration of scripting capabilities into Java applications typically revolves around the use of the `javax.script` package, also known as the Scripting API. This API provides a standard mechanism for integrating scripts into Java applications. Reflection adds another layer of dynamism by allowing runtime operations that are not predetermined at the compile time.

- The first step in dynamic script execution involves the identification and loading of the script engine corresponding to the scripting language being used. Java Reflection is employed to dynamically query and instantiate script engines based on their names or file extensions.

- Next is the evaluation phase where the script is directly passed to the engine and executed. This operation can be performed multiple times and can be applied to different scripts or even generated scripts at runtime.

- Finally, reflection is used to access and manipulate the script's environment, modifying variables or functions defined within the script from the Java application, or conversely, accessing Java methods and fields from the script.

Here is an example demonstrating the use of reflection for loading and executing a JavaScript script using the Nashorn engine, which comes standard with Java 8 and above:

```
import javax.script.ScriptEngine;
import javax.script.ScriptEngineManager;
import javax.script.ScriptException;

public class DynamicScriptRunner {
   public static void main(String[] args) {
      ScriptEngineManager manager = new ScriptEngineManager();
```

12.11. REFLECTION IN DYNAMIC SCRIPT EXECUTION

```
8          ScriptEngine engine = manager.getEngineByName("nashorn");
9          try {
10             engine.eval("print('Hello, World');");
11         } catch (ScriptException e) {
12             e.printStackTrace();
13         }
14     }
15 }
```

```
Output:
Hello, World
```

Reflection is particularly useful when the type of scripting language or the specific scripts to be executed are not known until runtime. This scenario is common in applications requiring high degrees of customization or in systems that support end-user scripting capabilities.

Dynamic script execution can be significantly optimized by using reflection to cache references to methods or fields accessed frequently. This approach minimizes the overhead associated with reflective operations, which might otherwise impact performance:

```
1  import java.lang.reflect.Method;
2
3  public class MethodCachingExample {
4     public static void main(String[] args) {
5        Method printMethod = null;
6        try {
7           printMethod = System.out.class.getMethod("println", String.class);
8           printMethod.invoke(System.out, "Hello, World with Cached Method");
9        } catch (Exception e) {
10          e.printStackTrace();
11       }
12    }
13 }
```

```
Output:
Hello, World with Cached Method
```

In terms of design considerations, it is crucial to handle exceptions and errors gracefully when working with reflection and dynamic script execution. Script engines can fail due to syntax errors, execution exceptions, or unsupported features in the scripting language. Robust error handling ensures that the host application remains stable and can recover or gracefully degrade its functionality in the face of such errors.

Dynamic script execution, empowered by Java Reflection, opens diverse avenues for developing adaptable and versatile applications. It enables the incorporation of script-driven logic that adapets dynamically to changing requirements or user inputs without the need for recompilation. This capability is instrumental in creating software that is not only resilient and adaptive but also forward-compatible with emerging technologies and scripting languages.

12.12 Concluding Thoughts on Persistence and Evolution of Java Reflection

Java Reflection remains an instrumental feature in the Java programming language, driving an array of dynamic capabilities that have influenced modern software design and development. Through the course of this chapter, we have explored the multifaceted applications and advanced techniques of Java Reflection, establishing not only its current significance but also its potential to adapt and evolve within the ever-changing landscape of software development.

Reflective techniques offer potent solutions to complex design and runtime challenges, facilitating late binding, dynamic invocation, and introspective capabilities, which are crucial for contemporary software systems. The use cases outlined in this chapter underscore the utility of reflection in achieving modularity, flexibility, and decoupling, ideals at the heart of modern software architecture.

The persistence of reflection as a core component of Java can be attributed to its continuous alignment with emerging patterns and paradigms. For instance, as we delve into realms like microservices and cloud-native applications, Java Reflection adapts to offer dynamic proxy generation and manipulation of bytecodes in real-time, ensuring that Java retains its relevance and efficacy.

Beyond current applications, the evolution of Java Reflection mirrors advancements in computing paradigms. With the onset of machine learning and artificial intelligence, reflection provides the necessary mechanisms for dynamic script execution and the seamless integration of AI models into Java applications. This adaptability not only revitalizes Java's utility across domains but also ensures that reflection remains a critical tool in the developer's toolkit.

The integration of reflection with aspect-oriented programming (AOP) also highlights its adaptive nature. AOP augments the modularity of Java applications allowing for cleaner, more maintainable code bases where cross-cutting concerns like logging and transaction management are handled more elegantly. Reflection's ability to dynamically manipulate and adapt class behaviors aligns perfectly with these requirements, further cementing its role in advanced application frameworks.

12.12. CONCLUDING THOUGHTS ON PERSISTENCE AND EVOLUTION OF JAVA REFLECTION

From a performance perspective, while reflection is often criticized for its overhead, optimizations in JVM and JIT compiler strategies have significantly mitigated these concerns. Enhanced class loading and caching techniques further improve the performance of reflective operations, ensuring that their benefits can be leveraged without disproportionate cost.

Finally, as Java continues to evolve, so does its reflective capabilities. Upcoming enhancements in language features and JVM improvements promise to expand the horizons for reflection, simplifying previously complex tasks and enabling more robust dynamic behaviors. This ongoing evolution speaks to the resilience and enduring relevance of reflection in Java's ecosystem.

www.ingramcontent.com/pod-product-compliance
Lightning Source LLC
Chambersburg PA
CBHW050048230526
45470CB00004B/1451